NIMROD
RISE AND FALL

Previous books by the same author

Flight Testing to Win (Autobiography paperback)
ISBN 978-0-9553856-4-3, 0-9553856-4-4
Published Blackman Associates

Vulcan Test Pilot
ISBN 978-1-906502-30-0
Published Grub Street

Tony Blackman Test Pilot
(Autobiography revised and enlarged, hard cover)
ISBN 978-1-906502-28-7
Published Grub Street

FICTION

A Flight Too Far
ISBN 978-0-9553856-3-6, 0-9553856-3-6
Published Blackman Associates

The Final Flight
ISBN 978-0-9553856-0-5, 0-9553856-0-1
Published Blackman Associates

The Right Choice
ISBN 978-0-9553856-2-9, 0-9553856-2-8
Published Blackman Associates

Flight to St Antony
ISBN 978-0-9553856-6-7 0-9553856-6-0
Published Blackman Associates

Now You See It
ISBN 978-0-9553856-7-4, 0-9553856-7-9
Published Blackman Associates

NIMROD
RISE AND FALL

TONY BLACKMAN

GRUB STREET | LONDON

Published by
Grub Street Publishing
4 Rainham Close
London
SW11 6SS

Original hardback edition 2011

Reprinted 2011

Copyright this edition © Grub Street
Copyright text © Tony Blackman 2013

Reprinted 2019

British Library Cataloguing in Publication Data

Blackman, Tony.
  Nimrod : rise and fall.
  1. Nimrod (Reconnaissance aircraft)--History.
  I. Title
  623.7'467-dc23

  ISBN-13: 9781909166028

Jacket and book design by Sarah Driver

Printed and bound by Finidr, Czech Republic

Grub Street Publishing uses only FSC (Forest Stewardship Council) paper for its books

Title page photograph courtesy Simon Thomas

CONTENTS

ACKNOWLEDGEMENTS

Writing this book has given me great pleasure as it has provided the opportunity for contacting many interesting people and recording their stories. In addition lots of people have got in touch with me on hearing that I was writing this book. However first and foremost this book could not have been written without the help given to me by Justin Morris. He has worked tirelessly, telling me where to look for information, writing personal accounts and putting me in touch with scores of retired Nimrod aircrew. It was a delight to work with him and I consider myself very fortunate. Incidentally, it only happened because David Gordon of *Knock News* put an advert in the paper and Justin contacted me.

It is impossible for me to list all the many people who have helped me with anecdotes, details and, sometimes, just encouragement. However, some deserve special mention: Ian Marshall who sent me verbatim accounts of his flying as did Andy Collins, Terry Earl, Jim Lawrence, Joe Kennedy, Wils Metcalfe, Colin Pomeroy, 'Roxy' Roxborough, and Paul Warrener. I have also been greatly helped by Brian Cushion, David Emmerson, Ian Hampton, Chris Herbert, Sir 'Win' Harris, Al Mackie, Sir Charles Masefield, Garry Porter, Robbie Robinson, Peter Rosie, Bill Speight, Drew Steel, Doug Torrance and John Turner, to name but a few! I must apologise for not listing everyone with whom I have been in contact, but I am so very grateful for all the help I have received.

As mentioned in the Introduction there is an enormous amount of information on the web but I would like to acknowledge in particular that I constructed nearly all the maps using Google Earth with some help from www.gcmap.com for distances. I also used some details from Aeroflight and Target Lock.

With regard to photos, the majority of which have come from retired Nimrod crew, I have tried to acknowledge copyright where it is known but inevitably there will be some omissions. Indeed it is probable that a few photos could be crown copyright but I have found it impossible to ascertain which ones and I can only apologise if I have inadvertently used those pictures without acknowledgement. As usual the Avro Heritage Centre (AHC) have helped me, this time by supplying some pictures of early Nimrods.

I would like to thank my publisher for all the support he has given me, with his suggestions and superb editing. Furthermore he has managed to turn my manuscript into hard copy in record time which is very much appreciated.

And finally, last but definitely not least, thanks to my wife, Margaret, who has supported me, given me lots of ideas and encouragement and edited the chapters again and again. Inevitably there will be some errors for which I can only apologise and take full responsibility.

AUTHOR'S NOTE

When I joined A.V.Roe and Co. Ltd in 1956 as a test pilot at Woodford we were still building the nosewheel variant of the Shackleton, the Mk3. When the Nimrod requirement arose in 1963 I was deputy chief test pilot and soon got involved with the development of the airframe, helping my boss Jimmy Harrison. In the end I flew 40 of the 46 aircraft we built. I never had the experience of flying in a fully equipped aircraft though I was fortunate enough to fly the aircraft four times at Farnborough and very much appreciated its viceless handling properties which made it ideal for low level searching over sea or land.

I decided to write this book because I felt that the general public has no idea what wonderful things the Nimrod did. The cancellation of the Nimrod MRA4 gave some people entirely the wrong idea of the aircraft and hopefully this book will help to put the record straight.

In my lifetime I helped develop the Vulcan, the Victor tanker and the Nimrod, all three of which helped to win the Falklands campaign. Sadly they have all now gone from front-line service and one has to wonder what the future will bring.

NB: Some of the stories quoted herein come from serving officers, so naturally cannot be attributed.

ALB
August 2011

DEDICATION

To the many Nimrod aircrews, some sadly no longer with us, who flew in the aircraft for over forty years protecting our shores, rescuing our sailors and supporting our armed services, both on land and at sea.

PREFACE

This book is about an aircraft which was arguably the best reconnaissance aeroplane in the world until it was scrapped prematurely by the government of the day under great financial duress but, unfortunately, leaving the country almost defenceless from a long-distance maritime reconnaissance point of view.

It is written especially for the general reader, rather than for Nimrod specialists, though I hope that they will read it with interest and enjoy it. Not many people realise what a great job the aircraft did because so much of its work was classified. Conversely they can't comprehend what a great loss it is to this country. My aim in writing this book is to let everyone know what a superb aircraft it was and tell a few stories of all the things it could do. It tells as much as is currently allowed about the fascinating task of anti-submarine warfare, explaining the challenges involved.

Writing this book was not made any easier because of the understandable security that surrounded some of the Nimrod flying and care has been needed not to breach any security regulations. Luckily, there is a mountain of information on the internet, some of which surprised me and in addition, manufacturers of equipment from BAE systems down to the smallest sonobuoy manufacturing firm understandably love to advertise their wares and tell how capable they are. However there is a lot more to be told when security permits but, regrettably, it must be for another day.

One major feature of the Nimrod which cannot be over emphasised is that it succeeded so well because of the tremendous teamwork between all the members of the crew. In the Royal Air Force, at one end of the scale is the high performance fighter/ground-attack aircraft flown by one person, the pilot. At the other end was the Nimrod with at least ten crew with each person having a vital part to play to bring a mission to its successful conclusion. Both tasks are essential but very often it was the 'speed jockey' who flew for a few alarming minutes who got the plaudits and the exhausted Nimrod crew flying for hours at a time which got forgotten.

The original Nimrod design was conceived in 1963 to prevent a French competitor being selected but, in the event, proved its superiority over all the others. It started as a maritime reconnaissance aircraft but as technology advanced it was able to have new sensors fitted which enabled it to provide vital support to the UK ground forces also in a reconnaissance role. Unfortunately in an effort to make the aircraft even more effective to fufil all its roles, the manufacturer failed to manage properly the changed wing design and new engine installation which they had proposed, with the result that the procurement costs soared and the programme was delayed by at least two years. However, just as the new aircraft was about to go into service, after all the investment had been made, the government was faced with a financial crisis and decided that Nimrod had to be sacrificed, perhaps not really appreciating why it was so vital to the UK to fulfill all its commitments and not facing up to the fact that it will, in the future, have to buy a foreign replacement aircraft costing just as much and probably more, while paying unemployment benefit to all the aerospace workers who could have been looking after the Nimrod in service.

The book examines all the Nimrod programmes from the beginning to the end and also tells just a few of the many, many stories of the very valuable work that the aircraft was able to do with its dedicated crews.

The airborne early warning variant which never worked satisfactorily is examined critically as is the MRA4 upgrade which turned into a horror story bringing credit neither to the manufacturer nor to the government. In both cases aircraft were destroyed and the beneficiary was and inevitably will be the American aircraft manufacturers.

Shortly after cancelling the Nimrod the government hastily had to issue a last-minute reprieve to the planned grounding of the Nimrod R1 electronic reconnaissance aircraft of 51 Squadron because of the need to monitor electronically the transmissions from all the countries who are involved or who are interested in the numerous Middle East democratic uprisings. Had the rather precipitate scrapping of the MRA4s not been authorized they could be helping right now, since the aircraft was working well and the crews were already being trained.

Finally, there have been many excellent papers written explaining the problem that the country now has to contend with in following the cancellation of the MRA4. Dr Sue Robertson's written evidence to the House of Commons Defence Committee is extremely cogent and all embracing: www.publications.parliament.uk/pa/cm201011/cmselect/cmdfence/writev/761/m18.htm

There is also an article by Lee Willet called 'Mind the Gap' in a RUSI Journal which concentrates on anti-submarine warfare: www.rusi.org/analysis/commentary/ref:C4D4C20CB26473

I would have loved to have included these articles in this book had space permitted since the arguments are so well expressed. However in my concluding paragraphs at the end of the book I do deal with some of the pressing issues.

PROLOGUE

THE HUNT

"'Radar to standby. Climbing'. As the airspeed bled back towards 230 knots and we started to regain the radio signals from the sonobuoys further away in the field on only our second climb to height, the lead wet underwater equipment operator came on the intercom, 'Captain – Jez. We've got an interesting line on buoy 14.' 'Yet another nuclear-powered Grimsby trawler' I cynically thought, instead of a submarine, wondering why we hadn't detected it visually or on radar as we laid the buoys.

"Maintaining RF contact, we gradually dropped down to low level, drew a blank on the radar, and supplemented the field around buoy 14, shortly after which the AEO came on the intercom reporting further buoys in contact and a classification of 'Possub, Confidence Level 4', and an identification of the suspected class of the Soviet hunter-killer submarine that we were firmly in contact with, and which was tracking in a south-westerly direction and presumably proceeding to its patrol area. 'This only happens in the Simulator', I thought. SOSUS, the US underwater sound detection system between Greenland and the UK, always puts us on to the target area first. Nobody ever gets an unalerted, underwater contact with a Soviet sub but the wet team and AEO were supremely confident that we had done just that! I didn't want to alert the submarine to our detection; equally, I didn't want to let him slip away, so we adopted a strategy of close tracking with passive sonobuoys and not using our active ones. We laid passive 1C buoys (bomb bay carried, and the only directional sonobuoys available to us in those days), obtained usable bearings and flew down these bearings to obtain some excellent confirmation measurements from our magnetic anomaly detector. Staying ahead of the target, we obtained some equally excellent tracking information, to confirm the submarine type. This was just too good to be true.

"With due respect to those controlling us from the MHQ, whom we guys on the squadron felt lacked a dynamic approach to ASW, I wasn't at all convinced that this unalerted detection would be prosecuted fully if we didn't take the initiative, so I instructed the radio operator to send back a message along the following lines: 'Intend to remain on task until PLE (prudent limit of endurance) and land at Kinloss instead of St Mawgan, the airfield we'd taken off from many hours before. Request ETA of our relief aircraft'. That might do it.

"With the flight engineer and routine navigator keeping a close eye on the fuel state, and the routine weather updates from MHQ being studied more closely than usual, we were becoming worried that we might have to go off task before our relief, of whom we had now been notified, arrived in the area. The weather in Scotland was completely clear, meaning there was no worry about Kinloss being fogged out or similar, but when our fuel state (which I had been happy to drop down to) meant that the only alternates from Kinloss became Lossiemouth or Inverness Airport, it really was time to go. The tactical team worked out a forecast CPA (closest point of approach) for the target and at the last possible moment, as we were climbing through 30,000' and the co-pilot tactfully advised me that the pressure launchers were only cleared up to 20,000', because I assured him that probably that was all that Boscombe Down had been asked to do, we dropped our point buoy and, shortly afterwards, established secure R/T contact with the second Nimrod just as he picked up the signal from the buoy which gave 200 yards as the CPA. Whew!

"The rest of the flight was uneventful. As dusk gathered, we crossed the beautiful Hebrides and Scottish Highlands, let down visually into the Kinloss circuit and touched down at the other end of the British Isles from whence we had started our day after a flight time of 10 hours and 5 minutes (quite a long Nimrod sortie). The sonics data was taken from us by the Kinloss Maritime Acoustics Analysis Unit (MAAU), and we set off home for a short night flight back to St Mawgan – and a celebratory couple of beers.

"Was it a true unalerted detection which had slipped by SOSUS? I don't know, for it could be that the long weekend off had meant that the St Mawgan MAAU plot was not fully up to date when we were briefed. I'm pretty happy in my own mind, though, that it was – but will probably never know for sure – for, if the target was already on the plot why wasn't it already being tracked; why were we relieved on task by a crew 'scrambled' from a routine day on the squadron; and why were we allowed to fly a sortie, which was only planned as a training sortie, precisely in the area which we had asked for?

"Whether it was or not, it was certainly an unalerted detection for us, a perfect tracking exercise and definitely a bonus."

Colin Pomeroy, Tactical Navigator,
4 March 1980, Nimrod MR1 XV262

1 NIMROD FROM START TO FINISH

THE LIFE STORY OF A MIGHTY HUNTER

INTRODUCTION

The Nimrod was a fantastic aircraft which operated for over forty years playing its part in the defence of the nation, but most people had no idea of all its capabilities because of the high security required for many of its tasks. During the Cold War the Nimrod squadrons worked flat out tracking Russian submarines but of course this vital undertaking was kept securely under wraps so that very few people, including a lot of decision makers in the Royal Air Force, knew what was being achieved other than those with the right security clearances. The aircraft hit the headlines occasionally when there was a search and rescue story such as the 1979 Fastnet race or the Piper Alpha disaster, but for the most part it soldiered on unremarked. When the Falklands campaign erupted everyone knew about the Vulcans and the Black Buck operations but hardly anyone knew that there were Nimrods there steering the Victors to the Vulcans as well as acting as a search and rescue trail if anything went wrong. Few of the many accounts of the Falklands campaign even mention the vital role that the Nimrod played.

The UK has an international responsibility for searching and monitoring a large area of the Atlantic, which was provided very effectively by the Nimrod using its superb search radar, better than any other air force in the world bar none. When our customs and excise boats were inter-

UK area of responsibility in light shade

cepting drug runners or when the navy was capturing them in the Caribbean, the fact that Nimrods may have been tracking the targets for days to obtain the necessary information never got a mention. Then, after the Cold War when the UK started fighting in the Middle East few people realised that the Nimrods had a new role, supporting the troops on the front line with the aid of their wonderful Wescam cameras. When in September 2006 that terrible accident occurred to the Nimrod in Afghanistan there was no explanation as to why it was there nor was it mentioned that, without the Nimrod, there was a terrible gap left for our land forces. Unfortunately, it is because of this very necessary security screen that people don't appreciate how much of a loss it is that the Nimrod programme has been stopped. However, now that the aircraft is history and has been cut up for scrap, it seems a good time to describe the remarkable things it did by studying documentation, recording interviews and collating all the information that is available on the internet and in the media. There is a great deal that can now be told.

The very successful operation of the aircraft was only achieved by team work. In a fighter aircraft it is the pilot who is in command and it is his/her skill that contributes to the country's defence. In the Nimrod the two pilots were part of the team, albeit a vital part, and the captain

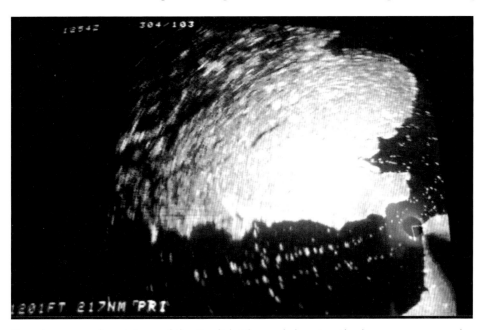

Searchwater radar picture of the English Channel showing the large area covered

of the aircraft was as often as not the tactical navigator, because it was the tac nav who took the decisions on how to chase the submarine or search for the target. This book tells the story of the aircraft, the history of anti-submarine warfare and the sensors that found the submarines, as well as finding the search and rescue targets. The book then goes on to explain the layout of the crew stations in the aircraft and how each operator played a part in the team and the hunt. After that there are the real stories of chasing submarines, search and rescues, the Falklands campaign and, finally, supporting the troops. The book finishes by discussing the very few accidents that have occurred to Nimrod over its forty-year life, then goes on to relate the failure of the Nimrod airborne early warning aircraft and, finally, tells the heart-breaking story of the cancellation of what would still have been the best reconnaisance aircraft in the world.

IN THE BEGINNING

When I joined A.V.Roe and Co Ltd in 1956 we were still building Shackletons for the South African Air Force as well as for the Royal Air Force. In fact my first job was to install the autopilot in the Shackleton Mk 3. Avros had a long tradition building maritime aircraft starting with the Avro Anson, which first flew in 1935. As a new boy somehow it never occurred to me that the RAF would ever need to go elsewhere for their coastal aircraft.

In 1958 there was a NATO specification for a long-range maritime patrol aircraft to replace the Lockheed Neptune, followed by a competition which was won by Bréguet with an aircraft that was called the Atlantique.

South African Air Force Shackleton 3

As in all European projects, a multi-national consortium had to be formed to build the aircraft and it first flew in October 1961. However, the UK did not feel the Atlantique specification was suitable for RAF needs since the MOD were looking for a bigger technological advance from the Shackleton Mk3. Air Staff Target 357 was therefore produced in 1963 which was mentioned in parliament in the Air Estimates, envisaging a new aircraft which would have the very latest equipment to defeat the Soviet submarine threat. It was quickly realised that such an aircraft could not be available until the 1970s and in those days it was unthinkable for the UK to be without a very powerful anti-submarine warfare (ASW) capability, and so a more realistic aircraft was defined, but not formally issued, called Air Staff Requirement 381. Of course, once the Western aircraft manufacturers realised that the UK was not going to agree to the NATO proposal they started mulling over the best and most effective way of replacing the Shackleton.

Bréguet Atlantique

Speed in itself is not vital for a maritime aircraft but on the other hand it is clearly desirable for a search aircraft to be able to get 'on station' as quickly as possible. What also is important is for it to have a long search time and be very manoeuvrable at low speed so that it is able to keep station over possible targets and be able to launch weapons as required. The key decision for the UK was whether to have a jet-engined aircraft or compromise and choose the propeller-driven Bréguet Atlantique, by now being operated by the French air force and looking like a very credible contender. There were other very capable aircraft as possibilities also, such as the Lockheed P3 Orion being operated by the United States Air Force, plus a variety of UK-sponsored drawing board designs such as versions of the BAC111, the Short Belfast, the Trident and the Avro 748.

The requirement was then refined to ask for a jet-engined aircraft to replace the Shackleton, since propeller aircraft were felt to be acoustically too noisy and thus easily detectable by submarines whilst they were submerged and so, just under a year later in June 1964, the Air Staff Target 357 was issued. The idea was to have a medium-sized jet-powered aircraft with the latest electronics and Hawker Siddeley bid the HS800 which was a trijet based on the de Havilland Trident. There were bids from other manufacturers also but the costs for the new aircraft were clearly far too high and so, in June 1964, the Air Staff Requirement 381 was issued specifying a much simpler and less capable aircraft based on the Bréguet Atlantique.

Gilbert Whitehead

Avros were determined to win the contract and, of course, were well aware that the RAF really wanted a jet aircraft. Under the leadership of their chief designer Gilbert Whitehead they decided, in just a week, that a modified version of the Comet Mk 4C would meet the ASR with an enlarged nose to accommodate a search radar, a long unpressurised skirt for a weapons bay to hold stores, droppable dinghies and other equipment plus a long boom or sting in the tail to house a magnetic anomaly detector (MAD). I was deputy chief test pilot at Avros while the bidding was going on and it was a very exciting time trying to optimise the submittal. To keep the costs down much of the electronics used in the Shackleton were specified for the aircraft, now named as the Hawker Siddeley 801. The front of the aircraft was basically a Comet 4 but with the latest Smiths automatic flight system; the detailed interconnection between the operating crew in the rear and the pilots was not an issue during the bid and was added later. We found that the latest Rolls-Royce Spey engines could be fitted instead of the more 'thirsty' Avon engines so that an acceptable endurance could be obtained. In order to get the necessary search time on station we proposed that low level searches over the sea could be done on three and then two engines depending on aircraft weight and the other engine(s) would be restarted when required at the end of the search. The basic rule for the bid and for everything we did later was that there would be minimum change from the Comet 4, because Gilbert Whitehead realised right from the start that any alteration would cost time and money.

In February 1965 the government announced that we had won the contract which, by MOD procurement standards, was really quite quick bearing in mind that ASR 381 had not been issued until June the previous year. What was unique in the contract, negotiated by January 1966, was that it was at a fixed price and that it was for thirty-eight production aircraft. It was the first large fixed price contract that MOD(PE) had ever given and the first that Hawker Siddeley had undertaken. The programme dates were clearly defined so that the company were taking a huge risk. At the time we at Avros were still developing the government-funded Vulcan, but most of our design effort was being spent developing the Avro 748 civil airliner which first flew in 1960. This programme was completely company funded with critical customer time scales and it is my belief that the experience and success of running this programme helped to give Hawker Siddeley management the confidence to allow Avros at Manchester to go ahead with the fixed price Nimrod contract.

FLIGHT DEVELOPMENT

The programme got off to a good start. As there were two unsold Comet 4C airframes at the de Havilland Hawarden factory near Chester, the decision was made to use them as prototypes for aerodynamic and systems test work. The first aircraft XV148 was fitted with Spey engines,

the new nose and weapons bay but not the MAD at that time. The second prototype XV147 also had the new nose and weapons bay but in addition had the MAD fitted; however the aircraft retained the Avon engines but was fitted with the avionics.

All the Comet fuselages were built at the de Havilland factory at Hawarden and the achieved time scales

Nimrod XV148 without MAD boom (AHC)

for the Nimrod development were very impressive by present-day standards. The first prototype, XV148, flew on 23 May 1967. The first flight was from Chester to Woodford and Jimmy Harrison who was Avro's chief test pilot at the time would normally have flown it. However, such was the eminence of de Havilland's chief test pilot 'Cat's eyes' Cunningham in the UK aerospace industry and the fact that he had test flown the original Comet 4, it was decided by

senior management that JC would be in charge and that Jimmy be 'second pilot'. The flight was uneventful and, in reality, was just a positioning flight from Chester to Woodford.

I flew the initial flight of the second prototype aircraft XV147 on 31 July 1967 before it was handed over for navigation trials to RAE Farnborough.

The basic Comet had become a very reliable aircraft once the original square windows which caused the initial pressurisation disasters had been removed and Avros were determined to make the Nimrod as reliable as its civil predecessor. In fact, the Royal Air

John Cunningham

Force already had considerable experience with the Comet in Transport Command, having initially Comet 2s and later Comet 4Cs. There were also some classified Comet 2s used as electronic reconnaissance aircraft on 51 Squadron.

The first flight and all subsequent flights were really uneventful from a testing point of view. I flew the first prototype aircraft myself a month later and it behaved just like a fully developed certificated aircraft. The new nose and bomb bay skirt had some negative effect on directional stability as the designers had expected; the dorsal fin area was increased a month or so after the

first flight of 148 and I notice from my log book that I did some of the confirmatory checks on the stability in August. The wing had been strengthened to enable the carriage of stores in the future and the under-carriage had been strengthened, permitting an increase of 19,500 lb in take-off weight over the 162,500 lb of the Comet 4C.

Second prototype XV147 *(AHC)*

The systems were basically unchanged from the Comet 4s, which was a very important safety feature since the systems were those of a fully certificated aircraft. However, in order to get the maximum endurance from the aircraft search mission, which had to be able to be flown on three or two engines, an air cross feed duct was installed connecting the air bleed and the starters of all four engines so that engines could be restarted in flight. Unfortunately, this duct many years later proved to be a subject of great controversy, possibly causing the crash of an aircraft and the grounding of the whole Nimrod fleet.

From an aircraft handling viewpoint the only difficulty that Jimmy and I found was with the ailerons which had rather a lot of friction and backlash and, together with the spring feel, made the aircraft unpleasant to fly. We went to John Cunningham and asked him about this rather unsatisfactory artificial feel and I well remember what he said: 'Yes, I don't know why they made them like that'. Jimmy and I looked at one another but said nothing until later; however, we were definitely unimpressed since at Avros we always felt that it was the test pilots who should determine how the flight controls should feel; clearly JC took a different view. However nothing was changed because we had to ask ourselves the question 'was the aircraft safe to fly with the ailerons as they were in the Comet?' and reluctantly we came to the conclusion that they were. Firms get no more money or credit for making an aircraft nicer to fly, it just has to meet the safety requirements, so maybe JC was right after all though we didn't think so at the time.

From an aerodynamic flight test viewpoint we had to check and adjust the pitot static system on the nose to correct for the effect of the new radome. We had to enlarge the fin slightly to improve the directional stability of the aircraft and then we did routine performance measurements and stalling checks. The functioning and operation of the radar and sensors were not Avro's direct responsibility though we had to ensure that the electrical connections were correct and that both the electrical and the equipment systems had adequate cooling.

The handling of the aircraft was in reality as viceless as one would expect from a fully certificated civil aircraft. Though I never had the chance to operate the Nimrod over the sea and to maintain station over a target, I did demonstrate it four times at the Society of British Aerospace Contractors biennial air shows at Farnborough; I really appreciated the new eyebrow windows that had been added to the Comet flight deck and the enlarged windows which helped me enormously in positioning the aircraft without crossing the 'dreaded' display line and being sent home for transgressing the rules. The improved visibility clearly helped the Nimrod pilots in operations, orbiting over a submarine or over sensitive areas in the Middle East wars and I was able to fly it 'low and slow' in front of the crowd without any problems.

Air shows of course always put great pressure on the pilots and as described later in this book a Nimrod was lost demonstrating at one in Canada. In addition, by a sad coincidence the competitor to the Nimrod, the Bréguet Atlantique, crashed at Farnborough in 1968 demonstrating single-engined operation but flying too slowly and too low.

The first production aircraft, XV226, flew on 28 June 1968 and was the first production aircraft to have the MAD boom fitted. Besides assessing the effect of the boom on directional stability, Avros were also responsible for making sure that the magnetic anomaly detector was far enough away from the fuselage so that it could function correctly and detect submarines, its primary task. In fact I did six flights on the first production aircraft to make certain that the MAD would work correctly on the Nimrod.

SQUADRON SERVICE

The whole flight test programme was remarkably trouble free and on 2 October 1969, just over three years from the granting of the contract, the RAF took delivery of its first aircraft, the Operational Conversion Unit (later 236 OCU) at St Mawgan in Cornwall being the first to operate the type. The first overseas flight occurred on 27 October 1969, when a crew flew to Gibraltar.

It cannot be emphasised enough that the delivery of the aircraft was on time and on budget. This was a remarkable achievement which was largely taken for granted at the time and would be unheard of in today's environment; by a strange coincidence it was made just as Coastal Command was being disbanded and No 18 (Maritime) Group of Strike Command was being formed. Production aircraft were soon being delivered to operational units at RAF Kinloss, Morayshire, and at RAF St Mawgan, Cornwall. The last unit to begin re-equipping was 203 Squadron at Luqa on Malta, which received its first aircraft in October 1971.

While production was getting underway, it was realised that the Nimrod airframe would make an ideal replacement for the ageing Comet 2Rs, still used by the RAF for electronic intelligence (ELINT) duties on 51 Squadron. The Comet offered ample internal space for electronic equipment and excellent cruise performance. Accordingly, three additional airframes called Nimrod

Below: Nimrod at Gibraltar

R1s were ordered, the first being delivered to 51 Squadron at RAF Wyton as virtually an empty shell in July 1971 without MAD booms or the opening weapons bay doors. It kept the same ASV-21D radar of the MR1 but the LORAN long-range hyperbolic navigation system and a periscopic sextant were fitted for more accurate navigation. Later the standard Doppler equipment was removed and two inertial navigation systems were fitted. Because some of the sorties were longer than on the standard Nimrod there was provision for two extra crew besides the basic crew of two pilots, a flight engineer and two navigators. In the main cabin there was provision for up to 23 SIGINT specialists to work all the special equipment fitted to the aircraft. The Nimrod R1 became operational in

42 Squadron Nimrod MR2s at Gibraltar

1974 after having been fitted with its special equipment, including extra antennae, the most noticeable being the extra small fins above and below the tailplane.

Over the next three years a complex array of sophisticated electronic eavesdropping equipment was fitted to the three aircraft, resulting in a large number of antennae appearing on the fuselage. The aircraft had dielectric radomes for more antennae in the nose of each external wing tank and also one in the tailcone replacing the MAD.

Over the years, the R1 aircraft have undergone numerous equipment upgrades as electronic surveillance has become ever more sophisticated. Some of the cabin windows have been blocked up to allow the installation of more equipment and the fuselage antennae have exhibited several changes. Around 1982 the three R1s had ESM (electronic support measures) pods fit ted to the wing tips and which were later fitted to the AEW and MR2s. One of the R1s, XW666, was lost in an accident after an engine fire following maintenance (see Chapter 8). To replace it, MR1 XV249 was converted to R1 standard. The R1 has kept a very low profile but has played a key role in many conflicts, from the Falklands campaign to the 2003 Second Gulf War and all the incidents since, identifying and classifying enemy air defence systems and gathering information on enemy activities.

In January 1972 eight more MR1s were ordered bringing the total order up to forty-six and bringing the squadrons up to full strength with the last three held back for the AEW programme. It should be em-

51 Squadron interior Nimrod R1

phasised again that Avros continued to deliver all these Nimrods on time and on budget, a fantastic tribute to Gilbert Whitehead and his team.

When the original requirement for the aircraft was defined it was realised that it would have

Nimrod R1 from Waddington

to be updated fairly quickly since, as mentioned earlier, a lot of the MR1 sensors were basically the same as the Shackleton though the crew operated in more comfortable conditions. The first Nimrod XV147 was used to develop the avionics for MR2 and it first flew with the MR2 system in 1977. The main change was the installation of the Searchwater radar which replaced the ASV 21 radar on the MR1; this change increased the search capability of the Nimrod dramatically and because the radar frequency was 'agile' it was much harder for a submarine to detect. The antenna was stabilised in pitch and roll and could also be controlled in pitch; in addition when a target was being tracked there was no need for the antenna to go round continuously since the radar could be made to sweep in pre-selected sectors, which made tracking much easier. The presentation was on a TV-like flicker-free screen with a single radar operator; the radar was so effective that a submarine's snorkel could be seen clearly, even in rough seas. The system continuously analysed the returns and a number of targets could be automatically classified at the same time. There was also a 'stand-off' mode to avoid the need for the aircraft to fly over the target for visual identification.

The first MR2 entered service in 1979 at Kinloss but, despite all the previous work the main computer, made by Marconi, did not function reliably. Luckily there was an RAF support team at Kinloss who had the details of the design software and were able to make changes to the main operating programme. Apparently this caused some contention in that the aircraft should not have been using unapproved software, but the Squadron claimed that only by doing this was the computer able to do its job. However, like a lot of software programme glitches in all sorts of equipment, the problems were eventually resolved and the electronics became extremely reliable. Certainly by the time of the Falklands campaign three years later the system was working well.

Thirty-one Nimrods were converted from MR1s, the last aircraft to go to Woodford for conversion being in 1984. There was very little difference in the outward appearance of a MR2 from a MR1; there was a change of colour scheme from grey-and-white to a NATO 'hemp' colour, almost beige. There was also an additional cooling air scoop on the port side just below the dorsal fin for the supplementary cooling pack (SCP) and ESM.

Coincidentally with the advent of the MR2s it was agreed that the UK would no longer keep defence forces in Malta and that 203 Squadron, which had operated from the island for many years with first Shackletons and then Nimrod MR1s, should be disbanded. This saved the UK government a considerable expense as the Maltese government had insisted on vastly increased rental charges after 1971 when the Labour Government came to power in the UK. Apparently the whole island turned out to say farewell to the aircraft and Royal Navy ships which had been based in Malta, as the last Nimrod and the RN warships left at the same time. The Maltese government called the departure on 31 March 1979 Freedom Day and printed some special stamps for the occasion. At the same time apparently they had also signed some commercial deal with Libyan leader Col Gadaffi who was in Malta for the celebration.

In parallel with the development of the Nimrod MR2s, the government awarded BAe the AEW contract in 1977 and eleven airframes were used to support the project, some of which came from the Nimrods returning from Malta, though in fact the AEW never came into service. This project is discussed in detail in Chapter 9.

Maltese commemorative stamps
31 March 1979

The next milestone in the life of the Nimrod was the Falklands campaign and the introduction of flight refuelling capability, discussed in detail in that chapter. Of course once this modification had been approved and fitted to the MR2 fleet the range and endurance capability of the aircraft was increased enormously. Initially the tankers used were Victor K2s but the aircraft later took fuel from all the other RAF tankers, VC10s, C130s and Tristars.

The Nimrod continued to operate successfully and relatively uneventfully for many years through the '80s, '90s and early 2000s and it proved to be a very reliable aircraft. Some of the more notable sorties are described in later chapters.

From 1985 the MR2s began to be fitted with wingtip electronic support measures (ESM) pods as developed for the R1, to enhance their surveillance capability; these pods were able to receive radio transmissions at a wide range of frequencies and the aircraft had a database to enable the source of these transmissions to be identified, friend or foe. In the late 1990s several Nimrod MR2s were fitted with an underwing infrared pod under the starboard wing, two BOZ defensive pods one under each wing and a towed radar decoy, under the unofficial designation MR2(GM) – where GM stood for Gulf Mod. Nimrods helped to secure the Arabian Gulf sea lanes during the 1991 Gulf War and returned in 2003 to take part in the liberation of Iraq.

While the British government was equipping the Royal Air Force with Nimrods the Australian, Canadian and New Zealand air forces were also buying and operating maritime aircraft for ASW as well as for SAR. In 1960 Mr and Mrs Aird-Whyte presented a silver tray in memory of their son Fincastle who was killed in action in 1943 in Coastal Command. This tray launched an annual competition between the four Commonwealth air forces, initially for depth-charge bombing but from 1971 it reflected the modern ASW skills required from maritime aircraft.

Only the RAF had a jet-powered aircraft; the Royal Australian Air Force had Lockheed Orions as did the Royal New Zealand Air Force. The Royal Canadian Air Force had first the Argus followed by the Canadian-equipped Orion called the Aurora. The Nimrod won thirteen times and shared the trophy once in the years up to 2005. The RAAF won six times and shared twice, the RNZAF won seven times and shared once whilst the Canadian Air Force won five times and shared once.

Nimrod equipped for Middle East operations

The form of the competition changed again in 2006 so that it was held during routine exercises. It is sad to think that the RAF can no longer take part, thus emphasizing the current deficit in the UK defence capability.

In 1976 a bit of realism was added to the competition. The host nation was the RAF at Kinloss, the search area was a notified 3,600 square-mile area near Rockall in the Atlantic and the submarine to find was HMS *Ocelot*. The Russians obviously wanted to watch the competition and check the detection methods being used so they sent along a diesel-powered submarine to observe the chase. However they clearly were not expected to be discovered on the surface in the middle of the night just after the Nimrod had found *Ocelot* and had dropped a small explosive charge to let the RN crew know their boat had been discovered. No wonder the RAF won the competition that year!

From time to time the RAF sent Nimrods to take part in air displays and there was a very fortunate air display in Chile in 1998, described in Chapter 5, when the aircraft was able to drop some stores to a dismasted British yacht in the Pacific crewed by thirteen girls trying to break a round the world non-stop record.

Russian submarine taking part in the Fincastle Trophy 1976!

In 1996 BAE systems won the contract to upgrade the capability of the Nimrod fleet by having a new variant called initially Nimrod 2000 and later Nimrod MRA4. The programme proved to be more challenging and expensive than forecast and so the planned in-service date of the new variants slipped steadily to the right. The story of the MRA4 is told in the last chapter of this book but meanwhile continuous improvements were being made to the avionics fit of the MR2 aircraft; in 2001 Ultra Electronics introduced an improved acoustics processor, followed by the AQS971 so that the aircraft could monitor and control thirty-two sonobuoys simultaneously. Some MR2s were fitted with the L-3 Wescam MX-15 electro-optical turrets under the starboard wing to enable the reconnaissance of ground targets to support the ground troops. These aircraft were also used, based in Seeb, Oman, to support the coalition maritime forces. A lot of these improvements were absorbed as later variants in the MRA4s. On 18 July 2008 the MRA4 order was confirmed for twelve aircraft with initial operation capability in 2010.

In July 2004 the Nimrod MR2 fleet was reduced to eighteen aircraft on the grounds that the anti-submarine task was severely reduced. The remaining aircraft were programmed for reconnaissance work plus search and rescue, though the scope of the reconnaissance was increased

Air display Guernsey 13 September 2001. Flt Lt Kev Hughes carrying out a splendid 'wing over' (*Ian Hampton*)

enormously for overland work by the fitting of the latest optical cameras.

On 2 September 2006 Nimrod XV230 crashed in Afghanistan killing all fourteen crew members. The aircraft had just flight refuelled and the accident is fully discussed in the accident chapter later. The report of the Board of Inquiry was published in December 2007 and the government charged Charles Haddon-Cave to conduct an independent inquiry, which came out on 28 October 2009. The inquiry found that the accident was caused by the fitting of the crossfeed duct in the basic design in 1969, by the addition of the supplementary cooling pack as part of the MR2 modification and by the introduction of the air-to-air refuelling modification in 1989. There had been a Nimrod safety case carried out in 2001-2005 and this NSC was severely criticised in the inquiry as it was felt that because the Nimrod had proved so reliable for thirty years the NSC had not been carried out rigorously enough. Showing perhaps a little too much hindsight, the inquiry also suggested that had the NSC been carried out properly the accident might never have happened. The inquiry criticised MOD, BAe and Qinetiq and felt that the accident had been avoidable, but it must be remarked that that comment applies to most accidents.

After the accident to XV 230 the decision was taken to switch off the supplementary cooling pack during refuelling which in reality prevented a similar accident again. However, when more cases occurred of fuel in the bomb bays after air-to-air refuelling, the decision was taken to stop flight refuelling altogether but, rather surprisingly, there was no suggestion of finding out from where the fuel was coming and trying to prevent it happening.

THE SAD CONCLUSION

On 9 March 2009 the MOD announced that the Nimrods that had not been fitted with replacement fuel seals and engine bay hot air ducts would be grounded after 31 March, which in effect grounded all overseas Nimrods. As a result of the inquiry the Coalition Government announced in December 2009 that the Nimrod MR2 fleet was to be grounded in March 2010 and that the introduction of the MRA4 would be also delayed until 2010.

One of the last operational flights of the Nimrod MR2 took place from Kinloss on 8 March finishing with a flypast of the warrant officers' and sergeants' mess where members of the Nimrod Line Squadron were celebrating all their long service to Nimrod operations. Justin Morris tells me that three final flights were planned for 29 March 2010 but in fact only two took place as the weather deteriorated with a 40kt cross-wind and driving snow but he did manage to get on the penultimate operational sortie. The Nimrod was finally removed from RAF service on 31 March 2010 and then XV250, XV226 and XV232 were flown to locations where they were going to be displayed in visitors' parks at Elvington near York, Bruntingthorpe and Coventry, some to be kept serviceable for taxiing. XV255 & XV231 were flown to Norwich and Manchester for their museums.

"The final Nimrod MR2 sortie took place on 26 May 2010 when XV229 left RAF Kinloss en route to the Defence Fire Training and Development Centre at Kent International Airport, Manston. This last flight had little of the publicity of the earlier disposals – 2,000 people had been waiting at Elvington for our arrival where they had started arriving at 0700! Maybe this was apt since for the last 41 years Nimrod aircraft had flown from RAF Kinloss and deployed to operating bases on operations with little, if any, fanfare; crews and support personnel simply completed their tasks to the best of their ability without fuss, although it has to be admitted that, on occasion, frustration was felt when our efforts went unnoticed and others took the credit for our endeavours. Nevertheless, we took off into a shower of rain and headed towards Burghead Bay before returning to say goodbye to the station with a waggle of her wings before heading off down south. I am led to believe that a freak dust storm appeared to have developed shortly after the flypast as some individuals were seen removing dust from their eyes! Little more than an hour and a half later, and without incident, the aircraft's Spey engines were shut down for the very last time and XV229 was handed over to the Defence Fire Training and Development Centre. We left Manston with the knowledge that, unlike many other visitors to this establishment, at least there was no intention to set fire to our Mighty Hunter! Incidentally, the return trip to Kinloss would take somewhat longer!"

On 10 March 2010 the RAF accepted the MRA4 for flight training its crews but on 19 October 2010 the government cancelled the aircraft. The last flight of the Nimrod R1 was planned for 31 March 2011 but as that date neared there was an uprising in Libya and the aircraft were needed to monitor the transmissions coming from Colonel Gadaffi and his men, to liaise with fighter operations and to monitor any transmissions from all the eavesdropping equipment of other countries, Russian and Chinese to name just two. Ironically the Coalition Government was forced to cancel the grounding of the Nimrod R1s and and delay it for three months.

Unwisely the Government decided, secretly and in great haste, to scrap the MRA4s which had been carrying out training with a completely satisfactory mission system; they also destroyed the perfectly good aircraft that were waiting for delivery. Had they delayed scrapping them so prematurely they would have realised that they could have been used where they were currently urgently needed in the Mediterranean, in June 2011.

NIMROD MR1 LOCATIONS

Squadron	Dates	Station
42 Squadron	1971-1984	RAF St Mawgan
51 Squadron	1971-2011	RAF Wyton, RAF Waddington
120 Squadron	1970-1982	RAF Kinloss
201 Squadron	1970-1983	RAF Kinloss
203 Squadron	1971-1977	RAF Luqa
206 Squadron	1970-1981	RAF Kinloss
236 OCU	1970-1985	RAF St Mawgan

NIMROD MR2 LOCATIONS

Squadron	Dates	Station
42 Squadron	1983-2010	RAF St Mawgan, RAF Kinloss
120 Squadron	1981-2010	RAF Kinloss
201 Squadron	1982-2010	RAF Kinloss
206 Squadron	1980-2005	RAF Kinloss

The United Kingdom has always been, and will always need to be, a maritime nation, trading, exploring and competing with the other nations of the world. Up to now the country has always had excellent military reconnaissance plus civil search and rescue capabilities, on the water and, since the early 20th Century, in the air. In times past, governments were in no doubt as to what was needed and spent the money as required to keep the country in the forefront as a leading trading nation, defending its interests but, as I write this in 2011, the UK's maritime and search and rescue capability is severely depleted and the vital support of our land troops which the Nimrod provided has almost disappeared. Hopefully this situation is only a transient one until the country once again purchases the aircraft it needs but, alas, the aircraft will no longer come from a UK manufacturer and will almost certainly cost more than maintaining the Nimrod programme would have done.

Retirement of Nimrod R1 28 June 2011 (*Crown copyright*)

Remembering the forty years of wonderful operations which the Nimrod has carried out and the dedicated service which the crews have given to defend and support the UK, I am reminded of Winston Churchill's immortal remark at the end of his introduction to his history of the Second World War. I have taken the liberty of paraphrasing it slightly:

'At the end of forty years, all our objectives having been achieved or about to be so, the aircraft was immediately cancelled by the British Government from all further protection of their affairs.'

2 HISTORY OF ANTI-SUBMARINE WARFARE

INTRODUCTION

Anti-Submarine Warfare (ASW), the original primary role of the Nimrod, is a very specialised form of warfare. This chapter, which starts by explaining the development of the submarine, is a brief introductory guide, written to introduce the layman to this fascinating and on-going subject.

Technology has always been the driver in ASW. As fast as the submarine hunters, originally ships and then aircraft, found a way to detect their prey so the submarines found a way of negating the attack, either with new equipment or by adopting different tactics, rather like a deadly game of hide and seek. This 'battle' between the hunter and the hunted is a never-ending one. Just because currently there is no active war between the nations who have submarines and those that want to track them, it would be wrong to imagine that this technological 'hide and seek' battle is not continuing. Though it is always desirable to know at all times where modern ballistic nuclear submarines are located since they can launch weapons almost instantaneously at the outbreak of any hostilities, it is perhaps even more vital at the present time, with hostilities occuring in the Middle East, to know where the smaller submarines are located, to which country they belong and, if necessary, to have the means to attack them.

The first submarine?

The submarine goes back many years and divers using tubes for breathing were used during the siege of Syracuse in 413BC according to the *History of the Peloponnesian War*. Probably the first reconnaissance submersible was used in Egypt in the 12th century AD judging by this 16th century Islamic painting (left).

Unfortunately, like many such inventions, it did not take long for people to recognize the military potential for these crude devices. In fact John Wilkins of Chester in *Mathematicall Magick* in 1648 described the characteristics of a submarine:-

"Tis private: a man may thus go to any coast in the world invisibly, without discovery or prevented in his journey.

"Tis safe, from the uncertainty of Tides, and the violence of Tempests, which do never move the sea above five or six paces deep. From Pirates and Robbers which do so infest other voyages; from ice and great frost, which do so much endanger the passages towards the Poles.

"It may be of great advantages against a Navy of enemies, who by this may be undermined in the water and blown up.

"It may be of special use for the relief of any place besieged by water, to convey unto them invisible supplies; and so likewise for the surprisal of any place that is accessible by water.

"It may be of unspeakable benefit for submarine experiments."

The next two hundred and fifty years saw the continuous development of the submarine as a useable weapon with various problems slowly being resolved, but navies at this stage did not feel immediately the need to develop ways to detect enemy submarines. In 1692 a French physicist, Denis Papin, made a submarine which was resistant to outside water pressure and air was pumped into the hull to facilitate breathing. There was also a water pump to control buoyancy but there was no means of propulsion. In parallel with this design the Ukrainian Cossacks were using a so-called riverboat, *chaika*, for reconnaissance. It was easily submerged so that the crew could breathe like a modern diving bell with air tubes and it was propelled by the crew walking along the bottom of the river. By 1727 fourteen types of submarines had been patented in England and in an issue of the *Gentleman's Magazine* of 1740 there was a description of a boat which had the facility of a ballast using goatskins to admit and expel water.

The first military submarine was the *Turtle* used in the American War of Independence,1776. It was designed by an American David Bushnell, with a single crew who had to propel the boat. It was the first true submarine propelled by screws and capable of independent underwater operation and movement. Apparently on 7 September of that year the *Turtle* operated by Sgt Ezra Lee tried and failed to sink the British warship, HMS *Eagle* in New York harbour but there is no record of the attack in the ship's log, probably because no-one knew there might be anything there.

Next came the *Nautilus* in 1800. Designed by Robert Fulton, an American living in France. It was human powered by a hand-operated screw propeller but it also had a sail for use on the surface. It could carry two mines which it did in a demonstration but the French gave it up a few years later as did the British when they tried the machine out.

In 1812 during the Napoleonic wars Silas Halsey lost his life while using a submarine trying to sink a British warship in New London harbour, Connecticut. The Russians built a metal submarine in 1834 in St Petersburg which carried six British-built Congreve gunpowder rockets. Then in 1851 a Bavarian artillery corporal, Wihelm Bauer, took a submarine to sea in Kiel harbour to break the Danish blockade; it was powered by a tread mill but sank and got stuck in the mud at sixty feet. Almost miraculously the crew of three escaped six hours later when the increasing water pressure from leakage enabled them to open the hatch.

There were quite a few submarines built and used during the American civil war, 1861-65, including the French-designed 1862 *Alligator*, the first submarine of the US Navy. However it was a confederate submarine, the *Hunley* which, on 17 February, 1864 sank the USS *Housatonic* off Charleston harbour, the first time a submarine successfully sank another ship, though it also sank in the same engagement. Submarines in fact did not have a major impact on the outcome of the war, but they did portend their coming importance to naval warfare and so generated an increasing interest in the need to be able to detect such machines.

The French navy made the great breakthrough when in 1863 they launched the *Plongeur* which was equipped with an air-driven reciprocating engine using compressed air from bottles at 180 pounds per square inch. This was followed by the *Ictineo II*, designed by Monturiol, which was the first combustion-driven submarine and the first fully functional one. It was made of wood and originally it was powered by sixteen men operating a screw propeller. It was then converted to a peroxide and steam-powered engine. It could dive to 96ft, had a crew of two and could remain under water for two hours. On the surface it was powered by steam but underwater the engine was peroxide driven so that oxygen was a by-product which helped the crew breathe. The boat pioneered the use of double hulls and also solved the pressure, buoyancy, stability, diving and ascending problems which had bedevilled earlier designs, but the company went bankrupt and the development came to a halt.

Jules Verne came next in 1870 but he had the advantage of not being hampered by reality and wrote his classic book *Twenty Thousand Leagues under the Sea* with his *Nautilus*. Though he cut no metal, he inspired the inventors of future submarines.

The first series production submarine was human powered by a hand turning a propeller and fifty were built for the Russian navy in 1881. Significantly the inventor, a Pole Stefan Drzewiecki, built an electrically-powered submarine a year or two later. However, 1888 was a big year for submarines as the Spanish navy received a Spanish-built electrically-powered machine, designed by Isaac Peral, which had two torpedoes, a new air system with a propeller and an almost modern hull shape. It could do 10 knots which was the fastest underwater boat yet but was very limited on range since the batteries could not be charged internally. It launched a torpedo and had an underwater navigation system; interestingly despite two years of successful trials the Spanish government terminated the programme when streamlining its defence budget, clearly 120 years ahead of its time! In the same year the French navy's electrically-powered *Gymnote* was launched and made 2,000 successful dives but like the Spanish submarine it was short on range.

It was at the turn of the 20th Century and later that submarines really became a force to be reckoned with. As usual advances of technology were the driving force and it was the arrival of reliable diesel engines, invented by French-born Diesel but patented in Germany, with the capability not only of propelling the submarine but also charging the batteries which provided a step change in design and manufacture. The Irishman John Philip Holland designed the *Holland VI* which was launched in 1897; bought by the US Navy in 1900 and rechristened USS *Holland*, the design was developed and a company formed called the Holland Torpedo Boat Company/Electric Boat Company which became part of General Dynamics, still probably the world's foremost builder of today's submarines.

The US Navy now started to build submarines in New Jersey and at their first Pacific base in Vallejo, California. Holland got a US patent and his designs were purchased by the US Navy and then by navies all over the world including the Royal Navy, the Imperial Russian Navy, the

Below: RN *Holland* submarine c1902

Royal Netherlands Navy and the Imperial Japanese Navy. In fact the *Holland VII* became the Royal Navy's first Holland class submarine. The Japanese ordered five *Holland VII*s from the US for use in the Russo-Japanese war and the Russians ordered German-manufactured submarines; however, neither side used them before the war ended.

As the world's navies equipped themselves with the latest submarines they were forced to start buying equipment to find and attack other countries' submarines. With the diesel engine, submarines could now submerge when needed and run almost silently on batteries. At the time of the First World War the solution to attacking submarines was to use depth charges but the chance of finding a submarine was extremely unlikely. In fact, the first known sinking of a submarine by a depth charge was in 1916 when a German U-Boat was sunk by the heavily armoured HMS *Farnborough*. Experiments were carried out using electrical loop cables to detect submarines magnetically and by the end of the war experiments with hydrophones had been started but were not continued. Seaplanes and airships were already being used to search for submarines but they were relying on visual sightings of the boats on the surface charging their batteries.

Between the world wars there were developments in hydrophones and then radar from aircraft. The submarine response to being detected by radar was to suck in air to run the diesel engine down a pipe sticking up just above the water called a snorkel or 'snort mast'. However, as radar improved even a target as small as the snorkel could be detected. In parallel with the radar as a sensor, acoustic detection was being developed for finding the submarine under water. Meanwhile nuclear power was starting to be used to power submarines which meant that there was no need for them to surface to charge the batteries, once again making it much harder for the hunter; they could also produce oxygen to breathe so they could stay submerged for long periods which made them very difficult to find. All this was instrumental in defining the specification of the Nimrod MR4.

Nuclear submarines are very expensive and only a few countries in the world have both the financial resource to buy them and the expertise to operate them. Diesel-operated boats are much cheaper but their effectiveness is spoilt if they are

Modern mast array

continually having to surface with their snorkels to charge their batteries. Consequently, a lot of development has been carried out enabling the diesel engine or a steam turbine to run on oxygen carried in the submarine and this approach is given the name air-independent propulsion, AIP. Such submarines are likely to be able to remain submerged for up to about fourteen days but inevitably advancing technology will enable this submerged time to be extended. In 2009 it was believed that about eight countries were operating AIP machines using different technologies but there were only four shipbuilders, French and German owned, offering upgrades to existing submarines.

Summarising the historical situation, submarines were being continually developed to become more effective and much harder to detect. Meanwhile radar and acoustic sensors based on the hydrophone, called sonobuoys, were becoming available and also more effective so that aircraft could detect submarines providing they knew roughly where to start looking. The submarines responded by making themselves quieter and so the sonobuoys and other detection aids needed to become even more capable. The Nimrod can no longer take part in this never-ending leapfrogging between the hunter and the hunted but the development of ASW technology continues remorselessly.

To understand what the capability of the Nimrod was, the rest of this chapter is devoted to explaining how, in general terms, submarine sensors operate.

ANTI-SUBMARINE WARFARE – THE TOOLS

For a submarine to be effective in its role it must remain hidden at all times which presents immediate problems in design and operation.

1. The submarine ideally should be able to leave and return to its base without being seen and identified.
2. The propulsion system has to be able to run without getting air/oxygen from the surface.
3. The engine and its supporting systems in the craft must not make a noise.
4. The propulsion system, meaning the propeller or water jets, must be as silent as possible.
5. For a normal crew-operated submarine there has to be a supply of oxygen.

The hunting aircraft of course is aware of all these problems and tries to exploit these weaknesses so that the submarine can be found and if necessary destroyed. To this end a search aircraft has to be equipped with the necessary sensors and weapons. These include:-

Sound detection equipment, sonobuoys.
Radar detection equipment in case the submarine surfaces.
Electronic support measures in case the submarine transmits electro-magnetic radiation.
Magnetic anomaly detection to detect and orbit immediately over the submarine.
Electro-optics for infrared detection.

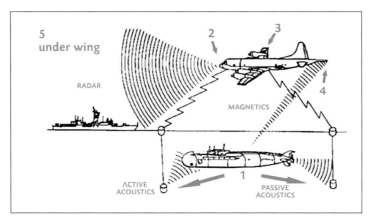

The search tools

In the next chapter details of the actual equipment that the Nimrod used during the years are given but in this chapter there is a general non-specific discussion on the development of sensors and an introduction to the methods of finding submarines.

ACOUSTICS AND SONOBUOYS

Although some animals, especially dolphins and bats, have employed sound for communication and object detection for millions of years, the use of sound in the water by humans is assumed to be relatively recent and initially recorded by Leonardo Da Vinci in 1490; a tube inserted into the water was said to be used to detect vessels by placing an ear to the tube. Lighthouses used this technique in the 19th Century by ringing an underwater bell and boats could hear the sound by putting an equivalent of DaVinci's tube into the water.

The use of sound to 'echo locate' underwater in the same way as bats use sound for aerial navigation seems to have been prompted by the *Titanic* disaster of 1912. The world's first patent for an underwater echo-ranging device was filed at the British Patent Office by English meteorologist Lewis Richardson a month after the sinking of the ship, whilst a German physicist Alexander Behm obtained a patent for an echo sounder in 1913.

The Canadian engineer Reginald Fessenden, while working for the Submarine Signal Company in Boston Mass, built an experimental acoustic system beginning in 1912, a system later tested in Boston harbour and, finally, in 1914 in the US Revenue (now Coast Guard) Cutter *Miami* on the Grand Banks off Newfoundland, Canada. In that test, Fessenden demonstrated depth sounding, underwater communications using Morse Code and by echo ranging (detecting an iceberg at a distance of two miles). The ten Montreal-built British H class submarines launched in 1915 were equipped with Fessenden oscillators.

During World War I the need to detect submarines prompted more research into the use of sound. The British made early use of underwater hydrophones, while the French physicist Paul Langevin, working with a Russian immigrant electrical engineer, Constantin Chilowski, worked on the development of active sound devices for detecting submarines in 1915 by using quartz oscillators. In 1916, under the British Board of Invention and Research, Canadian physicist Robert William Boyle took on the active sound detection project with A B Wood, producing a prototype for testing in mid 1917. This work, for the Anti-Submarine Division of the British Naval Staff, was undertaken in utmost secrecy using quartz piezoelectric crystals to produce the world's first practical underwater active sound detection apparatus. It is said that to maintain secrecy, no mention of sound experimentation or quartz was made – the word used to describe the early work ('supersonics') was changed to 'ASD'ics, and the quartz material to 'ASD'ivite: hence the British word ASDIC which everyone thought was an acronym. In 1939, in response to a question from the Oxford English Dictionary, the Admiralty made up the story that it stood for 'allied submarine detection investigation committee', and this is still widely believed, though no committee bearing this name has been found in the Admiralty archives.

By 1918, both France and Britain had built prototype active systems. The British tested their ASDIC on HMS *Antrim* in 1920, and started production in 1922 and the 6th Destroyer Flotilla had ASDIC-equipped vessels in 1923. An anti-submarine school, HMS *Osprey,* with a training flotilla of four vessels, was established in Portland harbour in 1924.

During the 1930s American firms developed their own underwater sound detection technology and important discoveries were made in the development of hydrophones and transmitting sound pulses. After technical information was exchanged between the two countries during the Second World War, Americans began to use the term sonar for their systems, coined as the equivalent of radar, while the UK was still using the term ASDIC.

Sonar (originally an acronym for SOund Navigation And Ranging) is a technique that uses sound transmissions (usually underwater) to navigate, communicate with or detect other vessels. Two types of technology share the name: *passive* sonar is essentially listening for the sound made by vessels; *active* sonar is emitting pulses of sounds and listening for echoes. Sonar may be used for measurement of the echo characteristics of 'targets' in the water and also as a means of location of the source of the sound. The term sonar is also used for the actual equipment employed to generate and receive the sound. The acoustic frequencies used in sonar systems vary from very low (infrasonic) to extremely high (ultrasonic); the study of underwater sound is known as underwater acoustics or hydroacoustics.

By the outbreak of World War II, the Royal Navy had five different sonar sets to equip five different surface ship classes and yet more for submarines, making a complete anti-submarine attack system. The effectiveness of early ASDIC was hamstrung by the use of the depth charge as an anti-submarine weapon. This required an attacking vessel to pass over a submerged contact before dropping charges over the stern, resulting in a loss of ASDIC contact in the moments leading up to attack. The hunter was effectively firing blind, during which time a submarine commander could take evasive action. This situation was remedied by using several ships co-operating and by the adoption of 'ahead throwing weapons' which projected warheads at a target ahead of the attacker while still in ASDIC contact. Developments during the war resulted in British ASDIC sets which used several different shapes of beam, continuously covering blind spots. Later came acoustic torpedoes.

With the United States entering the war British ASDIC technology was transferred for free to their ally. Research on ASDIC and underwater sound was expanded both in the UK and in the US and many new types of military sound detection were developed. These included sonobuoys, first developed by the British in 1944 under the codename High Tea, dipping/dunking sonar and mine detection sonar. This work formed the basis for post-war development to counter the growing threat from the nuclear submarine. Work on sonar had also been carried

Below: Catalina flying boat

out in the Axis countries, notably in Germany, which included countermeasures. At the end of World War II this German work was assimilated by Britain and the US into their own research centres. Since then sonar technology has continued to be developed by many countries, including Russia, for both military and civil uses; in recent years the major military development has been the increasing interest in low frequency active systems.

Aircraft only really came into their own as anti-submarine warfare vehicles in the Second World War. Early days of ASW primarily relied upon visual lookouts to detect submarines. The United Stares used aircraft like the Catalina seaplanes and, at one stage, various airships (or blimps). Their weapons systems were limited to guns, depth bombs, and rockets. Unlike the present day, submarines then carried guns because they had to spend a lot of time on the surface charging their batteries. In June 1943 a US airship sighted at night and attacked a German surfaced submarine, U134 in the Western Atlantic. The airship was shot down but the submarine was forced to return to base and it was finally sunk by British bombers in the Bay of Biscay.

As explained, early submarines used battery-powered engines when submerged and these batteries could only be recharged by the submarines surfacing and running their diesel engines. This gave the searching ships and aircraft a very good chance of finding them even though they usually surfaced at night. The ASW aircraft used searchlights, flares and, later, radar systems. However, when the submarines fitted snorkels so that they could suck air into the diesel engines without surfacing completely whilst, at the same time, 'listening' for searching radars so that they could submerge completely when they sensed they were under attack, it made the task of finding them much harder. It was the development of the technology that made sonobuoys small and light that really enabled the aircraft to become an effective submarine finder and destroyer.

A sonobuoy is a device which is dropped into the ocean and used to gather acoustic data which is transmitted back to the aircraft. There are a number of different types of sonobuoys, designed for a variety of applications from anti-submarine warfare to whale research. All sonobuoys are characterized by being very rugged, built to withstand severe weather, waves, extreme temperature and pressure; for ASW airborne work they are not recoverable which is clearly an expense issue.

As already explained, there are two main types, active and passive. The active sonobuoy has the advantage of being able to locate a submarine with some accuracy but because it makes a noise the submarine is aware that it is being hunted and can therefore take avoiding action.

ACTIVE SONOBUOYS

Active sonar gives the range to a target, also the bearing which tends to be less precise. It works in a similar way to radar in that a signal is emitted as a short pulse and the sound wave then travels in many directions away from the emitter. When it hits an object, the sound wave is reflected back in many other directions. Some of the energy, but only a very lit-

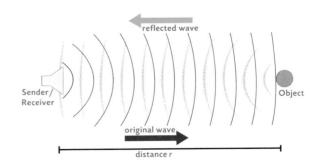

Active sonobuoy transmitting sound

tle, will travel back to the emitting source. The timing of the echo return will enable the sonar system or operator to calculate the distance of the reflecting object though for accuracy allowance has to be made for many factors such as the depth, the water temperature, salinity of the water etc. Active sonar is used when the searching aircraft decides that it is more important to determine the position of a possible threatening submarine than it is to conceal its own position, since a submarine will always hear active sonar. Furthermore, active sonar also suffers from the disadvantage that a submarine can hear the signal at a greater range than the sonobuoy can detect echoes, colloquially known as the 'ESM advantage'.

PASSIVE SONOBUOYS

Passive sonobuoys listen using hydrophones without transmitting. The sonar has a wide variety of techniques for identifying the source and position of a detected sound since the nature of the sound is very important as different sources, for example engines, cooling systems, or propeller noise, have different noise characteristics which can be recognised. The computer processing the noise will have large sonic databases, but it is the sonar operator who usually finally classifies the signals manually, identifying the nature of the transmitter and the country of origin, for example French submarine or a USN frigate. A modern computer system frequently uses these databases to identify classes of ships, actions (i.e. the speed of a ship, or the type of weapon released), and even particular ships. Databases of unique sounds, engines, turbines, shafts, pumps and other machinery are part of what is known as acoustic intelligence or ACINT. For this reason submarines like to operate as silently as possible since amongst other things acoustic operators can measure how many blades are on a propeller and how many revolutions the shaft is making per minute. High-speed propellers often create tiny bubbles in the water and this cavitation has a distinct sound so to help silent operation the propellers are designed and precisely machined to emit minimal noise. It is also possible to assess the speed of the boat by measuring the difference in frequencies being received by different passive sonobuoys (the Doppler effect) as well as its course and speed without having to use active sonobuoys. Nuclear submarines, even though they do not have to surface, always make a noise, even the very quiet ones but the diesel boats when on batteries are virtually silent.

SEARCH RADAR

Airborne radar is an absolutely key tool carried by aircraft to find shipping and submarines. During the Second World War aircraft started carrying air-to-surface vessel (ASV) radar, for detecting shipping and submarines; the history of this radar and the detection of submarines is a very good example of the continual struggle that takes place between the searching aircraft and their prey.

The Avro Anson is considered to be the first aircraft, in 1937, to carry radar capable of finding ships but the power generated was very small and the operation was not 'operator friendly' in that it was a nightmare to control and interpret; the RAF's Short Sunderland was chosen to carry early operational ASV radar because it was large

Avro Anson

enough to carry the antennae. The direction of the target was determined by steering the aircraft so that the returns from two antennae matched in amplitude on the operator's cathode ray tube. This radar, ASV Mk1, was not very effective in detecting small returns and only about 200 sets were produced. However, it enabled the aircraft to track convoys and helped navigation by seeing the coastline returns.

Short Sunderland

The problem with these early radars was that submarines could only be seen at six miles and the aircraft had to be at 6,000 ft. As the range was reduced the aircraft had to lose height so that the echo from the response was not lost in the returns from the sea itself, known as surface clutter, and, at 200 ft, the submarine echo could only be held down to half a mile. After that only the eyeball Mk 1 was available to detect the submarine! The next development was to use sideways-looking ASV, called at the time Long Range ASV, added to the forward-looking aerials. This approach meant that the whole length of the aircraft could be used for the transmitting and receiving antennae. With this system a submarine could be detected at up to 15 miles and then, as the aircraft got close the operator would switch to the forward-looking ASV.

The next big breakthrough came with the invention of the cavity magnetron by two British men, John Randall and Harry Boot in 1940. These devices could transmit not only a lot of pulsed power, 10kW, but very significantly the frequency of the radio transmissions could be reduced so that the antennae sizes could not only be made smaller but the beam could be directed more accurately. Up to 700 sets of this ASV Mk II were fitted to Catalina flying boats and other aircraft. The submarine detection rate was not all that high as there were only two kills in 1941; however the sinking of the *Bismarck* was achieved using this equipment. This radar definitely gave the British an advantage over the Germans until, unfortunately, a Wellington bomber fitted with the equipment crashed in enemy territory and the Germans were able to determine the operating frequency of the equipment. The submarines were then fitted with a receiver called Metox, the name of the French manufacturer of the equipment, which could detect the radar when it was transmitting. When the radar operator selected a shorter range as the aircraft homed in on the target, the 'pulse repetition rate' would

Leigh Light

be doubled, the submarine would hear this, know it had been spotted and would crash dive.

A lot of the ASV Mk II aircraft were then fitted with a 22 million candle power light, called the Leigh Light after the RAF officer who campaigned to have these lights fitted. The submarines charging their batteries at night on the surface suddenly found that operating on the

RADOME

Shackleton Mk 1

surface to keep the batteries topped up without being discovered no longer worked, which meant that they were much less effective chasing and harassing convoys since their range on batteries was reduced. By the end of 1942 3,500 ASV Mk IIs had been manufactured and the number of submarine losses increased steadily. German statistics showed that 35% of submarine losses were from aircraft attacks while on their way out to the convoys, 20% were lost due to aircraft near the convoys and 19% from a combined air/sea attack. The remaining 26% were said to be due to naval attack but in fact most of these attacks were only successful because of the initial locating of the submarines by aircraft.

The next radar to be developed was the ASV Mk III called centimetric radar and the size of the scanner reflector was reduced to just 28 inches. From then on the Battle of the Atlantic was won and in April/May 1943 the Germans lost fifty-six U-boats. At this stage of ASW the aircraft definitely had the upper hand and largely ensured the success of the Allied forces.

After the war the Avro Shackleton Mk 1 flew in 1949 carrying ASV 21 radar in the nose but the Mk 2 carried the radar underneath the fuselage to give a 360° sweep.

MAGNETIC ANOMALY DETECTION

Exploration of the earth by measuring and studying variations in the earth's magnetic field had been conducted by scientists since 1843 in order to locate iron ore deposits and Thalen's 'The Examination of Iron Ore Deposits by Magnetic Measurements', published in 1879, was the first scientific treatise describing this practical use.

In World War II it was decided to use the fact that iron distorts local magnetic fields to try to locate submarines with ships and aircraft. The technique is basically to use a magnetic coil of wire called a magnetometer to sample the earth's field while the vehicle is moving to determine if there are inconsistencies.

However, it was important that the vehicle making the measurements did not interfere magnetically itself with the measurements being made so that on a boat, to be effective, the magnetic sensor had to be towed behind it. For an aircraft, a long boom was fitted to the tail but the sensor needed calibration to allow for the aircraft's own magnetic properties.

For ASW purposes, the MAD-equipped aircraft must almost be overhead or very near the submarine's position to detect the change or anomaly, since the detection range is normally related to the distance between the aircraft sensor ('MAD head') and the submarine. Naturally, the size of the submarine, its hull material composition and its depth normally determined the strength of the anomaly. In fact, though titanium is a difficult metal to use for construction, the Russians did build some of their hulls with this metal in the Cold War which affected MAD detection per-

formance adversely. Additionally, the direction travelled by both the aircraft and the submarine relative to the earth's magnetic field was also a factor. Nevertheless, the close proximity required for magnetic anomaly detection made the MAD system an excellent sensor for pinpointing a submarine's position prior to an air-launched torpedo attack.

Magnetic anomaly detector P3C

ELECTRONIC SUPPORT MEASURES

The acronym ESM is actually a misnomer since ESM is really the gathering of electronic intelligence, ELINT. All radio transmissions have their own particular characteristics which are recognisable and can be logged in databases. However, initially ESM was just listening to see if there were any hostile transmissions and taking the necessary avoiding or attacking action. ESM started seriously in World War II as radar was being developed and installed on boats and aircraft. For example, when the German battleship *Scharnhorst* was being chased by the Royal Navy it listened to the British transmission and turned away. Again forty years later during the Falklands War the Argentinians were very careful not to switch on their radar if they thought their navy would be discovered prematurely. Gradually the emphasis switched to logging and classifying all transmissions and the current equipment as fitted to modern aircraft is extremely advanced.

SEARCHLIGHT

As mentioned earlier, airborne searchlights were fitted to UK aircraft during the Second World War as a result of a Wing Commander Leigh who realised that submarines charging their batteries at night could only be attacked if the aircraft could see the submarines. Nowadays all ASW aircraft have searchlights.

AUTOLYCUS

This equipment was fitted to the Shackleton Mk1 so that it could analyse the air it was flying through to detect diesel fumes. It was an effective tool except that it was really too sensitive detecting fumes from ships that had long since gone. With the advent of nuclear submarines the sensor was phased out.

WEAPONRY

Early airborne weapons against submarines were depth charges and torpedoes. The depth charges became nuclear and the torpedoes became more effective armed with the latest homing technology. Later aircraft were fitted with under-wing attachment points for attacking ships and surface submarines but the weapons could also be used to support land forces. In addition sidewinders for attacking other aircraft could be carried.

CONCLUSION

Summing up submarine and subsequent anti-submarine development, the problems that had to be solved by the submarines were crew breathing, boat propulsion, buoyancy control, battery charging, noise, communication and navigation, to name but a few. By the start of World War II airborne ASW efforts began in earnest to counter the dangerous submarine threat which by now had mastered a lot of the design challenges. The devastation and terror experienced from submarines early during the war during the Battle of the Atlantic, when the U-boats caused havoc to the shipping convoys, made it very clear that the vital requirement for effective ASW forces included the use of aircraft. Since then the duellists, the aircraft and the submarine, have been locked together in an intense chess match. For the submarine hunter, life became a lot harder when the snorkel started to be used and harder still with the advent of nuclear submarines. For each procedure or system the submariners came up with, a new tactical or technological innovation for ASW had to be developed from the air. The three distinct historic phases of air ASW include the World War II years, the Cold War period and the post-Cold War era; the technical battle between aircraft and submarines is still being fought as keenly as ever and the advent of AIP machines has not made things any easier.

We no longer have the Nimrod and, at the moment, it is impossible therefore for the UK to track globally the location of submarines from the air. Almost certainly the Boeing P8 will be just another step along the ASW trail. Technology is endlessly altering the scene and the nature of the defensive and offensive tools required. In the years ahead it may well be that there are other ways of tracking submarines besides the use of aircraft. The United States Defense Advanced Research Projects Agency, DARPA, is looking for unmanned underwater vehicles, some that will track and follow submarines and others that will operate in very deep oceans listening for sounds thousands of miles away. Clearly a chain of fixed sensors between Greenland, Iceland and the UK is a very effective defensive barrier as was used in the Cold War but with the advent of much quieter submarines perhaps other protective means need to be found.

Further discussion of this fascinating subject is outside the remit of this book but it can only be a matter of time before unmanned aircraft, friendly submarines and satellites are all enlisted to keep a 24/7 global watch on all the world's submarines. The situation could even become more complex if submarines follow the example of aircraft and become unmanned. We already have pilots thousands of miles distant controlling their airborne machines gathering reconnaissance information or attacking targets; it does not take much imagination to conceive of submarines being controlled in a similar way, a rather frightening thought.

3 NIMROD MR2

The Nimrod was a complex aircraft and it only succeeded as well as it did because of near-perfect crew co-ordination and co-operation. It carried both sensors for the crews to find submarines and shipping and also the weapons to destroy them if needed. These sensors included radar for finding targets, acoustics for listening underwater, ESM for identifying radars, and MAD for finding a submarine's magnetic presence. To find the submarine the information from all these sensors had to be analysed, which required teamwork from the separate operators using a lot of computers and supporting software. There were the flight deck crew who flew the aircraft and put it in the right place, the tac team (especially the tac nav who was frequently the captain and mostly drove the whole effort by assimilating and utilizing all the information) the wet team who monitored the sonobuoys and operated the cameras and the dry team who operated the radar, ESM and radios. A good crew was a lesson to all in teamwork, it seemed there was no finer working machine.

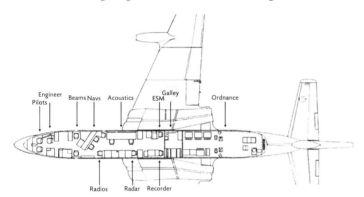

Nimrod MR2 crew positions

To help the reader understand what all the crew members did, this chapter first shows each position with an explanation of his/her crew function. The actual tools, that is the sensors and weapons, are explained in the second section.

FLIGHT DECK

The MRs 1 and 2 pilots' panels were conventional for the time with a Smiths Mk 6 instrument system, attitude indicator and horizontal situation display. The engine control cocks were between the seats on the central console and the hydraulic control system levers were in the panel above the pilots' heads; however the rest of the systems were controlled by the flight engineer.

Not visible is the searchlight

joystick, just to the right of the straps over the top of the right-hand (RH) seat. The 70M candlepower carbon rod, once struck, turned night into day and scared the living daylights out of many a drug smuggler. It couldn't be operated on the ground as it needed flying speed airflow to cool it. Once struck it had to stay on for twenty seconds with a maximum of sixty seconds and then had to cool for four times the time it had been on before re-use (normally the time it took to get back around to the target or survivor in the water).

PILOT'S INSTRUMENT PANEL

For convenience the RH (co-pilot's) panel is shown – although the left-hand (LH) seat was designated as the 'first pilot' position and the RH seat as the co-pilot; the basic layout was the same on both sides and in practice the pilots would alternate on each sortie as the nosewheel steering was only operable from the LH seat. This meant that only 'rollers' or touch and go circuits could be done from the RH seat; taxiing, take-offs and final landings were all done from the LH seat, so if the pilots didn't alternate, the co-pilot would miss out on practising a large part of the duties but a lot depended on the nature of the sorties, the experience of the co-pilot and the weather at the airfields.

At the top was the ever useful stopwatch, surrounded by various warning lights – from an era before a central warning panel became the norm. Below that were the routine basic instruments which displayed no tactical information. It was up to the pilots to build their own situational awareness from the information gleaned over the intercom. Of note, on the yoke are two buttons: 'C' was to release conventional weapons, and 'N' was to release nuclear weapons – obviously this was wired into several fail-safe switches.

BANK ANGLE LIMITATIONS

RH (co-pilot's) panel. A typical view through the window (top right)! When manoeuvring over submarines and other objects, large bank angles were not unusual. The rules were no more than 30^0 at 200ft above the sea or the ground, 40^0 at 300ft, 50^0 at 400ft and 60^0 at 500ft.

FLIGHT ENGINEER'S STATION

Engineer's panel – the air engineer was responsible for managing all the aircraft's systems: engines, fuel, hydraulics, electrics, air conditioning, oxygen and air-to-air refuelling. He carried

out his initial aircraft preparation, pre-flight checks and fault diagnosis, liaising with the crew chief and his team long before the bus arrived at the bottom of the steps with the full crew. He also worked with the route nav for on-task planning and fuel calculations.

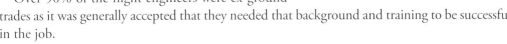

The first pilot was in charge of the flight deck but it was the engineer who generally had the greatest knowledge of all the systems, especially during emergencies, resolving them often in conjunction with the whole crew, especially when the four Ds were carried out: Drills, Discuss, Diagnose, Decide.

Over 90% of the flight engineers were ex-ground trades as it was generally accepted that they needed that background and training to be successful in the job.

TAC AREA

The 'tac area': shown closest is the routine navigator (route nav) whose duties were mostly of the traditional type, managing the navigation equipment – using GPS and other systems for positioning, monitoring the pilots, ensuring the aircraft didn't stray out of its area or into someone else's territorial waters, maintaining communication with any other aircraft in the vicinity, maintaining a graph paper plot for the sortie records and as a backup, liaising with the engineer concerning fuel calculations, sonobuoy management, managing the datalink (Link 11) system and aiding the tactical navigator with his duties.

Behind him is the tactical navigator (tac nav), running the whole show. With help from the crew, he managed all the sensor inputs to produce the 'end effect', a successful mission. He directed the pilots to put the aircraft in the place he wanted it to be to carry out his wishes. He was responsible to the captain (if it wasn't himself) for the efficient application of the crew and aircraft to the task it was set. He also controlled the bomb bay contents, switches and settings – he was the man who 'pushed the button' (unless he let the pilots do it!)

Behind him, standing, is the air electronics officer (AEO) who co-ordinated and quality controlled the sensors in conjunction with the lead operators. He was the only crew member without a specific sensor or equipment to operate, hence was best placed to stand back from the action and apply level-headed decisions to situations where sometimes everyone else was operating to their maximums.

To the right is the radio operator, looking after most of the communications in and out of the aircraft, ranging from Satcom, HF, V/UHF, FM, utilising teletype, voice and, in the worst of eventualities, a morse key was retained as the final backup!

In the background is the acoustics station.

Above left to right: nav bench; route nav; tac nav

NAV AREA

GENERAL VIEW

The blank panel above the tac nav screen was where the nuclear weapons switches were positioned. To his right were the switches and settings panel for the bomb bay stores and weapons, all made live with the master armament safety switch (MASS) (unseen).

ACOUSTIC AREA

AQS 901 MR2(left) facing forwards. Two complete processors enabling sixteen sonobuoys to be monitored, half in green (monochrome) and half in full colour with the late addition of the replacement screen. This

was the last processor to use paper printouts, seen either side of the operator's keypad. Each of the two printers per station printed to 28" wide paper as an addition to the screen information. To utilise fully this facility the printouts had to be allocated across the whole of the paper and if the 'checkers' were stood behind watching then any unused slots would have a tree drawn on them to symbolize the waste of paper!

AQS 971 in the MR2 after 2000 (right) facing aft. Again, two complete processors enabling thirty-two sonobuoys to be monitored in full colour. Obviously two less screens seems like a step back but the processor and the displays more than made up in the leap forward that was taken. The system was generally easier to use but because there was a great increase in the options available to the operator, losing the third acoustics operator was a definite drawback.

In both cases extra equipment was stored above the operators' heads, for the 901 the panel concealed the black boxes (line replaceable units – LRUs) that drove the screens as well as the tape unit where the software was loaded; this had been sourced from the Chieftain tank, used by them to load the gun stabilization programme! The units in the case of the 971 were the LRUs that drove the whole processor. Also housed there were the Wescam processor, software and tape recording unit.

WESCAM

Wescam station – aft of acoustics. The large central screen was the master screen to which all the equipment could be slaved. The three small screens were for each of the lenses: IR, EON, EOW with a master control panel below. To the left a standard keyboard with a joystick to the right. On the far right is the moving map panel.

In this position previously had been the acoustics laptop (training and programming unit, TPU) used amongst other things to provide synthetic training. The 'clockwork mouse' as it was known was a computer-generated submarine target de-

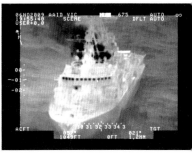

signed to allow ASW training to take place on the 971 with which the whole crew, apart from the dry team, could then interact.

RADAR STATION

Searchwater radar was designed to detect a submarine mast breaking the surface in a sea state 3 to 4, out to thirty nautical miles, which it usually succeeded in doing. The range scales were

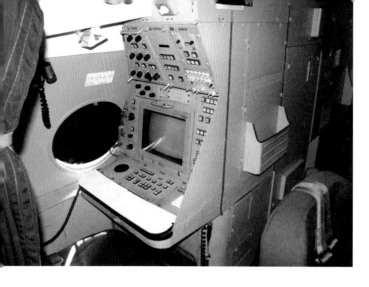

28, 50, 100 and 200nm. Whilst it wasn't a synthetic radar using extensive computer processing, the use of high resolution displays enabled operators to identify the generic type of ship, merchant vessel etc, and measure it and its visible features to an accuracy of fourteen feet. Despite Searchwater being 1950s technology, at its withdrawal from service in 2010 it was still the most effective maritime radar in the world.

ESM STATION

Yellowgate was a software-driven ESM system which was designed to tune to the frequencies of known radars and dwell long enough to detect them if they transmitted. Its frequency coverage was sufficient to cover all radars of interest. The two wingtip pods containing the receivers were joined to each other by a very expensive continuous cable. Also at this station was the magnetic anomaly detector (MAD) consisting of the 'sting in the tail', the MAD boom, a magnetometer which was located as far as possible from the plane's ferrous components, a black control box and paper trace located above the two main screens. This system was used to pinpoint the location of a submerged submarine by identifying its magnetic footprint. In times of war this sensor was accurate enough on its own strength to allow a torpedo drop. The Nimrod self-defence suite was also managed here for operations in hostile airspace. It consisted of four external ultra-violet sensors controlled by various computers and chaff/flare dispensers.

RECORDER STATION

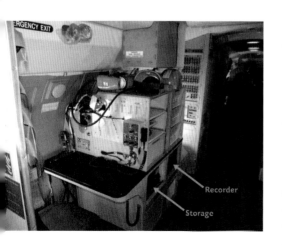

The recorder station was where the recording devices for the mission data were installed. The 'black box' (which was in fact orange/red) was in the tail as per most aircraft for survivability and only recorded a limited amount of data. The mission data went on a 28-track tape to allow most of the flying and sensor information to be replayed in the greatest of detail on the ground. Some MPAs had the ability to do short replays in the air but not the Nimrod. The enormous dual 'one inch' Ampex tape-recording system was replaced in the early nineties by a much smaller singular system in the format of a large VHS cassette. A much lighter and more easily maintained machine than it replaced, the black storage box and recorder itself can be seen in the bottom right of the picture.

Ancillary equipment such as the TICMS (thermal imaging common module system) repeater screen, explained in the next section, and, subsequently, the AIS ship-tracking system laptop fitted after 9/11 were also installed. AIS is a system for tracking ships which are fitted with AIS equipment for transmitting GPS position and other data on VHF marine channels. Above the stowage positions can be seen the emergency portable oxygen set and above that the HF aerial tuning units. In the latter was also the aperture for pulling in the long external HF aerial wires should one break (lightning strike etc). Also shown with the curly lead attached was the MICS remote station, another supplementary comms system explained in Chapter 10.

GALLEY STATION

The galley table was fitted with the video streaming equipment before it was all integrated into the Wescam position. Its normal appearance is on the right and it would be covered in sausage rolls in foil trays or steaks ready for the oven. On SAR callouts the long life dry rations (tins) were opened here with the aircraft tin opener or a curved aircrew dinghy knife to be poured into the big cooking pot or mixed into individual trays to cook up a 'Honkers stew'(see Glossary), the Nimrod staple diet on SAR, named as it looked the same going in as it did coming out. If on a long transit from one place to another with groundcrew, then the table would be covered in newspapers, playing cards, HM Customs declaration sheets, coffee cups and sweets. Smoking was only banned from Nimrod aircraft in the early nineties so paper cups half filled with water and fag butts were the order of the day up until this time as well.

In the top right corner of the picture (right) can be seen the three sockets for the underfloor CO_2 fire extinguisher, plumbed to the hydraulic, aileron and elevator bays.

ORDNANCE

The Nimrod had four sonobuoy launchers, two fixed and two rotary. The fixed launchers had a door hinged near the floor which opened up, allowing the buoy to be loaded and a rubber seal allowing it to be used at any height with the aircraft fully pressurised. When the buoy was

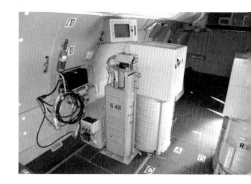

due to be launched another pressurised door opened up at floor level to allow the buoy to fall free (similar to a submarine's torpedo tubes). The other two launchers held six buoys each but because they rotated like a six-gun to position the selected buoy over the release tube, they could only be used when the aircraft was depressurised at relatively low level. All the launchers could be loaded at any stage of the sortie, sometimes even on the ground, but normally only when the radio frequency spectrum in the operating area had been checked to ensure there was no stray RF to block the channels of the sonobuoys the crew intended to use. The Nimrod fleet was allowed to drop buoys on any one of ninety-nine allocated channels in the VHF band.

The photo below shows an operator loading a DIFAR buoy into one of the two fixed launch-

ers. Over his shoulder is the aircraft entrance ladder. On the left are the multiple buoy storage racks.

Beyond are the two larger rotary unpressurised launchers. All the settings to enable the operator to load the buoys as the navs required were shown on the sonobuoy loading displays (SLDs), a small screen, one of which can be seen in the top of the picture at the bottom of page 45.

Additional ancilliary equipment was also installed in Ordnance such as the talk-through equipment, a system installed to allow the Nimrod to be used as an autonomous re-broadcast platform.

A number of other equipments resided in Ordnance; the LOX bottle/s, Link 11 hardware crate, various communications gear, the avionics cooling fans and, until it was made obsolete in the mid nineties, the awesome retro launcher. This was an eight-bar-relled gun that fired flares backwards out of the fuselage at the same speed as the plane was flying forward so that the highly flammable phosphorous flare dropped into the sea exactly where the Nimrod was for positioning purposes pre-GPS. This was the cause of more than a few nasty (but small) fires that could be very difficult to put out.

BOMB BAY

The bomb bay, one of the largest in NATO, had seven positions where bomb carriers could be placed to enable the aircraft to carry a large arsenal of weapons including amongst others nine Stingray torpedoes! Ordinarily for flying operations the bomb bay would always contain at least an ASR pack (dinghy plus a pair of survival packs) so that the aircraft was always able to take up airborne SAR duties at a moment's notice. This add-on was what really changed the look of the Comet, culminating in the point at the nose where the radar was positioned.

SENSORS AND WEAPONS

In this section the sensors are discussed together with the supporting analysis systems and the weapons carried. As will be seen, the capability of the sensors and the integration of their in-formation improved considerably between the MR1 and the MR2 and again between the MR2 and the MRA4. The information in this section is deliberately quite detailed to illustrate the enormous amount of work that was involved in constantly improving both the technology and the operating techniques to maintain the Nimrod's capabilities in all its roles, anti-submarine, search and rescue and reconnaissance over land and sea. If it seems a little complex that is because it was and required highly skilled operators to maximise the results.

NIMROD RADAR

The radar in the Nimrod was in some ways the primary sensor for the aircraft since it was used in most of the aircraft's tasks: SAR, land battles and searching for submarines, though in the latter case it could only look out for snorkels; once a possible target had been located the primary sensor system was the sonobuoy.

The original radar in the MR1 was the ASV21 inherited from the Shackleton Mk3 but it was the introduction of the Searchwater radar in the MR2 that really made the Nimrod a world-leading reconnaissance aircraft. Situated over the wing on the port side, the radar operator was the aircraft's eyes and, unlike any other sensor, the radar would usually be employed from take-off to landing, albeit with its priorities changing as the flight progressed.

Searchwater was a processed radar system, meaning that although in essence it worked as any other radar, transmitting a pulse and timing its return, the system would analyse several returned pulses before a positive return would be displayed to the operator. This, combined with frequency agility, reduced the number of false returns (clutter from rough seas for example) on the screen, thus lessening the operator's workload and allowing him to work more effectively, since the exact processing techniques employed would vary with the mode selected to optimise the system for each specific task.

Because one of the main roles of the radar was to spot submarines, it had a special feature to enable the radar to display 'unprocessed' data instantaneously. This was required because a submariner is never keen to stick anything out of the water, although on occasion this would be necessary since, as previously explained, a diesel boat has to draw in air for the engines when charging its batteries or when it is necessary to have a peek through the periscope. Whatever is protruding out of the water will be as small as possible and be there for as short a time as prudent. However, though the radar's pulse compression techniques ensured that a small contact would always be received, this processing might either disregard it as unwanted clutter, or it might take too long to be displayed to the operator so that by the time the aircraft could react the submarine had gone.

This extra feature introduced a second route from scanner to display which cut out almost all of the processing, enabling the operator to see 'processed' and 'raw' returns overlapping on the same display (or select one or the other) thus having the best of both worlds. To discriminate between the raw and processed returns they were displayed in different colours (red for processed and green for raw) as opposed to the old monochrome display, therefore the upgrade is often referred to as the introduction of colour Searchwater.

The radar operator had three different types of display available known as the Plan Position Indicator (PPI), B-Scope and A-Scope:

a. Plan Position Indicator (PPI) – a ground-stabilised, north-orientated display, used to show contacts on 28, 50, 100 and 200 nm ranges. The display also presented track and heading marker, range rings, IFF and other target markers.
b. High Resolution Display (HRD) B-Scope – provided an expanded view of a selected area on the PPI display under the direction of the rollball, resulting in a square with sides of several miles length depending on the selected range scale.
c. HRD A-Scope – used in conjunction with the 28, 50 and 100 nm ranges to obtain target length measurement, to an accuracy of ±14 feet, and target classification.

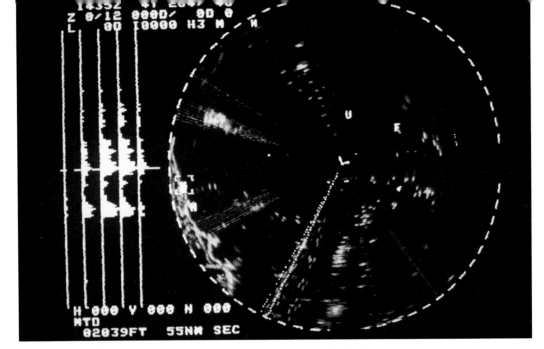

B Scope   PPI Mode

Above: Searchwater radar display; *Below:* Searchwater radar antenna

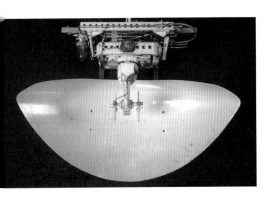

The first priority for the radar operator, as for all crew, was always flight safety. Flying around as low as 200 feet, over sea as well as land, presented some real dangers. In the United Kingdom area there were many oil rigs scattered all over the North Sea which presented the most obvious danger. Another risk, but not to the crew, was spoiling some innocent mariner's day by dropping any one of the required stores on or through their vessel. Whatever the task being carried out the radar operator always needed to be alive to these risks.

SONOBUOYS USED IN THE NIMROD

Once the submarine was underwater the radar could not be used and the primary sensor was the sonobuoy with its supporting processing computation. When really close to a submarine there was the additional MAD detector. The manufacturers of sonobuoys were continually having to sell their wares and all the information below on sonobuoys is available from marketing pamphlets. This section explains how the sonobuoys improved through the years from the MR1 to the MR2 and MRA4; for the aficionado some of the sonobuoys are identified by their numbers.

In the beginning sonobuoys were five feet tall, nine inches wide, weighed up to 38.1kg ('C size' buoys) and had to be carried in the bomb bay; furthermore they were very expensive and were evaluated by the crew as costing the same as a mini car. As technology advanced during the life of the Nimrod the buoys got smaller, lighter and more capable at the same time. Once the buoys could be carried in the aircraft they all had a common diameter size of 124mm so that they would fit in the launchers. Their length varied and for the record there were A size (CAMBS, ALFEA, Ranger, Barra) – 914mm , G size (DIFAR, HIDAR) – 419mm, F size

(LOFAR, Bathy) – 305mm.

The buoys drifted in the ocean so it was important for the operator to know their position. The later ones solved this problem by having on-board GPS receivers transmitting their positions but all the earlier ones required the aircraft to home to its transmissions for position updates.

The buoys weighed between 4kg and 18kg which required no mean effort when loading them into launchers for seven hours solid in a busy ASW sortie. During the tracking of a difficult target the aircraft had to be thrown around the sky to maximise the chances of keeping hold of the target, frequently resulting in up to 2g being pulled making the 18kg buoy weigh 36kg! Couple that with a trip in a storm or a bumpy dark night and the result was that

Loading the buoys

heroics were sometimes needed to load the buoys, especially when one considers all 200 plus sonobuoys could be used on a single busy trip. No wonder the operators loading the buoys were called wet men!

The Nimrod's later sonobuoys were all made by Ultra Electronics who are pre-eminent on both sides of the Atlantic for designing and making sonobuoys, both passive to listen without the submarine knowing it was being located and active to close in for the kill.

PASSIVE SONOBUOYS

Passive buoys which did not alert the quarry were the preferred method of starting a search. The early ones used in the MR1 were called Jezebell sonobuoys but since they could not identify from where the sound was coming, that is they were non-directional, the task of determining the submarine's position was not very easy. These American-built buoys were called LOFAR (LOw Frequency And Recording), resulting in the SSQ41 Jez buoy in 1965; the fact that 213,000 of these 'A' size buoys were built for use by the Nimrod MR1 (between 1969 and 1978) nevertheless shows how effective they were. Ultra Electronics obtained the licence from the American company Sparton and produced the UK version of the Jez buoy, T30059 (T30068 – calibrated version).

80s style sonobuoy

The Jez buoy was used for area searches and localization only. It processed sound information by analyzing the sounds in the sea into their frequency components and displaying the information on a continuously moving paper printout in a frequency versus time format. Because each type of surface ship and submarine has a unique frequency, 'fingerprint', the operator would be able to identify the type and possibly the nationality of the target, given the best of conditions. This was a highly skilled, scientifically based art. The operator could identify a target as ship or submarine (or marine life), identify the propulsion system as nuclear, diesel, steam, gas, or combinations thereof etc as well as the number of engine cylinders, propeller shafts, blades, pumps, generators, motors etc. Tactical information such as speed and, in the case of submarines, depth, could be ascertained by application of a bit of science and maths! The output from Jezebell went on to four side by side 3" printouts. Once a submarine was detected with Jezebell, then Julie, an active system described below, could be used to help refine the position when cleared to do so.

There were quite a large number of different buoys at this time made by different countries with their own national identification. The LOFAR (SSQ904) British buoy, introduced in 1980, was the basic evolution of the modern small G-size buoy which contained the aerial, electronics package, cable for selectable depth and hydrophone which evolved into the SSQ906, basically a

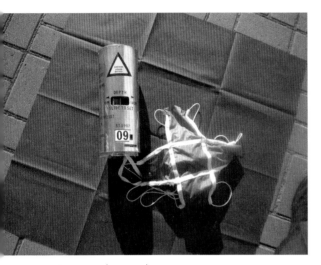

much better engineered buoy. To locate the submarine efficiently it was necessary to be able to process the information from the buoys simultaneously and, initially, sixteen was the maximum number possible but this was increased to thirty-two in the later years of the Nimrod as further improvements to the airborne processor became available. Other British buoys were the Bathy, Ranger and the Australian buoy called Barra.

The next improvement was to introduce direction finding ; the British DIFAR (Directional Frequency Analysis and Recording) (SSQ954, latterly the SSQ955) was introduced in the 1970s. In 1985, Ultra Electronics introduced the improved performance and reliability G-size DIFAR sonobuoy, ef-

Buoy with parachute

fecting the gradual phasing out of LOFAR. The buoy had two extra hydrophones giving a total of three enabling the two new directional 'ears' to compare the signal strength of a given line and display a bearing on the operator's screen. This was a massive leap in passive technology as a processed bearing from two displaced buoys gave an instant AOP (area of probability) where the

submarine must be: effectively triangulation. Over the years the buoys, the technology and the operating techniques advanced considerably to increase the accuracy of these bearings, but at the same time the opponent's submarines were getting ever quieter. This wasn't helped by the intervention of the American Walker-Whitworth spy ring, passing the secrets of the West directly to the Russians, leading to the Victor III, Akula, Sierra and Oscar generation submarines.

Meanwhile the Australians had developed a buoy called the Barra (SSQ801) in the 1970s, called the 981 when built in Britain; it was a very sophisticated device which deployed twenty-five hydrophones on five 9ft arms when submerged in the form of an array. This gave great accuracy at the higher frequencies and, in addition, the buoy had the ability to sample large bands of the acoustic spectrum, enabling it to exploit a wide broadband and diffuse data very well thus making it possible to recognise different ships and possibly submarines. Unfor-

DIFAR buoy with control panel

tunately the Russians managed to quieten their submarines in response which rendered the buoy much less useful compared with its ever-improving rival, the DIFAR, which relied upon signal strength rather than frequency. There was an associated difficulty with the Barra in that the large amount of data that was transmitted from the buoy to the aircraft due to the number of hydrophones resulted in a burden on the analysing computer's processor, which meant extra work was required to display meaningful information from the buoy. Altogether it was more labour intensive in comparison with the DIFAR for a similar result which meant that it had only a relatively light use by the Nimrod fleet.

Because the speed of sound varies significantly with water temperature, it was also desirable to measure the temperature at various depths to enable the range calculations to be carried out as accurately as possible, particularly with active buoys. To this end the Bathy buoy (SSQ36 to SSQ937) was developed which determined the local speed of sound in water. The temperature sensor would descend from the buoy's surface electronics package at a pre-determined rate and transmit the measured temperature to the aircraft, allowing the processor to display a simple SVP (sound velocity profile) trace to the operator which could be interrogated and saved for reference. This data, together with ambient noise measurements, could also be fed into another algorithm in the processor to determine accurately any changes to detection ranges, ex-

Barra depth and life settings

tremely useful in the airborne environment and a new feature with the introduction of the more advanced processor, the 971 (see below).

ACTIVE SONOBUOYS

It was necessary to use active sonobuoys transmitting audio pulses when an echo was required from the submarine. In the very early days Julie was in effect the active sonobuoy system and its function was to listen to the returns from a small explosive charge called a 'practice depth charge'. The system used audio and paper tape recording with the results calibrated for water temperature. Unlike later buoys the Julie was said to be expensive and a 15-buoy Julie circle was nicknamed 'the Cadillac pattern' as one could allegedly buy a car for the price of the buoys, but of course in wartime it would have been cheap at the price.

The American Ranger buoy (SSQ47) was the next active buoy to be developed in the 1970s and was the last buoy to be deployed from the Nimrod without a parachute. It had four aluminium spring-loaded blades at one end of the buoy, so that they opened up upon deployment into the airstream and slowed the buoy to avoid damage on water entry. The asymmetric design of the blades caused a rotation effect which added stability in the air. Unfortunately for the inexperienced, it was quite easy to load the buoys into the launcher the wrong way up so that when it was released, the blades would jam inside the launcher which often required a fire-axe and much effort to resolve! Upon receiving information back from the buoy, the processor displayed it in a simple raw format which meant it was just as effective to simply monitor the ping aurally and do the measurement with a stopwatch and brief the contact on intercom. Being an omni-directional buoy there was no bearing information, so unless there was a good idea of the sub's position through other means (DIFAR or visual) another Ranger had to be used which resulted in two fixes where the tac nav's two fix circles, one from each buoy, would overlap.

Without any more information being available from acoustics, a MAD run was required to resolve the ambiguity.

The British CAMBS buoy, Command Activated Multi-Beam Sonobuoy (SSQ963), was developed in the early 1980s. This buoy could be sent to various depths and its ping was controlled by the wet men so it could be started, stopped or its type changed depending on the depth of

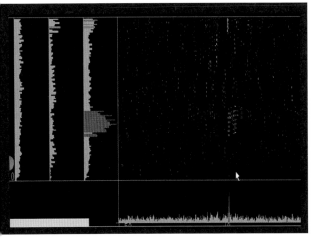

CAMBS display – target in pink

the submarine or its range from the buoy. This was initially carried out by the operator using buttons, but later via the software as it evolved. Eventually four depths could be utilised to enable the operator to send the hydrophone array through the oceanographic layers, since they could act as barriers to sound waves and therefore mask the returns. Additionally, depending on the distance of the submarine, the operator could alter the timing between each ping and the length of the ping, known as the refresh rate, to improve the accuracy of determining the submarine's position. All this relied upon relative movement being observed from the submarine, which meant it had to either be going towards or away from the buoy to display Doppler movement. If this wasn't the case and the target displayed relatively low speed then the ping frequency could be increased to provide its own Doppler. CAMBS was a fantastic buoy – the guys in the submarine knew generally that with two of them nearby, one in each of the two main modes, with an update rate of up to three seconds then the game was up and a torpedo would be the next thing to listen for.

The final development in active sonobuoys was MSA (multi-static active). Trials had taken place where a field of digital passive buoys was deployed, which had embedded GPS and were called HIDAR, High Instantaneous Dynamic range Analysis and Recording (SSQ955), a British development of the DIFAR. They received returns from a handful of special active 'pinger' sonobuoys in the pattern, the ALFEA, Active Low Frequency Electro-Acoustic (SSQ926) buoy. This technology relied upon the passive buoy receiving the active ping as it was reflected from the target. The beauty of this system was that the ping didn't have to travel

Mk84 SUS

all the way back from the submarine to the active buoy, having only to travel to the nearest passive buoy, hence reducing the submarine's chance of knowing from where it is being pinged, the 'ESM advantage', and effectively producing much greater detection ranges. This new system is possibly the biggest step forward in decades but alas cannot be used by the UK as there are now no marine patrol aircraft to utilise it. A demonstration of its use can be found on web site www.ultra-sonar.com/play_video3.php.

Two more deployable products available on the Nimrod were the SUS and EMATT. The

Mk84 SUS (signal underwater sound) was a device a little smaller than a LOFAR weighing only 2.7kg, which was used to signal one of five different codes to a friendly submarine by means of a two-tone acoustic signal. Mostly it was used to signal a practice torpedo attack, a request to surface for communications or, more importantly, to signal the proximity of a fishing boat.

EMATT, the Sippican Expendable Mobile ASW Training Target, was used for training as it simulated a submarine sailing the seas. It was launched like a regular sonobuoy and was a dynamic target, following a pre-programmed 'run-plan' for several hours, transmitting an acoustic signal to allow tracking, being designed to react to active sonar and also to transmit a signal to replicate a MAD mark. It was utilized by Nimrod crews for several years but it finally succumbed to the more flexible and much greater range of options offered by the aircraft's own on-board laptop-based acoustic simulator.

EMATT

Sonobuoys are clearly vital to catch and if necessary destroy submarines. Practising is also necessary and it was not unusual for Nimrods to take off with 200 sonobuoys. It is difficult to establish how much these buoys cost the Ministry of Defence but allegedly the DIFAR buoys were £450 and the CAMBS £6,000; clearly the loss of the Nimrod was a blow not only to the defence of the country but also to the sonobuoy manufacturer, since on a training sortie as many as 30 CAMBS might be dropped and occasionally 100 DIFARs.

NIMROD ACOUSTICS PROCESSING

The returns from the sonobuoys had to be processed and again as technology advanced the processing of the sonobuoy information increased dramatically.

Mk1C sonics – The Mk1C system (which included both the processor system and the sonobuoys) evolved in the 1950s when the then Ministry of Aviation decided to develop directional passive and active sonobuoys. Entering service, first on Shackletons then on Nimrod MR1, it was phased out after some twenty-eight years with the introduction of the Nimrod MR2. On the MR1, the Mk1C was located in the forward acoustics station (ie starboard, to the rear of the AEO's position).

The signal from the buoys was fed to a small double beam CRT screen which could display either one active or two passive buoys, the audio from them being fed to the operator's headphones.

AQA-5 – acoustic processing system; manufactured by Western Electric and Emerson; it was used in the American P-3, S-2 aircraft and the MR1. The AQA-5 received the Emerson modification in the mid 1970s which was a major advance in capability, providing an increase in the frequency cover from 310Hz to 1280Hz and two windows to 'zoom in' on frequencies of interest: however, it could still only monitor eight buoys on the paper printout display, the only directional information, which was not hugely accurate.

AQS 901 – This was the first system with proper screens to display data. Later in its life it gained a colour screen per system for colour DIFAR data. There were two systems fitted side-by-side in the aircraft with an operator per system and a co-ordinator (lead wet) positioned in the middle. As the submarines became progressively quieter there was a requirement for patterns of up to thirty-two buoys to locate them, resulting in 'dual aircraft prosecutions' to enable this as the Nimrod 901 fit could only monitor sixteen buoys at a time. This of course was very expensive, having two aircraft and two crews 'on task' at one time to locate a target, so the requirement for a new, thirty-two buoy capable processor was issued.

AQS 971 – This was the selected processor, based on the Canadian AN/AQS 503 and fitted to the MR2 in autumn 2000. Luckily the RAF had put the right people in place to write the requirement, shortlist and choose this processor with the correct amount of interaction with the supplying company. The result was a tremendous machine with a British interface (front end), developed with the aid of Nimrod acoustic operators, a true success story. Not only did it give the crews the first advance in submarine detectability for decades, it gave the Nimrod fleet a look into the future, as this was the basis for the selected acoustic suite for the MRA4. The Canadian 503 is still in use today and is described in its promotional write ups as being developed partly by the RAF.

The signals received from the buoys at the processor were displayed to the operator in a number of different ways but with different methods of displaying target strength, Doppler and bearing from the buoy. The three lines (or 'tonals') seen below emanating from the target (submarine, ship – anything transmitting sound in the water) could be seen to change colour over several minutes from green through blue to pink and orange. Utilising the colour wheel on the left the operator could see that the 'target' had passed from the SW of the buoy to the NE giving a rough track. The laws of Doppler allowed the crew to measure the change in frequency of a particular sound observed from the submarine which in turn gave a speed. Knowing this speed it was then possible to work out distance from the buoy. The situation is analogous to listening to a train passing close by with the eyes shut; you can tell how fast it is travelling by the change in the engine note (frequency) as well as the volume. Voila, submarine tracking!

When the techniques of using Doppler were fully understood, submarine tracking became

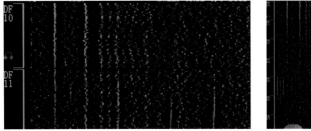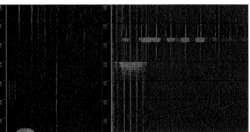

AQS971 passive buoy display (*left*); 8-buoy display with greater frequency range hence more data/colour (*right*)

easier but basically a reasonably close-range CPA (closest point of approach) on one or two buoys was required to get a good fix on the sub's position. Once it had been located any other sonobuoys in the water which had been sown as part of that 'pattern' were then disregarded from the processor as the submarine wasn't there!

From there on the crew analysed the information being received in the aircraft to determine the PCS (position, course and speed) of the target so they knew where to lay the next pattern of sonobuoys.

During the tracking of an actual submarine the lead wet man, the route navigator, the AEO and the tac nav would all have to assess the information available to come up with an independent position, course and speed, all within a small percentage of each other to enable a compromise to be calculated for the final solution. Should any one person differ from the others, another conversation would take place to thrash out the reason and hopefully refine the com-promise. Should this process falter then the next buoy pattern might go in the wrong place fol-lowed swiftly by losing the submarine! This decision making was repeated very rapidly, normally every ten to twenty minutes. Communication between the operators in the MR2 (and the MR1) was very much a labour-intensive process as it was the main method of sorting out prob-lems. It was probably a little easier in the MR2 as the sensors were able to pass much more data to the nav screen in the form of symbols, confidence level categories, directional trackers etc but these still needed to be backed up by a verbal report.

AQS 970 – This development took quite a while and finally had many advantages over the 971, not least the ability to monitor sixty-four sonobuoys. Unfortunately, as with most large con-tracts, a line had to be drawn in the sand somewhere in the development programme to allow the project to actually be built. This had the effect of almost allowing the MR2's 971 to steal a march over the 970 as it continued to be developed while the latter was frozen in time.

All this changed with the MRA4 which was a much more integrated aircraft in that the in-formation flow between the sensors and the tacco (name change from tac nav) required much less talking. There was therefore a marked difference in the intercom, the MR2 being sometimes hectic when the situation was difficult, the MRA4 being much quieter – almost serene. With the MR2 especially, and indeed the other marks, this was all aided by the standard operating procedures (SOPs), a written set of methods and working practices for every situation as a proper rigidly enforced structure, which made life so much easier. If each crew member knew exactly where and when their input was due then everyone else knew what to expect and this did make life very much simpler. The trouble came when the crew was swamped with data, which is where a solid, professional, worked-up crew came into their own.

Anti-submarine warfare using these tools and computer analysis was very much considered the 'Sport of Kings' by Nimrod crews in that only a good crew could excel requiring an enor-mous demand on brain power. Crews had to efficiently figure out exactly what the target was doing, agree completely amongst themselves without exception or re-analyse the whole deal, choose the best tactic for each given situation, fly the aircraft around the sky within the given airspace and geographic limitations to 'sow' the correct sonobuoys in the correct places, and do that all without error every twelve minutes or so. Crews would do this for up to seven hours at a time, quite tiring at 300ft over a pitch black ocean being buffeted during a storm for night after night. It was important to remember that the submarine foe was trying its best to evade the aircraft at the same time, utilizing their own skills – they lived in this environment for weeks at a time, their lives depended upon it, the Nimrod crew just went out for eight hours at a time! It was the bread and butter of the submariner, if they messed up they had much, much more to lose. All this isn't to say that the other Nimrod disciplines were any easier, just that ASW tended to concentrate many minds for long hours on occasions.

SIMULATION

Nimrod crews needed to be able to practise finding submarines, but real ones which were avail-able to help training were few and far between. Obviously a real submarine was ideal for prac-tising ASW, but only when it could be communicated with to provide exactly the amount of training the crew required at that moment. The only place available was in the Bahamas at the Atlantic Underwater Test and Evaluation Center (AUTEC) where communication between the Nimrod and the submarine was continuous and reliable via the NASA-like US Navy setup.

This however was enormously expensive so other ways to train had to be found.

A very clever substitute trainer, during the MR1 era called stage2, was installed opposite Hangar 3 at Kinloss in a small building and on a table 6ft square with simulated sonobuoys representing actual buoys which the aircraft had dropped in the Moray Firth close-by, the positions of which had been reported to the simulation team. A moving target was placed on the table connected to the sonobuoys and the 'bearings' of the target from the simulated sonobuoys were transmitted to the aircraft. Very Heath Robinson but definitely better than nothing. Records were kept so that there could be a debriefing after the flight.

With the MR2 came a new and integrated airborne crew trainer (ACT) that simulated submarine signatures for acoustics. It was located at the AEO table and was superseded with the advent of the 971 by a laptop-based simulator, this one sited at the aft acoustics station. All this meant that acoustics could track a fake submarine and the crew could react as if it were for real.

In addition to airborne training there was ground-based simulation in the purpose-built simulator building, where extensive training could take place and the pressure on a crew could be wound up to breaking point. At least the crews were still fed rations!

ASW TACTICS

Whilst, given a favourable target and lots of luck, the acoustics team could track a submarine effectively, prior to this the target had to be located. Good intelligence could sometimes allow sonobuoys to be laid in the correct position but given the low detection ranges that submarines offer (a figure that reduced throughout the life of the aircraft as submarine technology improved), this either required spot-on accuracy, or a huge number of buoys. Therefore radar would often be nominated as the primary initial detection sensor.

This obviously depended upon the target being decent enough to stick something above the water. As already discussed, a submarine captain will be reluctant to do this unless absolutely necessary. A further complication was the fact that submarines have their own ESM receivers and prior to commencing a snort, or protruding anything above the waves for any length of time, they would listen out for the presence of a hostile marine patrol aircraft (or any other hostile) radar. Therefore, despite the excellent performance of the radar, the chances of catching a submarine on the surface were much reduced.

In order to swing the advantage back a little in the hunter's favour the tactic of 'intermittent' scan was developed. Simply this meant that the radar would not transmit all of the time. The idea being that the target submarine would 'hear' no hostile radars and then commit to having to spend time with something above the waves. Having done so the operator would switch on the radar, and checkmate! Despite the apparent simplicity of this tactic, apparently an enormous amount of time was spent on the squadron discussing the finer details of exactly when and how to employ it.

Ultimately, ASW on radar was a simple task, but the operator still needed to remain alert, set the radar up correctly and investigate any new contact that appeared on the screen. When investigating small contacts it was up to the operator to decide, using the B and A scopes, whether it was worthy of further investigation. This was quite a responsibility as calling a 'non-sub' could compromise the integrity of the search plan (although as discussed, the integrity of any plan was always a matter for debate) whilst the other option, missing a real target, could have huge consequences. Unfortunately there are many things in the ocean that can appear very similar to submarine masts including any debris from shipping and fishing buoys. Schools of dolphins also looked surprisingly sub-like on a radar screen, and were even cheeky enough to move at about the same speed. Experience of live targets (and live dolphins) was the only way to build confidence in the analysis of radar contacts and it was noticeable in later years, with the drop in flying hours available, how much longer it took new operators to gain that familiarity. In any case it was always preferable to mistakenly have a look at some dolphins than mistakenly ignore a submarine.

So, having argued and decided upon a tactic, and possibly spent several hours remaining alert employing it, sustained by copious cups of coffee and doughnuts, finally the operator spots what he believes to be a sub. It was necessary to shout over the intercom: "CAPTAIN RADAR, HIGH CONFIDENCE SNORT, BEARING 275, RANGE 15, FILE 23". Ideally the shout would be made as loudly as possible, since the aircraft could have been on task for several hours with nothing to investigate, and thus levels of alertness might have dropped a little.

The whole crew then had tasks to carry out; initially the pilots would be turning onto the bearing and descending the aircraft ready for MAD procedures. The teapot would be abandoned mid brew as the two-man camera team raced to the port beam window, the radio operator would send out a FLASH message to the controlling authority and the navigators would be getting ready to drop sonobuoys as the aircraft approached the target.

Having indicated the radar file number on the initial call, the nav selected this file as the 'steer' thus giving the pilots an accurate indication and continuous update of the range and bearing to the target. If there were any technical problems then the radar operator would take over the homing manually, talking the pilots onto the target.

During the homing the radar operator would be watching the contact on the screen to check its course and speed and whether it remained on the surface. Should it remain there then, hopefully, the pilots would confirm a certain submarine and identify its type from whatever was above the water and get some intelligence photographs from the now open port beam window (the window was opened for photography to prevent distortion of the image, therefore the aircraft would be depressurised at low level).

More often than not however the submarine would go 'sinker' at some point during the homing. This was often the more difficult scenario, not least as at this stage there was no certainty that what the crew had homed to was a submarine. At a certain point on the run in the navigator would begin dropping sonobuoys, allowing the wetties to begin an underwater search. Additionally the aircraft would 'fly for MAD' which is described in the following paragraphs.

NIMROD ESM (ELECTRONIC SUPPORT MEASURES)

The MR1 ESM was called ARAR/ARAX and consisted of two large black boxes which were actually considered superior to the equipment which replaced it in the late 1980s, the early Yellowgate system, due to the lack of any delay in the computer-processing chain. It was fed by a large aerial in the top of the Nimrod's tail, which was the reason for the fibreglass 'canoe' up there, a much repaired piece of aerodynamics as any lightning strike often chose to exit here taking a chunk of it away at the same time.

The MR2 ESM system – known as Yellowgate – was operated from the same station as the MAD. ESM used antennae fitted on the wingtips to 'listen' for radar emissions. On receiving a signal the system would measure various parameters (frequency, pulse repetition frequency, pulse width, direction of arrival, signal strength). Each different radar design outputted a different set of parameters, and hopefully the operator, with some help from the system, would be able to identify which particular type of radar was being received and thus make some decisions about what platform was emitting the signal. For example, if a Type 996 radar was identified then the operator could be confident that a Royal Navy vessel was somewhere along the reported bearing as only the Royal Navy used that type of radar.

ESM operator's displays – note MAD display above

One challenge for the operator was remembering all of the parameters for those radar types likely to be encountered. Whilst the equipment did hold an electronic library which it would use to carry out automatic identification, it was not an exhaustive library and ambiguities did exist. Therefore operators were required to have a thorough knowledge of all the parameters of those radars likely to be seen, this requirement basically being the same as having to commit the phone book to memory.

ESM was something of a limited sensor. Firstly, submarines would very rarely switch their radar on, preferring to rely on their sonar systems to resolve the surface picture. Secondly, the radars used by submarines usually had nothing to distinguish their electronic signature from those used by civilian vessels. Additionally, the scenario most likely to cause a submarine to use its radar was in a busy surface environment when its radar was most likely to 'look' just like the radars coming from those same fishing boats so that the ESM would be of no help.

Finally a submarine is unlikely to leave its radar switched on for more than a couple of scans or rotations. Therefore even if the operator did receive and identify it the chances of having anything more than a bearing from the aircraft were slim; this therefore left a huge area of ocean to investigate (however receiving a radar signal did prove that the submarine was near the surface and thus there was a fighting chance of converting it to a radar homing).

NIMROD MAGNETIC ANOMALY DETECTION

MAD was very much a short-range submarine detection sensor. Due to this fact it was almost always employed in following up cueing from another aircraft sensor (such as a disappearing radar contact or acoustics). Its advantages were that it provided a very accurate position and, as it could search beneath the waves, it provided supporting evidence that what was being investigated was actually a submarine.

MAD was a superbly simple sensor, relying upon the earth's magnetic field. In basic terms the earth can be thought of as having a huge bar magnet inside it running from the North Pole to the South Pole. This creates a magnetic field across the surface of the earth which varies in intensity, being strongest at the poles. However, when considering an area of only a few square miles (such as when using MAD) then this field can be considered uniform. What the MAD system does is measure this magnetic field. Therefore under normal circumstances the reading would be constant (or a flat line on the paper trace that was used for the display).

If a lump of ferrous metal (like a submarine for example) is placed in this magnetic field it has the effect of creating a very local distortion (or anomaly) to the strength of the magnetic field. This would be detected by the MAD system as the aircraft flew over the top of the distortion giving a very accurate position. There were limitations to the system however, the strength of a magnetic field diminishes exponentially with distance, therefore the aircraft had to fly as low as possible over the water, ideally at the minimum height of 200ft. It also had to be pretty much right on top of the target, although this did have the advantage that any detection by the MAD system gave an accurate position. Finally, submarines are not the only lumps of ferrous metal that may be found in the water – pipelines, wrecks and ships could cause confusion and for this reason a map of known permanent features was carried.

The cry of 'MAD MARK!!' at the end of a radar homing was always a welcome sound, particularly to the radar operator who now knew it was unlikely that he had been deceived by dolphins and a real target had probably been detected.

NIMROD CAMERA – ELECTRO-OPTICS

The first evolution of this on the Nimrod was the Nimtan. This sensor was used in the beam positions and was succeeded by the hand-held TICMS (Thermal Imaging Common Module System), a large, heavy green lump that had to be man-handled into position and secured by means of a pin in the socket on the beam shelf, but only when the beam window was open! This was therefore a two-man operation, with the aircraft at a relatively low level and de-pressurised; the first operator would be handling the camera with its awkward bipod, the second operator opening the window and acting as safety man. This was all exacerbated by the fact that the first man couldn't communicate with anyone having his hands full leaving only his head to nod and gesticulate with. Of course the reason the sensor was being used was darkness, all helped by being stood next to an open window with the wind screaming past at 200mph – a little stressful sometimes! This piece of kit worked surprisingly well provided it was serviceable and set up correctly with electric cables and nitrogen cooling tubes spread across the floor to control boxes and TV repeaters further down the aircraft.

The next generation was a remotely mounted system called Sandpiper bolted to the underside of the starboard wing. Its controls were situated at the route nav position which was a little impractical if he was busy so more often than not a spare wet man ended up sitting on an upturned camera box to work the controls. This camera only had one IR lens.

During Operation Telic and the invasion of Iraq, an urgent operational requirement (UOR) was written to upgrade the system to provide a picture of increased resolution for intelligence gathering and/or a live overview of operations. Consequently in 2002, five Nimrods were fitted with the L-3 Wescam MX-15 (15" wide turret) electro-optical system in the same position Sandpiper occupied. It had three lenses; infrared (IR) with four zoom settings, electro-optic wide (EOW) with continuous zoom and electro-optic narrow (EON), a long fixed-length telephoto lens, the latter two in full colour. There was space for a further item, the laser rangefinder but this was not part of the UOR. The larger MX-20 was fitted with this item as standard. The whole system was situated at the aft end of the acoustics suite after the resident laptop and cradle had been moved. This was a more logical siting which also allowed for expansion and utilised the acoustics team whose role prior to this was much reduced during overland ops.

Wescam camera

During 2005 the Bendix observer king moving map system was fitted to the aircraft, another tremendous tool to aid the operation of the Wescam. The camera could be slaved to a position on the map and, equally, the place the camera was pointing at would be displayed on the same map, which could zoom in to a scale 'better than' Ordnance Survey mapping. Longhorn II, an Enterprise Control Systems product, was then installed, allowing two streaming video outputs of any of the Wescam images to be transmitted to a ground station, which might even have been a laptop in a Land Rover. This was absolutely invaluable to the troops in the thick of the action at the start of a conflict as nothing else could provide them with this information.

The whole system was known simply as Wescam for ease of reference on the intercom. Operation was a combination of the three lenses, moving map and screens to provide intelligence or simply additional information for the task at hand. The sensor took primacy on the mission, as opposed to being a secondary sensor, for instance when people or vehicle tracking, or pattern of life (POL) missions, which meant observing a scene over the course of many hours or days to ensure everything about the target was known, or at least as much as the time allowed. Typically the IR lens or thermal camera would be used to initially acquire a target as its picture appeared less cluttered than the other two cameras. During daylight a combination of the two EO lenses would then be employed and even at night-time they could be useful to view strong light sources. Obviously during night-time the IR lens was mostly prime.

The system was intended for use during the Nimrod's overland role but was a huge addition

MRA4 electro-optical search and detection retractable turret

to most Nimrod roles, providing another valuable set of eyes in most conditions except above cloud cover. In ASW, when already short of operators, it could be set to look ahead or scan side to side so that anyone near the main position or the route nav repeater screen could spot a submarine mast or a feather in the water (the wake remaining from a diving sub). Occasionally however, the person who was taking the teapot or choccy-bars around the aircraft for the crew, often someone with fresher eyes or just in the right place at the right time, would be the first to see the target, either using the 'mark one eyeball' through a window or by spotting it on another person's screen before they had. This obviously earned that person large amounts of brownie points, the reverse being true for the operator of the sensor at that moment.

The MRA4 was fitted with the Northrop Grumman nighthunter electro-optical search and detection system (EOSDS), a retractable turret installed in the old MR2 Doppler bay just be-

hind the nosewheel. Perversely it was procured for the MRA4 more than six years before the MX-15 for the MR2 and hence in some ways was an inferior sensor, one missing feature being the colour lenses.

VISUAL LOOKOUT

The Nimrod was well equipped for visual lookout and taking pictures manually. The port and starboard beam windows, just aft of the flight deck, were convex for extra visibility and opened for imaging in flight. The AEO window about 10 ft further back, on the starboard side only, was also convex but was fixed.

For night work the aircraft had a 70M candlepower light, steerable by use of the right-hand seat pilot's joystick.

View through night vision goggles

NIMROD WEAPONRY

TORPEDOES

Authentic/accurate figures on torpedo performance are still classified but some types with details are available.

Mk 44 Torpedo
Type: Active homing torpedo
Launch weight: 195kg (432lb)
Speed: 65k/h (30kts)
Range: 5,500m (3·4 miles)

Mk 46 Torpedo
Type: Active/passive homing torpedo
Launch weight: 235kg (517lb)
Speed: 83 k/h (45kts)
Range: 8,000m (5 miles)

ARMING WIRE

BATTERY PORT
COVER LANYARD

PRESETTER
CABLE

PARACHUTE
LANYARD

(GOLDEN YELLOW
BAND – HIGH EXPLOSIVE)

NOSE   WARHEAD   ELECTRONICS   POWER SUPPLY   MOTOR AND CONTROL

Stingray Production Warshot Torpedo (PWT)

Stingray Torpedo
Type: Active/passive homing torpedo
Launch weight: 267kg (589lb)
Speed: 83k/h (45kts)
Range: 11,000m (7 miles)

Three variants: Warshot / Exercise Variant Torpedo, EVT (behaves just like a warshot but warhead replaced by recovery and instrumentation section) / Training Variant Torpedo, TVT (inert and recoverable purely for exercise and drop purposes)

Above: B57 depth bombs;
Below: Sidewinder on Nimrod pylon

BOMBS

B-57 AS 550lb (not WE177) nuclear depth bomb
Type: Nuclear weapon
The Nimrod aircraft was certified for carriage of American nuclear depth charges from its entry into service in 1969. It has never been certified to carry British nuclear weapons. (Hansard 1993)

MISSILES

Sidewinder AIM 9G
Type: Air-to air-infrared guided missile
Weight: 87kg (192 lbs)
Diameter: 12·7cm (5in)
Fin span: 63cm (24·8in)
Range: 18km (11·2 miles)

HARPOON

Type: Radar-guided anti-ship
missile
Weight: 661kg (1,470lb)
Diameter: 34·29cm (13·5in)
Fin span: 91·44cm (3ft)
Speed: 855kph (531mph)
Range: 111+km (60+nm)

CONCLUSION

As can be seen the MR2 had
a very comprehensive crew
with wet and dry men and
was extensively equipped with
sensors and supporting computers being continually updated. This chapter clearly
demonstrates how the infor-

Nimrod dropping torpedo (*Crown copyright*)

mation from all the sensors was integrated in order to find the target and it was the teamwork
of all the crews that made the Nimrod so successful. As will be seen later, with the introduction
of the MRA4 not only was there a more efficient and effective mission system but a much better
simulation, including links between the pilots and the sensor operators, so that not only would
it have been first class in its performance but also very efficient in total operation since there
would have been the very minimum of training required in the air.

4 NIMROD ANTI-SUBMARINE AND ANTI-SURFACE UNIT WARFARE

INTRODUCTION

The Nimrod could do so many things but primarily it was conceived to fight the submarine which in later years it did extremely well as the radar and other sensors were improved, though as has been said, the task became harder as the submarines became quieter and took other defensive measures. Anti-submarine warfare is a fascinating subject and the very best of technology has to be used for the hunters to find the submarines and for the submarines to avoid being found. A lot of the sensors and techniques are still classified and as the older methods and tools are disclosed so new ones are invented. This chapter gives the reader just a brief insight into what the aircraft did and what it was like being a Nimrod operator. Towards the end of the chapter there are some recollections of tracking surface ships including drug runners.

Submarines come in all shapes and sizes and it would be a mistake to imagine that they are all nuclear powered and capable of firing ballistic missiles like the Trident SSBNs. There are submarines which fire cruise or guided missiles (SSGNs), nuclear attack submarines (SSNs), and diesel-powered hunter/killer submarines (SSKs). The method of propulsion is also vitally important since the more noise a submarine makes the easier it is for the aircraft sensors to detect; submarines that are diesel-electric powered can be almost absolutely silent if necessary

Below: Nimrod and Russian submarine (*Crown copyright*)

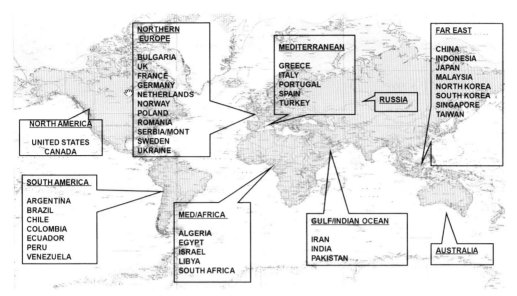

NORTHERN EUROPE	MEDITERRANEAN	FAR EAST
BULGARIA	GREECE	CHINA
UK	ITALY	INDONESIA
FRANCE	PORTUGAL	JAPAN
GERMANY	SPAIN	MALAYSIA
NETHERLANDS	TURKEY	NORTH KOREA
NORWAY		SOUTH KOREA
POLAND	RUSSIA	SINGAPORE
ROMANIA		TAIWAN
SERBIA/MONT		
SWEDEN		
UKRAINE		

NORTH AMERICA
UNITED STATES
CANADA

SOUTH AMERICA
ARGENTINA
BRAZIL
CHILE
COLOMBIA
ECUADOR
PERU
VENEZUELA

MED/AFRICA
ALGERIA
EGYPT
ISRAEL
LIBYA
SOUTH AFRICA

GULF/INDIAN OCEAN
IRAN
INDIA
PAKISTAN

AUSTRALIA

Countries with submarines worldwide

when on batteries underwater while nuclear-powered boats, which enable the boats to stay submerged for very long periods, require circulating pumps at all times to control their reactor temperature. However nuclear submarines were getting quieter and quieter and the later diesel-powered boats could run their engines underwater with on-board oxygen, so the task of the Nimrod was getting harder all the time.

While the Cold War was being fought the fact that the Nimrods were spending long hours tracking Russian submarines was kept absolutely secret as was the way the tracking was carried out. However, with the end of that war information was gradually released and so it is now possible in this chapter to relate some of the stories that previously have been classified. Of course, just as the Allies were trying to track Russian submarines, conversely the Russians were always trying to track the UK's nuclear ballistic missile submarines, SSBNs. Russian submarines would loiter off Faslane in the Clyde waiting for the SSBNs to depart or arrive and one of the Nimrod's roles then was the protection of UK SSBNs which can no longer be carried out.

Nevertheless it would be a mistake to imagine that it is no longer necessary to be able to track submarines since, for example, small submarines in the Strait of Hormuz for instance could wreak absolute havoc. One has only to imagine what might happen in the busy waters of the Gulf with all the oil tankers going backwards and forwards if hostile submarines were being operated in these crowded waters.

Most people do not realise how many countries in the world operate submarines. Clearly the Russians and the United States have the largest nuclear fleets with intercontinental missiles but there are a lot of other very capable submarines being operated by smaller countries.

Iran is a good example of a small country with submarines and it is situated right next to

Iranian Russian-built Kilo SSK submarine. The fleet had three Kilos and three North Korean midget subs

the Strait of Hormuz, reinforcing the need for anti-submarine capability. All navies are continually developing their submarines and making them harder to detect. Consequently the United

States is developing the Boeing P8 as its new anti-submarine aircraft fitted with the latest equipment and it cannot be long before this aircraft or a close equivalent is ordered by the UK to replace the cancelled Nimrod MRA4.

SEARCHING FOR SUBMARINES

As an observer and ex-test pilot it seems to me that searching for a submarine has one thing in common with test flying – hours of boring monotony plus occasional bursts of excitement. I found that this verbatim account by Justin Morris of chasing submarines seemed to describe the situation very well:

"Sitting on a barrier.

"In 1985 when I went to the careers office to put my papers in for AEOp (air electronics operator, now WSOp, weapon system operator) the sergeant there had a bit more of an idea about the job than most folk who hadn't a clue what we did. He sat me down and questioned my commitment by asking me how I would cope with the spying game, long hours of boredom waiting and hoping for the 'end-game'. A few short years later I was there, sitting watching my screen with twelve other brains sat around me, at low level over a vicious sea at night, pitting our wits against the opposition, trying to out-fox the Russians, week in week out, endlessly, for the short period of the Cold War that I was involved with. Ivan had stacks of submarines, some better than others thanks to the Walker-Whitworth family in the USA passing over our secrets to the other side (very much a two-sided game though) and we'd be out on 'Ops' sometimes for a month, each one for days and days at a time, Nimrods and our allies flying continuously, 24-hour coverage on one bit of ocean hundreds of miles away without any intended gaps. Days and days and days. The station infrastructure would groan at the seams under the relentless pressure of continuous flying; fuel (lucky we had that pipeline from Inverness installed in the Eighties), servicing, sonobuoys by the truckload, tons and tons of in-flight rations, the list goes on. Ivan had his job to do and we had ours, we couldn't afford to lose our grip on his whereabouts for a moment because he'd get away and become a nuisance. Yes, the perceived wisdom was that they had a huge organisation to run up which meant no one occurrence happened overnight, there was a build up. But we were dealing with a big bad bear, that had a temper and could indeed snap, so we had to be careful. That's not to say we didn't wind him up occasionally….

"We would fly to an area and figure out where was best to search according to a number of things, history, intelligence, geography, conditions at the time, a gut feeling possibly. Our tactics, worked out and evolved since the first marine patrol aircraft, MPA, in WWII, would guide us and our Lords and Masters in London to figure out exactly how and where to do it. The game was hard fought and hundreds of aircrew would spend hundreds of hours waiting for the 'enemy' to sneak past one of our sonobuoys and fall into the trap. Of course the flip-side to this was the mission tape being spun at base and someone else (in the luxury of a static, quiet office) finding the submarine you missed. Everyone wanted to be the person who shouted 'Contact In' when a line you were expecting appeared on your screen. If it was the correct thing and not a whale fart then the game was well and truly on, the whole crew (often at 4am, at their lowest ebb) would rise to the task as if they'd been injected with something. The teapot would be thrown aside, doughnuts might hit the floor, crew members would run to their stations, sonobuoys in the launchers would need to be changed, the aircraft would rack around the sky and the 'coals would be poured on' to get us to the right spot to start prosecuting the foe. One might regret finding the contact as a cosy quiet night on a 'cold barrier' would use less energy but by God the hours passed in a heartbeat when the work started for real. Once we got to our fuel limits for home-time and had handed over to the next crew some of the crew relaxed but others had paperwork to fill out, jobs to do, teapots to fill, curries to eat, and as long as the transit was, some of us would still be sweating on the bus back to the Operations Block to debrief the mission and ensure the next crew could take all the information available with them, not missing out on some crucial nugget that could scupper the whole effort."

As mentioned above there are various types of submarines. Nimrods were built initially in order to find the Russian submarines and to simplify the many types they were all allotted codenames by NATO. These submarines were continually being developed to make them more dangerous and harder to track; for example in the diesel-powered category Foxtrot was an attack submarine, Juliet was a guided-missile submarine and Golf was a ballistic missile submarine. The nuclear category submarines were improved during the life of the Nimrod so that for example for the attack submarines the names went from November to Victor (I to III), and then Mike. The guided-missile submarines went from Echo to Charlie and Oscar. The ballistic nuclear submarines started at Hotel and then Yankee, Delta and Typhoon.

The Russian navy had four main bases for their submarines to watch over the world. Murmansk by the South Barents Sea was used to cover the Atlantic while the Pacific submarines were based in Vladivostok on the extreme eastern edge of Russia opposite northern Japan. The Baltic port was Kaliningrad between Poland and Lithuania and Sevastopol, now in the Ukraine,

Below: Sevastopol submarine base in the Black Sea

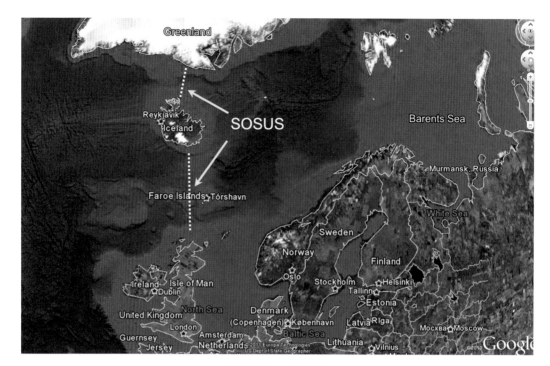

SOSUS and IUSS

was used as the base for the Mediterranean submarine fleet. NATO and the Nimrod tried to keep check on the European-based submarines and as described below there was routine tracking of the Murmansk submarine fleet. In addition for six years in the 1970s No 203 Squadron was based at RAF Luqa in Malta and frequently tracked Juliet, Foxtrot, Tango and even an Echo 2 nuclear machine; however the end of the Cold War, combined with Turkey being a member of NATO, made the use of the Black Sea by Russian submarines less attractive, particularly as they could only go through Turkish waters on the surface.

Looking for a submarine, Russian or anyone else's for that matter, which is probably submerged most of the time, from an aircraft or a ship is virtually impossible without some definite aids and so during the Cold War to assist detection of Soviet submarines six arrays of hydrophone were installed between Greenland and Iceland and between Iceland and the islands north of Scotland, the system being given the generic name SOSUS (sound surveillance system). The arrays were connected to the mainland with electric cables and the combination of locations within the ocean and the sensitivity of the arrays allowed the system to detect tiny amounts of acoustic sound at ranges of several hundred kilometres. In 1985, the system was improved and the name for the overall system became IUSS (integrated undersea surveillance system) and was used until the end of the Cold War in 1991. Once a submarine had been detected there was a chance of being able to find it and track it providing the search resources were available.

As soon as the Nimrod aircraft entered operational service with the RAF in 1969, besides watching the Atlantic it was in almost daily contact with ships of the Soviet Baltic and Northern fleets who were collecting intelligence on UK armed forces by listening on all radio and radar frequencies and even sometimes watching. These vessels, normally converted medium-sized trawlers, would loiter for extended periods, just outside territorial waters, in various locations around the UK. They established an almost continuous presence in the Clyde approaches, principally monitoring USN ballistic missile submarines from the US Navy base on the Holy Loch and RN ballistic missile submarines from the UK submarine base at Faslane on the Gare Loch.

Clearly the Russians wanted to know and if necessary track both the US and RN submarines.

In return the Allies, besides trying to ensure that they always knew when Russian submarines were going out into the Atlantic, needed to be aware of submarines leaving Murmansk, particularly if they then 'loitered' north of Norway and Scotland. The Barents Sea is in international waters and interestingly with the recent cancellation of the Nimrod it has become clear in public statements that the aircraft were used to monitor the submarines coming out of Murmansk. This is hardly surprising since the Russians in their Bear aircraft fly into British-controlled airspace with impunity, so it would be rather naïve to think that the Nimrod wouldn't do the same into the Barents Sea.

Of course, the Royal Navy would have been able to send warships including submarines to the Barents Sea any time for intelligence collecting, as did the Comet R1s operating from Bodø followed by the Nimrod R1s starting in the late '70s. Unfortunately I have not been able to obtain a first-hand account of the Nimrod R1s flying into the Barents Sea with its latest sensors but the earlier Comet R1 operation is described in this article on the internet and gives a flavour of the task though hopefully the crew were more comfortable in the Nimrod.

http://www.spyflight.co.uk/51sqn.htm
"51 Squadron operated very loosely as two flights. When one aircraft was away on detachment the other aircraft would carry out all the base duties and training. One of these duties was a three-day detachment to Bodø, north of the Arctic Circle in Norway. This was the land of the 'Midnight Sun' and for nearly six months of the year our trips from Bodø would be in daylight irrespective of the time of day and likewise for the other six months of the year would be in complete darkness. Transit to Bodø was undertaken covertly and the aircraft was parked in the secure aircraft park away from prying eyes. Only one trip was flown from Bodø and the timings for this trip were varied each month both during the winter and summer months. Our route varied slightly each time from the accompanying diagram [overleaf] but in general was very similar. Only one pass was ever made and we were under radar surveillance from the Norwegian radar situated at North Cape, at the very top of Norway, for the whole trip. The Americans, who also carried out this type of radar reconnaissance with B-47 aircraft had lost one of their aircraft (believed to have been shot down), on an earlier occasion in this area but that aircraft had reversed track at the northernmost point and was returning on a reciprocal track when it had disappeared from the Norwegian radar.

"Murmansk was the headquarters of the Soviet Northern Fleet and many of our intercepts were of shipborne radars but Novaya Zemlya was one of the two main Soviet testing grounds for new surface-to-air missile systems, SAM, and new fire control systems (the other being the Sevastopol peninsula in the Black Sea), and was a source of many new intercepts.

"Whenever we flew from Bodø on this route there was always a flurry of activity from the Soviet radar sites and we were regularly acquired by their fire control radars and by the search elements of the SAM sites but there was very little air activity and Soviet fighters never intercepted us. We heard the occasional air interrogation but it was always at long range and was of a type that we knew. Occasionally the SAM radars would lock onto us but only for brief periods. We were convinced that they quickly recognised what we were up to and closed everything down once they were convinced that we were no threat to them.

"During the winter months the outside air temperature at altitude was in the region of -50°C and because of the partial pressurisation the temperature inside the aircraft wasn't very much higher. For these trips we were issued with Arctic parkas and fleecy-lined underwear to wear under our flying overalls but even with these it was still extremely cold working in the aircraft. The floor got so cold that if any hot coffee was spilt on it, this turned to ice almost immediately. We used to hook our feet up on top of one of the black boxes under the rack to try and obtain a little warmth from the equipment. It wasn't very much but it did provide a little bit of comfort. We were always glad after we had landed to soak up the heat in the sauna in the Mess. Our accommodation with the Royal Norwegian Air Force was excellent. All the buildings were double-glazed and heated by steam from a central boiler house. The blankets for our bedding were contained in a linen cover and this was our first experience of duvets. Food was another thing! The Norwegians seemed to live on a diet of fish and cod liver oil. They put cod liver oil on their cornflakes at breakfast and lunch was always a fish dish. For dinner there would be fish soup followed by either a fish or reindeer main course and a sweet that was usually mostly raw yoghurt. We managed to convince the powers that be to allow us to eat in the airfield restaurant where we could obtain the kind of food that we were more used to at home.

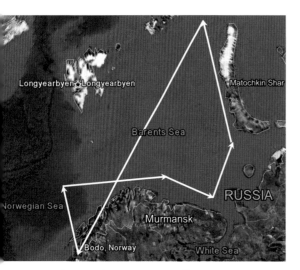

Comet R2 arctic surveillance

"As we were only there for three days it wasn't too much of a hardship and the results we obtained were well worth the small inconveniences. The Norwegian servicemen made us very welcome in the Mess and providing we weren't flying that night they treated our visits as an excuse for a party. They also organised outings for us during the summer months to show us the splendour of some of the local fjords and visits to local villages where the main occupation was woodcarving and furniture making. During the winter months everywhere was icebound but a few of the more hardy members of the Squadron did try their hands at sledging and skiing."

In the beginning the Nimrod R1s would only have been able to have any useful time in the Barents Sea if they refuelled in Norway but after 1982 both the MR2s and R1s were fitted with flight refuelling so it was possible to have quite long times on station north of Murmansk. Presumably authorisation for these flights couldn't be given from MHQ Northwood but had to come from the Foreign Office to avoid upsetting the Russians since the Barents Sea has long been regarded, by the Soviets, as their 'home waters'. These flights would almost exclusively originate from RAF Kinloss and preparation would commence with the selection of a suitably qualified crew at least forty-eight hours prior to the mission, which allowed the crew ample time to plan and rest prior to the flight. A senior, aircrew, station executive would closely monitor the crew's preparation and attend the final briefings prior to the crew's departure.

To achieve a useful 'on station' time within the Barents Sea, air-to-air refuelling was obviously essential and was provided by an RAF Tristar or VC10 aircraft. The flight plan for the sortie would terminate at the boundary of the Scottish flight information region and the Nimrod would continue covertly through the Norwegian Sea and subsequently 'round the corner' in to the Barents Sea. For the crew, it was usually a very early start with the intention to be on station off the Russian coast, normally in the vicinity of the Kola Gulf, at day break, hopefully this would coin-

cide with the Soviet navy commencing their daily training cycle. The refuelling tanker aircraft would depart RAF Brize Norton prior to the Nimrod leaving RAF Kinloss and the two aircraft would RV off the northern coast of Norway, transferring around 30,000 lb of fuel before the Nimrod broke off and entered the designated sensitive area.

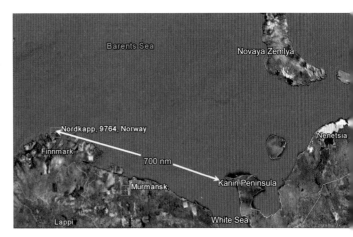
Southern Barents Sea

Two thirds of Russia's naval nuclear forces were based with the Russian Red Banner Northern Fleet, with its HQ at Sevoromorsk in the Kola Gulf in the Southern Barents Sea. In the Soviet era, prior to 1991, the Soviet navy could muster almost 200 submarines from their main bases in the Kola Gulf, notably from Litsa Guba and Sayda Guba, the Russian equivalent to Gare Loch and Holy Loch. In Soviet, and subsequently, Russian times, the units of this fleet would depart the Kola Gulf and conduct all manner

of trials and training in the 'home waters' of the Southern Barents Sea.

Once on station, the Nimrod crew would locate and photograph all Soviet air, surface and sub-surface units within their assigned area. Crews would often witness, and record, Northern Fleet training events which would rarely, if ever, be seen except in the Barents Sea. These events would often include the firing of live munitions, be it small-calibre cannon or submarine-launched ballistic missiles. It was not part of their remit for the Nimrod to interfere in any way with any missile launch or training event; however, on occasion Russian surface

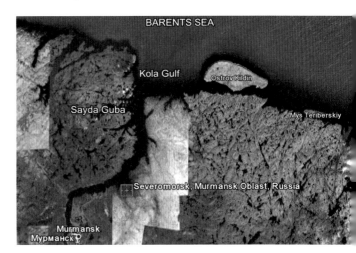
Kola Gulf leading to Murmansk and submarine bases

ships would fire flares to warn the Nimrod that they, the Russians, considered the Nimrod was approaching too close or interfering with their training. On very rare occasions, Russian interceptor aircraft would approach the Nimrod although it was not uncommon for May, Mail, Badger and Bear aircraft to approach for a closer look.

It was not unusual to find other NATO units doing intelligence-gathering missions in the same area. It really was the ideal place to observe Soviet tactics and hardware in action and bring

Above: Submarine *Kursk; Below:* Kirov Class nuclear-powered heavy cruiser *Peter the Great*

back as much information and quality crew records as possible for our analyst people. In 1987 a Soviet SU-27 intercepted an Orion P3B patrol aircraft of 333 Squadron RNoAF. The SU-27 clipped one of the P3's propellers. Damage to both aircraft was light and both aircraft landed safely. After this incident, Soviet fighter aircraft kept a respectable distance.

It is worthy of note that the Nimrod operating area was the main training area for the Russian Northern Fleet. It was in these waters on 12 August 2000 that the Northern Fleet were carrying out one of their largest training exercises since Soviet times. The units involved included four attack submarines, one of them, the ill fated *Kursk* SSGN, no stranger to the Nimrod fleet. The senior ship was the Red Banner Northern Fleet flagship, *Pyotr Velikiy (Peter the Great)*, a Kirov Class nuclear-powered heavy cruiser. At 11:28 local time there was an explosion. The only credible report is that this was due to the failure and explosion of one of the *Kursk's* tor-

pedoes. Despite the fact that the overall length of the *Kursk* exceeded the water depth at which it sank, by 150 feet, there were no survivors from the 118 crew.

In the absence of any obvious contact of interest, the Nimrod crew could 'loiter' just north of the Kola Gulf. It would be out of this waterway that the Red Banner Fleet nuclear submarines would transit, whether to conduct their training in the Barents Sea or enroute to their assigned patrol areas. The Nimrod could venture east to the entrance to the White Sea or north towards Novaya Zemlya, but, as the bulk of the activity seemed to be centred on the Kola Gulf, crews rarely ventured far afield. Despite the fact that these flights only took place in the summer months, weather in the Southern Barents Sea was often hostile, sea fog could blanket the whole area, frustrating the crew's attempts to identify and photograph vessels in the area. To add to their problems, in later years, large oil rigs, towering some 200 feet above sea level, would transit the Barents Sea. Nimrod crews would normally attempt to visually identify surface units whilst at 200 feet.

These sorties required a great deal of effort from the crews who were selected to carry them out and although the mission, from pre-flight briefing through to the conclusion of a lengthy debrief, could often stretch to eighteen hours there would always be no shortage of squadron senior staff struggling to get one of their crews selected to carry out the mission. Legend has it that a 'Squadron Tote' had to be maintained to ensure an equal distribution of these missions between the available squadrons.

Long-range Russian naval and air force aircraft continue to approach the coastline of the United Kingdom. Photographs of these intercepts by RAF air defence aircraft, from Lightning through to Phantom and Tornado, and now Typhoon, regularly appear in our national newspapers. One has to wonder how many pictures there were of Nimrods off the Murmansk coast in the Russian tabloid press?

Clearly both the Nimrod and the RN submarines had to be very careful of the territorial boundaries, particularly as the Russian method of calculation not altogether surprisingly resulted in the boundaries being further from Russia than the United States method of calculation. This was evidenced when the USS *Baton Rouge* nuclear attack submarine collided with a Sierra class submarine in February 1992, allegedly more than twelve miles from the Russian shore but classed by the Russians as within their coastal area.

Russian Delta IV. Note hatch open after firing missile, presumably taken in Barents Sea

One of the problems of these sorties in to the Barents Sea had to be having a suitable diversion if things went wrong. Clearly a Norwegian airfield was always a possibility if the aircraft could get there but presumably another option in extremis for the MR2 would be to land at a Russian airfield having jettisoned all the paperwork and any special gear if necessary. Landing in the sea would almost certainly result in the loss of all the crew as well as the aircraft.

The other main ASW sorties were tracking submarines detected by SOSUS and Ian Marshall describes what went on during the Cold War:

"Covert tracking of USSR submarines from the 1970s through the 1990s was probably one of the most important jobs the Nimrod crew performed. The operation was given a codename, like all military operations, and like all military operations the codename was frequently changed to ensure there was no loss of security. The Nimrod fleet was one of the very few military units that got to practise the exact tactics directly on the enemy and not on friendly blue units simulating red hostiles. With the exception of dropping a torpedo, which we were occasionally cleared to practise, all procedures were wartime procedures.

"It appeared early in my career that almost every second weekend was taken up with tracking Russian submarines; this procedure usually started on Friday night when they would enter into waters controlled by the UK, somewhere north of the Iceland - Faeroes Gap. The Russians usually left Murmansk, their northern fleet homeport on Mondays for deployment in the Atlantic or en route for the Mediterranean. As bad luck would have it the submarines usually took five days to reach UK waters, perfect timing for screwing up our weekend.

"In the early days there was no ATC communication at all, even take-off was autho-rised by an Aldis lamp, our IFF squawk would be known to the ATC service who would keep other traffic clear, the same would be true of our return transit from the ocean, just an IFF squawk to see us home until we would pick up Lossie radar. Occasionally some air trafficker would have forgotten to have read his briefing sheet for the day and would try to raise communications with the unidentified radar return but we would never answer. As the years progressed, the covertness of the missions decreased, until there was almost normal air traffic procedures.

"The operation would normally commence with the target being located by SOSUS, now replaced by IUSS, a system of fixed array underwater hydrophones that could pro-vide a reasonable area for an MPA to search; without the SOSUS clue it was indeed like searching for the proverbial needle in a haystack. Depending on target type, the crew would lay a field of sonobuoys to locate a diesel sub or a barrier of buoys to locate a nuclear submarine.

"The buoys in the water were monitored by the wet men (acoustic operators) and the general shipping noise would be noted. Most ships make a large amount of noise that would appear on almost every buoy; what the operators were looking for was very distinct known frequencies appearing on only one or two buoys which was the clue that we were now hot and into a localisation situation. To localise a submarine its position, track and speed had to be known. To achieve this, many closely spaced buoys would be dropped in a pattern around the target, each buoy in contact would measure a slightly different frequency from the Doppler difference emitted by the submarine. By understanding the Doppler difference in relation to the perceived speed of the targets a fairly accurate lo-calisation could be achieved. After localisation, the crew would then covertly track the target for the remainder of their on-station time. Tracking was also achieved by dropping closely spaced buoys around the sub, usually in a chevron or a straight line or a box, later on when directional buoys became the only type carried, the pattern shape of the sonobuoys was not so important, but as our buoys became better the targets became a lot quieter. For instance, in the early 1970s an Echo 2 class nuclear submarine might make noise out to twenty-five miles all around him but, by the turn of the century, the noise produced by a Delta IV SSBM was significantly reduced. Of course, the noise unfortunately was not a circular pattern since that would have made things much easier; in reality, there was usually a very quiet area on the sub's bow, a bit more noise on the beams and even more from the stern; plotting this pattern of noise was a fairly important job, both for tracking purposes and for future intelligence purposes. It was always a game of cat and mouse, each one improving equipment and tactics to take a short tactical lead.

"After tracking the target for several hours a relief aircraft would arrive; again, in the early days there was no communication between the aircraft, each had been assigned a designated height band and nominated handover buoys, the positioning of the four handover buoys told the oncoming aircraft all that he required, target position, course and speed and where and when it was safe to descend to take over the tracking. The worst nightmare of a Nimrod captain was to receive a hot handover from one aircraft, lose the target and have to provide a cold handover to his relief. It was also for me as the navigator and captain, the most exciting part of flying in the Nimrod, controlling the tactics and the crew to achieve the aircraft's primary mission of locating, tracking and on paper at least, destroying the target. Of course it could all too easily go wrong, the Nimrod could be tracking one very distinct noise source like a generator, then that generator is switched off and momentarily it all goes quiet until the acoustic operators reconfigure the system and track a different noise source. Another reason for losing a target was counter detection. Like the submarine, the MPA in general and the US P3C in particular made a very detectable and distinct noise if the aircraft was allowed to wander too close or over the top of the target; through its own acoustic systems the submarine would detect us; he could then speed up, slow down or go into a very quiet mode all of which would cause tracking problems for the crew. Counter detection became very big latterly when the targets were much quieter and therefore the buoy patterns had to be dropped much closer to them to get into contact.

"Very occasionally the aircraft was cleared to make a simulated attack following the passive buoys by dropping active sonobuoys. By attacking, this allowed the aircraft to go right over the top of the target, to gain a Mad Mark, which alone would probably startle the submarine crew, and then they would hear the pinging of active sonobuoys. I can only guess that this did not enhance the career prospects of any submarine captain on his return to Murmansk.

"At the end of a submarine-tracking sortie all records and magnetic tapes would be sent south to the Joint Acoustic Analysis Centre (JAAC, latterly ADAC and then MDAG) for analysis, this unit would then keep track of individual submarine noise sources and also replay every Nimrod sortie; lessons learned at the end were very important to the continued success of the Nimrod to be able successfully to track hostile submarines, something that the crews were very proud of – being universally accepted as the best in the world."

Normally a crew would consider themselves very fortunate to find one Russian submarine but on 26 March 1985 they struck lucky. Garfield Porter who was tactical navigator tells the story:

"In the 1970-80s, crews on training missions in the Shetland-Faroes Gap often strung eight or so sonobuoys *'the lucky eight'* across the transit lanes; this reflected both the need to train operators in distinguishing the ASW wheat from the surface chaff and the fact that we didn't always know whether or not a Soviet submarine was there – sometimes crews were not informed for good intelligence reasons and sometimes because simply no-one knew they were there! Although it did not start with the use of sonobuoys, a sortie on 26 March serves as a good case in point.

"Captained by Flt Lt Wally Allaway (AEO), 206 Squadron Crew 8 was tasked into the Gap to search for a Soviet Kilo class diesel submarine thought to be in transit. The crew took over the area from a 201 Sqn crew and, after some discussion, the tactical navigator, Flt Lt Garfield Porter, decided to maintain a long silent posture until near midnight (Moscow time) in the hope of catching the target coming to the surface for a broadcast at that time. The radar was subsequently turned on and after a few seconds the operator called a possible contact; it was approached in the dark and after striking up the searchlight upgraded to Certsub (category of 'Certainly a submarine') much to the delight of the entire crew. The target was then surrounded with a variety of sonobuoys, primarily for training purposes. A few minutes later, the acoustics team asked for confirmation that we had been tasked to find a Kilo class; Wally replied in the affirmative only to be met by the comment *'well that's interesting skipper, because this is a Foxtrot!'*

"After some discussion, the crew decided to move right across the area, again with the radar silent, on the basis that two submarines would be separated by a reasonable distance for safety purposes. Fifteen minutes or so later, the radar was called on again only to hear the operator announce *'this looks just like the last one, so I've got to call it'*; the crew closed the contact to find a second submarine this time at periscope depth. A similar period of frenetic activity followed before it was concluded that sufficient detail had been collected to declare that the Kilo had been detected.

"So, in less than an hour, two Soviet diesel submarines had been localised – one expected and one most certainly not. Ample evidence that in those days there was always room for a lucky eight!"

The Russians were always trying to get through into the Atlantic undetected and Operation Atrina, known in the West as the Victor Surge, described by Fleet Admiral V.N. Chernavin (Ret.) was an apparently successful sortie by five Victor class submarines. In fact it is not clear how successful the operation was since there is no rebuttal document written by the United States or UK authorities immediately available on the net. Chernavin sets the scene in the beginning of his (translated) account:

"Geographic peculiarities of the Northern Fleet operation zone force our submarines to proceed to the Northern, Central Atlantic and then to the Mediterranean Sea or other regions of combat activities and patrolling along the only one direction in the Norwegian Sea with its three arms: either between the Faeroes and the Shetland Islands, or between the Shetland Islands and Iceland, or between Iceland and Greenland (the Denmark Strait). This notorious Faeroes-Iceland line with its underwater hydrophones of the SOSUS American stationary anti-submarine system and mobile NATO anti-submarine warfare (ASW) forces is well known to our submariners and has always been a real headache. NATO anti-submarine warfare forces have always tried to intercept and track our submarines at this line. It was necessary to find, train and practically test the effectiveness of secured deployment methods of first of all nuclear submarines in the Atlantic as well as to demonstrate that if required we can become undetectable, ready to covertly deliver strikes as well as to deliver nuclear weapons counterstrikes at the surface targets located in the hostile territory. Such methods were trained and approbated by carrying out continuous fleet special operations. The most significant and effective among them was the operation with the 'Atrina' codename performed by a group of multipurpose SSNs in 1987. Leaping ahead we should say that this operation carried out in early 1987 raised a big stink in the Pentagon, caused numerous queries in the Congress and somewhat shocked the US Navy Command. But first things first."

He goes on to describe how he hand-picked five of the most up-to-date submarines and well trained crews who had unique experience of submarine operations in the Atlantic. In June 1985 a preliminary operation called Aport was carried out near the Newfoundland Bank to determine the US submarine's patrolling routes and the NATO ASW tactics and to prepare for Atrina. Apparently the preparation of operation Atrina was personally controlled and supervised by Admiral I.M. Kapitanets, the Northern Fleet commander taking into account the experience and the intelligence obtained by the submarines which had taken part in Aport. Never before had such detailed planning taken place and even the commanders of the nuclear submarines did not find out their ship's missions and details of the operation until the very last moment. Chernavin goes on :

"Operation Atrina started in early March 1987: all five SSNs left the base in sequence. Usually nuclear submarines went on combat duty alone, less often in pairs. This time nearly a whole division of multipurpose SSNs was going to the ocean. The Americans of course registered their disappearance from the base. But, apparently they didn't worry too much knowing that the SSNs would proceed along the usual route. But this time the Americans brought their eggs to a wrong market. On a certain day and at a certain hour all the nuclear submarines

Russian Victor III class submarine

'suddenly' turned. And from the rather stretched column a hydroacoustic screen of SSNs was formed, which was going west at full speed. The nuclear submarines 'disappeared' without being detected by ASW forces."

Chernavin alleges that the Pentagon leaders and US Navy Command were very nervous about 'losing' a whole SSN division that was approaching the US coast with an unknown mission and that they therefore sent dozens of anti-submarine planes and powerful forces of ASW ships to find the missing submarines. Every resource and sensor was used to find the boats using sonar, land-based planes sowing barriers, thermal direction finders and magnetometers. Apparently the density of the Allied forces was so great that the Russian submarines were unable to surface for communication with their control centre.

The Russians were convinced that as far as the submarine chasers were concerned their missile-carrying nuclear submarines had vanished without a trace. In fact they had gone through the Sargasso Sea and then skirted round Bermuda into the area of the notorious Triangle. Apart from the routine US submarine on patrol, a further six submarines left Norfolk, Virginia to search for the missing task force plus three squadrons of ASW aircraft, three hunter-killer ships with allegedly the UK *Invincible* aircraft carrier armed with long-range sonar capability. Whether the Russians included Nimrods in their assessment is not known.

Chernavin concludes:

" Our SSNs operated in the Atlantic for almost three months without being detected or tracked by US and NATO ASW forces. The missions were fully accomplished: US and British submarines deployed during the operation in the Atlantic were detected; underwater and surface navigation positions in the Atlantic region insufficiently described by other naval intelligence means was disclosed. All our SSNs successfully returned home. Their commanders and the division commander were awarded with the Red Banner Orders. Other officers, warrant officers and sailors of the SSNs' crews distinguished in this operation also got governmental decorations."

Unfortunately, as remarked at the beginning of this account, it has not been possible to verify this Russian account. It is interesting to note that the Russians knew full well that their submarines were being tracked from Murmansk by allied assets – ships and aircraft.

In anti-submarine warfare both the hunter and the hunted rely on sensors and electronic intelligence. Certainly in 1968 there were no holds barred when John Anthony Walker Jr started giving the Russian intelligence organisation based in Washington the critical key codes for encrypting messages so that when the Nimrods were working hard in the Atlantic tracking the Russian submarines, the Russians must have been mostly aware of what was happening. Walker was not discovered until his wife gave him away in 1984 and he was only caught and stopped in 1985. Regardless of who knew what it was obviously very good training for the Russians as well as for the Nimrod crews.

Before leaving ASW here is a general account by Jim Lawrence of what it was like chasing a submarine in the early days using a MR1.

" *'Would OC A Flight please come across to an urgent planning meeting in Ops'* – a call often received by the duty crew on Nimrod squadrons at Kinloss and St Mawgan throughout the 1970s and 1980s. Usually either late morning or early afternoon on a Friday, just in time to start yet another full working weekend, and the precursor to starting submarine-tracking operations on the latest southbound Soviet nuclear submarine either bound for the Mediterranean or heading into the Atlantic to the WAMPA, the 'Western Atlantic Missile Patrol Area' the loosely defined area in mid-Atlantic which was the usual patrol haunt of the Yankee and Delta Class SSBNs based in the Russian North Fleet.

"To be on a Nimrod squadron in those days was to be part of an unsung elite, engaged in 'The Deep Cold War'. The Panorama programme of that name was the first indication many in our own service, and certainly the public at large, had that such operations were taking place. The extreme sensitivity of anti-submarine operations and the strategic intelligence sources that initiated them, led to tight security constraints on all mention of 'live ops'. The general public knew little more about such activities until in later years Tom Clancy's *The Hunt for Red October* became a best seller. On the Nimrod force of those years it was a common boast that we were 'the only force in daily contact with the enemy'. As such it was true that, outside our magic circle, few people really knew the technological battle being fought daily many miles off the UK west coast with Nimrods, Soviet submarines and the exploitation of underwater sound propagation. The other players in this sub-surface game of cat and mouse were the Royal Navy Submarine Force and the Towed Array Frigate Force. Although, with its ability to get to the scene of the action at 400kts rather than 15kts as a ship could, the Nimrod was always the jewel in the UK's ASW crown.

"The codewords for such operations were so sensitive in those early days that back in the 1970s we were not even allowed to record the word itself in our flying logbooks. In our drive to be super secret for a brief period we even took to getting airborne on a green light from the tower. Shades of WW II and something of a fallacy of course as it immediately became obvious that something special was going on, when all these aircraft started departing Kinloss in radio silence and returning home some nine hours later in the early hours of the morning, especially over a weekend.

"It was all more primitive in those days. The prime means of communication with RAF Brawdy – the secret base on the Welsh coast at the bottom of Cardigan Bay, purveyor of all 'most secret' underwater intelligence from SOSUS, the underwater sound surveillance system of hydrophones laid on the ocean floor – was via an odd-shaped black phone known as the 'Bat Phone' located in a cabinet in the Kinloss or St Mawgan Maritime Acoustic Analysis Unit or MAAU. Line quality on this early generation scrambler phone was never the best and required a practised ear to ensure the latest positions were recorded accurately. Access to the backroom plot, perspex boards, tracing paper and chinagraphs, no electronics then, was fiercely guarded by the MAAU team and only those with the necessary SOSUS security clearances were permitted to see the large grid board with the little plastic stick-on symbols that showed the latest intelligence estimate of the position of the 'Red' submarine contacts. The only thing more sensitive than the 'Red Plot' was the 'Blue Plot', a source of enduring interest to our own crews as the RN rarely owned up to exactly what HM Submarines were really up to, and even if they did tell you, you knew you only had part of the story.

"The early acoustics equipment in the 1970s Nimrod would seem primitive now; we had no VDU screens or laptops. On the AQA5 processor all the acoustics signatures from the sonobouys were displayed on hard copy units, which burnt the frequency versus time printouts onto rolls of electro-sensitive paper, the 'Jezebel Grams'. The background 'click-clack' 'click-clack' as the electro stylus swept back and forth was just part of the background noise in the aircraft that you had to endure for up to nine to ten hours at a time. Our missions involved locating and maintaining a constant track of the Soviet submarines as they passed through UK waters, or loitered on patrol off the north-west coast of the UK. Lines of sonobuoys were dropped, with the individual buoys sometimes spaced miles apart, so noisy were those early nuclear boats. With these tactics we maintained track and speed on the submarines, sometimes for days at a time, with relays of Nimrods going on patrol one after the other at six-hourly intervals.

"The west coast of Scotland was an area of prime interest to the Soviet navy of those days, being astride the main sea route into Faslane and Holy Loch, home to both British and American missile boats (SSBN). Any indication that an 'intruder' submarine was getting into the UK's 'back-yard' would provoke an immediate reaction. Nimrods would be scrambled, the duty 'towed array' frigate (ship with a mile of hydrophones streamed from the rear) would be sailed, the nearest 'hunter killer' (SSN) would be diverted to the area, Sea King ASW helicopters would be repositioned. All available stops would be pulled out and close tracking maintained on the intruder, every minute of the day. Sometimes, if he came too far inshore a deliberate blast of active sonar would make the unwelcome addition to UK waters aware that the UK ASW team were right on his tail, and would he kindly disappear or words to that effect. And these operations could continue for days, weeks on many occasions.

"Such operations were the peak of the Deep Cold War and scrutinised closely by our admirals and air marshals. Some air officers took an especially keen interest and were even known to have their own set of dividers by the air ops centre plot! The intelligence analysts also pored over all the charts and tapes from these sorties, looking to distil out anything tactically useful that would give us an edge over our unseen opponent.

"Ex Nimrod aircrew will remember the dreaded debriefs from the experts at the Joint Acoustic Analysis Centre (JAAC) at Farnborough who analysed all our tracking operations. Sometime after an op they would visit Kinloss and St Mawgan where crews would attend the debrief in trepidation that they would be criticised for having used the wrong tactics, or not seen a closest point of approach (CPA) – one of your best targeting solutions on an unfriendly submarine, or worst of all, and a crime worse than adultery in the Nimrod Force of the day, having lost the submarine target. Political correctness had not been invented then and we were not invited to consider the 'challenges' and 'potential for greater efficiency' of our ops – we just got bollocked for getting it wrong, and if you had really screwed up, the Group Standards Unit took a special interest in you next time around.

"Lots of 'Honker stew' was eaten on those long trips. Health and Safety and Food Standards were all in the future and we just tipped most of the flying rations into the large stew pot set on the hot plate in the aircraft galley and made Honker stew, the quickest way to get some food into the crew when we were all too busy to concoct a proper meal. Vital ingredients included all the proper rationed food plus apricots, curry powder, tabasco sauce, dust, crumbs and stuff accidentally from the bottom of the rations bag and a splash of brown sauce. We then served it in foil trays and ate with a plastic spoon. Preferably at 300ft at night over a Sea State 9. It was surprising how tasty it actually was and how few people turned it down. We sometimes had the 'guess the ingredients' game on the intercom. Sounds revolting but it always tasted really good. A crew's most prized possession was a half-gallon teapot: you drink a lot of tea during nine hours over the sea. The smell of the Nimrod is also a memory, that unique blend of hydraulic fluid, oxygen, hot electrics and burnt Avtur. Guaranteed to make most passengers throw up after an hour or so at low level.

"The 'Malin Head AGI' (intelligence-gathering ship made to look like a trawler), 'Shetlands Contingency Tug' (rescuer of broken-down Soviet vessels), and the 'West of UK Whisky' – a Soviet diesel submarine that patrolled west of the Hebrides – were all regular features around our coastline and regular targets that required almost daily updates by a patrolling Nimrod. Operations were directed from the bunkers at Pitreavie Castle outside Dunfermline, and Mount Wise at Plymouth, home respectively to HQ NORMAR or Northern Maritime Air Region and HQ SOUMAR, Southern Maritime Air Region until the advent of the Joint Headquarters at Northwood in 1984.

"The seabed in the Iceland-Faeroes and Shetland-Faeroes gaps must be littered with the remains of tens of thousands of sonobuoys, the accumulated detritus of years of submarine-tracking operations. We used to joke about the cost of some of the more complex we dropped, the equivalent of throwing overboard the cost of a new Mini for each one. And over the years we must have dropped tens of thousands of sonobuoys of various types. As nuclear submarine power plants got progressively quieter and tracking ranges decreased from miles down to thousands and then hundreds of yards, the buoy consumption rose accordingly. ASW of this intensity was always something of a combination between science and art and a highly perishable skill. It is to the immense credit of the crews that with its sheer professionalism the Nimrod Force always maintained its tactical edge in comparison with our American colleagues who inevitably always had more money for the latest wizard tactical gadgets and processors.

"But after around twenty years this Deep Cold War just faded away. Operations diminished rapidly after the Berlin Wall came down in 1990. As the Soviet Union gradually disintegrated the simply enormous effort required to maintain the huge Russian submarine force was just too much. It's not gone away totally, but I doubt we will ever conduct pure ASW to that intensity again.

"This was a very protracted but highly successful campaign in the defence of the UK, conducted over many years by a few hundred dedicated aircrew and their equally dedicated groundcrew, but the sad thing is that outside the Nimrod community very few people even know that it happened. We need to remember that the UK's maritime aircrew and their ground engineers made a significant contribution to winning the Cold War, so I hope this brief vignette helps set the record straight.

"P.S. You know the old saying about those who fail to appreciate the lessons of history being doomed to repeat them – anybody note the recent (2008) Russian statements about their intentions to bring into service a new class of nuclear submarines, as a move to re-establish Russian 'Blue Water' capability?"

ANTI-SURFACE WARFARE

ASuW (anti-surface unit warfare) describes the techniques Nimrod would use to find something on the surface of the sea, from the interception of a lone yacht to the shadowing of an entire carrier battle group. Given this large range of tasks it was sometimes more difficult to have a rigid set of standard operating procedures to apply to ASuW.

TACTICS

ASuW was usually a 'long game' meaning that over a period of time a defined area of ocean would be surveyed which allowed the crew time to build a picture of what was happening. Standing off from the area was often necessary, either because of the threat posed to the aircraft or a desire to avoid counter detection. The downside was that unless the vessel was visually located there could never be any guarantee of its identity, just varying levels of probability. Of course there were circumstances when the situation allowed the crew simply to fly past all the contacts visually ID'ing them, and this was often the quickest way to achieve some tasks.

Surveilling an opposing force meant using techniques to try to overcome their attempts at concealment or covertness. The larger the capital ships in that force the worse the threat to the Nimrod normally, resulting in having to carry out the task with more limitations, usually at a greater range from the missile or aircraft threat. The lesser the threat, the easier the task, from singleton warships, to unopposing vessels including merchant vessels, fishing boats and pleasure craft. All of them had their own difficulties; merchant vessels all looking similar using the radar profiling facility, fishers being normally in a crowd of others and pleasure craft (yachts especially) being difficult to detect. There were various methods employed to whittle down the 'suspects' to 'likelies' which often depended on the contact density in that area. Finding the right one wasn't always guaranteed, although spending a whole training sortie narrowing down an area full of ships to a handful of likelies that may have been the practice 'target for the day' and then winning the target sweepstake amongst the crew members was extremely rewarding!

During the Cold War of course, the effort was biased towards thoughts of locating and tracking Soviet ships breaking out into the Atlantic along idealistic routes. Over time, ASuW evolved to search for Argentinian warships hiding along their coastline during the Falklands campaign, blockade-running merchants during the Balkans and Middle Eastern conflicts and drug runners in the various places Nimrod was sent to find them. Arguably the most important role the aircraft carried out was looking for suspect terrorist vessels which posed a threat to the UK, one of the roles the crews were acutely aware no-one else could carry out anywhere near as effectively as they could.

RADAR

The Searchwater radar was almost always the primary sensor for ASuW tasks. Its ability to spot submarine snorts also meant that it was ideally suited to find small surface vessels, or those with a small radar cross section. Searchwater had some limited 'imaging' capability. Because of its pulse compression techniques it could, given the correct aspect, use its high resolution A-Scope display to measure a vessel's length, and even give rudimentary outlines.

The other great capability of the radar was to carry out autotracking of contacts. Once raised the radar would maintain a file on the vessel and, over time, derive course and speed. This reduced the operator's workload and allowed a greater area of ocean to be worked at one time.

ESM

This was the Nimrod's ears, listening for any radars being emitted. Once received the operator and machine would combine to decide on the make and model of radar being received. This would then be matched to a list of vessels that were fitted with this radar. Once received the ESM system would take a number of bearing measurements allowing an estimate of its originating position to be made. This position could then be matched to any radar files.

All of the information from radar and ESM would be provided electronically to the tactical navigator on his or her screen, along with amplification on intercom when required. As ever, the tactical navigator ran the show down the back controlling the tactics and making the decisions.

CAMERAS

There normally came a point where a probable contact had to be turned into certain and therefore the crew had to get 'eyes on'. At its most basic this meant looking out of the window as they flew past. Whilst this could often provide a positive (or negative) ID, it did mean that everything had to be taken in and remembered in a couple of seconds. Therefore throughout the life of the Nimrod a number of imaging methods were used. Over time the cameras improved from large clunky slow things to the conventional SLR, all operated from the beam positions. Additionally, at the very rear of the aircraft a pair of external camera doors concealed thick glass windows through which the vertical camera could image the top of contacts, which allowed photography from directly above a vessel. Whilst the imagery using these devices would provide good intelligence and in-depth analysis, the downside was that the results were unavailable to the crew until after the sortie. With the advent of digital cameras the results were available instantly to the crew by using an on-board laptop or the camera's integral screen, thus allowing confirmation or further analysis of what had been seen from the window.

Apart from the vertical, phased out in the late 1990s, all photography was carried out from the beam windows, almost always with the beam window open to avoid any distortion on the image (the opening of the windows in flight was always the one thing any visitors refused to believe happened, many convinced they were being wound up!)

The Gulf War started when Saddam Hussein decided to enter Kuwait on 2 August 1990 and the UK responded with Operation Granby. Almost immediately it was decided to send Nimrods to Oman to patrol. Below is an account of patrolling the waters of the Gulf of Oman and the Strait of Hormuz. Three Nimrod MR2s were prepared and in case the Iraqis had ground-to-air missiles the aircraft were fitted with a self-defence tail pack containing chaff and flare cartridges. Some of the aircraft were fitted with Sidewinder rails for firing missiles at aircraft but in the event no Sidewinders were carried. The aircraft left with supporting groundcrew, NLS (Nimrod Line Squadron) engineers, and refuelled at Sigonella in Sardinia which was full of US naval aircraft.

"We were greeted on the south military pan at Seeb by the searing heat of the Arabian summer and a small ops team from Kinloss. A tiny single-story concrete building hosted our flight planning, safety equipment and ops rooms. Cramped certainly, but still adequate for our needs. The groundcrew had a small area to work from and various stores were kept in part of a SOAF (Sultan of Oman's Air Force) hangar a few yards along the ramp. That was it. All of it. Nothing like the enormous footprint that was generated nearly a

Below: Google map of the Arabian Gulf

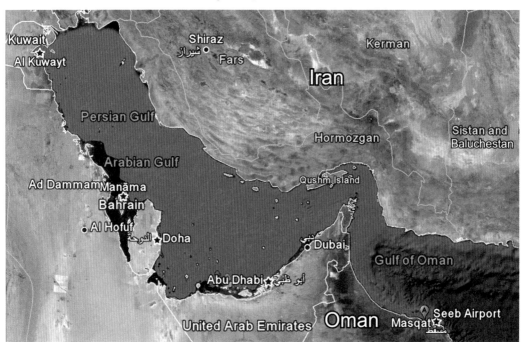

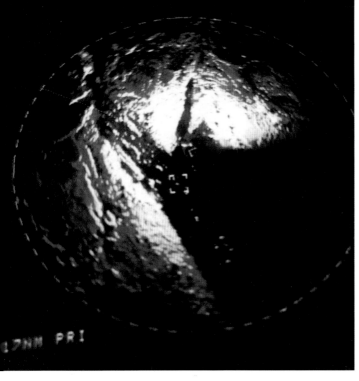

Searchwater map of the Red Sea

dozen years later for Episode 2.

"August 18 and we have an early start for the first sortie in the Gulf of Oman (GOO). With the sun rising we walked across to the Nimrod with our kit. Respirators carried onboard as that nasty man used gas. Guns? Oh yes we had guns. Pistols and ammo down the back and a handful of SLR rifles stuffed under the galley table. More importantly, rations were by Gulf Air – at least in the beginning.

"Launch and a sharp turn out over the Gulf of Oman. Locate, track, identify and challenge all merchant shipping moving through the Gulf. Record all details and pass back to HQ Northwood on landing. It was hot and very humid on the jet throughout the sortie. With only the new 35mm SLR camera for photography we stayed at low level for the most part, the usual shot or two on each tanker seen. Wet film processing was done by the 'next day service' in downtown Ruwi!

The amount of moisture meant water running over a lot of the panels, leading to the installation of a foil tray and paper cup guttering system above the navigators. This technique has kept the Navs dry for many subsequent detachments in hot countries of the world.

"The routine became a sortie every day or every other day. At first we were logging over forty vessels per trip. Bear in mind that at this stage the Western powers and UN were doing a lot of politicking to try and oust Saddam from Kuwait. As the verbal sparring became ever

Note Sidewinder rails under wing but no missiles carried

more heated the shipping numbers dropped as quickly as the value of Gulf currency. By the end of October as the crew prepared to leave, the daily 'take' was around a dozen ships, less than the number of coalition warships out there challenging them.

"It was the AEO's job to challenge the ships. Varying levels of English made for some

Soviet Kresta 2 warship and a suspect vessel

interesting results. A cargo of 500 tons of 'mice' was finally resolved to, 'I spell for you sir, Mike Alfa, India, Zulu, Echo'! On another occasion, the AEO's call of 'Confirm cargo is two hundred tons of gold?' had the local pirates launching left, right and centre until the panicked ship's captain shouted 'No sir! No sir! Coal! Coal, I spell . . .!' We were even asked by a Soviet Kresta 2 warship to investigate a suspect vessel.

"Night flying was very rare, just one full night trip and one day-into-night during our time in theatre. Seeing at night was a very different ballgame then than now. TICMS (later called TIS) was a starboard beam-mounted thermal-imaging camera. Cooled by two high pressure nitrogen bottles behind the beam seat it had to be held steady by the AEO in the beam, whilst the control of focus etc was managed on a monitor sat at the recorder position facing the ESM operator. Not pretty, but it gave fair results at low level.

"We had left with only fourteen days kit. One RAF blue holdall with flying kit and one with a few clothes and washkit. Additional clothes were bought using our allowances. News was gleaned from the Omani radio or the UAE TV station, whose reception in the hotel varied with the odd radio propagation that the Gulf experiences. Phone calls home were paid out of our rates, an expensive proposition in the hotel. The routine became to ring home, let it ring five times and hang up. That way the hotel didn't charge the call. Then your partner would phone from the UK at a cheaper rate.

"The first crew out were replaced after a month, the second crew a month after that. We finally departed Seeb towards the end of October, replaced by a St Mawgan-based 42 (torpedo bomber) Squadron crew. Our Nimrod was greeted by our families and, at that time, by the much less welcome customs inspectors. The war itself didn't kick off until the following January. By then the crews were accommodated in far less salubrious accommodation on a military base. Their more aggressive wartime exploits are stories for another day."

BETWEEN WARS

In 2001 Nimrods were involved with Operation Resinate. There were naval patrols in the Arabian Gulf and the Nimrods were based in Bahrain in a former RAF base called Muharraq. There was a small RAF detachment there and a VC10 tanker for flights that required air-to-air refuelling. The United States Gulf Fleet was based there so Britain needed Bahrain support for the joint operations taking place.

The Nimrods were there to stop Iraq illegally moving oil out of the Gulf as part of the United Nations sanctions. Every tanker would be photographed, questioned on the radio and, if the answers were incorrect or fishy then the naval forces would intercept and board the ship. Occasionally the Iraqis would take the desperate step of sailing inside Iranian territorial waters and therefore out of reach but they then risked being boarded by the Iranian National Guard who would demand monetary payments, bribes, to let the tanker continue. There is a probably apocryphal story of the Royal Navy boarding one side of a vessel while, unknown to them, the Iranians were boarding the other side and firing their weapons to encourage the tanker to stop. The navy beat a hasty retreat.

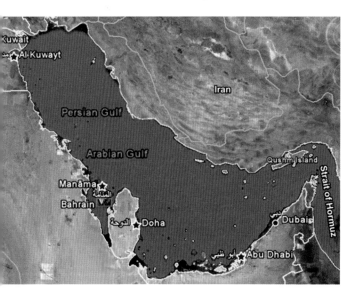

Arabian Gulf

The Nimrods fulfilled a second function which was to assist in 'force protection', an American euphemism for giving direct support to their fleet. They could then task the Nimrods as they so desired. Keeping a look out for hostile acts by the Iranian navy was a high priority but, probably more important, was keeping a look out for the Iranian diesel Kilo class submarines. The threat to the fleet from these submarines was immense and if Iran had decided to use them properly the fleet could have been in very serious trouble. The Strait of Hormuz in particular could be blocked up by the presence of just one hostile submarine. Luckily the Iranian navy never did operate these former Russian submarines very well, usually staying on the surface within territorial waters and moving between different naval bases.

Operation Resinate was possibly the first time that the Nimrod made full use of its recently fitted high frequency (HF) Link 11 system. Although the USA had been using this system for decades, the RAF Nimrod was late into using it. The system was slow and depended upon the navigator assigning manually the contacts who were going to use the Link. It took a lot of practice and skill to get the most out of the link and put valuable information onto it. By attaching contacts (radar, ESM, acoustic etc) to the Link, every unit with a receiver could see the whole picture in the whole Gulf. Even as old as the system was, it was a superb way of sharing information and it greatly reduced contact reports over the radio. Link 16 has now replaced 11 but the MR2 was never scheduled to be fitted with it; the MRA4 would have had both link systems fitted.

ANTI-DRUG MISSIONS

At first the use of Nimrods to detect drug running was not widely known but gradually it became clear that they were very effective in their task as evidenced by these quotations at the time of the cancellation of the project.

Mrs Moon House of Commons 4 November 2010
Let us also remember the use of maritime surveillance capabilities against drug smuggling, human trafficking and piracy. The new maritime patrol aircraft, of which the Nimrod was the mainstay, had the capacity to counter drug-running operations in the Caribbean, fight pirate activity in the Gulf of Arabia and form a crucial part of maritime counter-terrorism operations.

Defence Management 10 February 2011
Simple, Nimrod could have scanned the UK every 10 seconds. Nothing else we have can do that. We have no maritime air patrol, so should the drug cartels decide to use semi-subs as in the Gulf of Mexico for drug running, we have sod all way of detecting them or any other naval threat apart from line of sight, ship radar (with the small coverage area it affords) and pure bloody luck.

For example, in 1997 the aircraft was sent to the Caribbean instead of tracking boats about to land their contraband in the UK. Presumably someone in the relevant ministry decided that it could be more effective if the drugs were stopped before leaving the Caribbean in the first place. Of course the aircraft could not be hidden so that whenever and wherever it appeared in the area everyone including the drug runners would know what was happening.

At first the aircraft were based in Key West at the US Navy air station at Boca Chica, which meant a long transit into the middle of the Caribbean, reducing the on-station time looking for drug runners but apparently the advantage was that there could be face-to-face contact with the controllers and the local RAF liaison officer.

Later sorties were conducted from the US Navy base at Roosevelt Roads in Puerto Rico. This location was used for many years, being closer to the likely areas of interception, but around early

Below: Nimrod in Curaçao

2003, this base was shut as part of the US Navy cutbacks. In 2004 the Nimrod was seen in the Dutch Antilles on the island of Curacao which must have been ideal from the interception viewpoint since it is very close to Colombia, the origin of most of the drugs. On the other hand the 'down side' must have been that the island with its casinos renowned for money laundering of drug money was perhaps too close to Colombia since anyone with a pair of binoculars would have been able to sit and watch Nimrod or the USAF P3C aircraft taking off and warn the drug runners.

Apparently the drug boat traffic would normally leave from the Colombian coast just as it was getting dark. Presumably the aircraft, P3Cs or Nimrods, from co-operating air forces, searching for the drug runners would on occasions get information of the boats leaving. In nearly all cases the drugs would be heading for Europe or the USA but there was no way that these small Colombian boats could go all the way so they had to make intermediate stops in Haiti or Jamaica to allow the drugs to be transferred to a larger ocean-going vessel. The Nimrod must have been ideal to locate the very fast open-decked fishing vessel, usually fitted with very large outboard engines as it departed the Colombian coast; the aircraft's superb Searchwater radar was obviously perfect for this task and must easily have found these small fast vessels; presumably the aircraft was operating from there because of its radar in spite of the availability

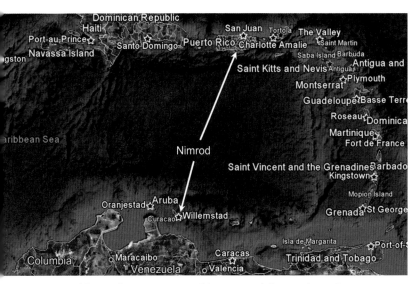

Caribbean showing Nimrod bases used for tracking drug running

of the USAF P3Cs and occasionally UK AWACS. The word in the restaurants was that on almost every night that the Nimrod was airborne detection was made, weather permitting.

The drug-running boats could do fifty knots so spotting the boats must have been only half the battle. Allied naval ships would be needed to actually intercept the vessels and of course they would not have been able to match the speed of the drug runners. Presumably if the naval ships were very lucky they could catch the boats if they came close and an arrest could be made. If the Nimrod spotted a boat it would have been able to tell the closest naval vessel the position, speed and direction of the drug runner; a helicopter could be launched and vectored by the Nimrod to the boat and if it did not stop then a sniper on the helicopter might try to hit one of the engines so that the boat would slow down and could be intercepted by the naval vessel.

Nimrods were equipped with either a Sandpiper or Wescam infrared camera and so if the boat was forced to slow down the Nimrod crew would have been able actually to see the drugs being thrown over the side in an attempt to get rid of the evidence before the warship could arrive; anyway it is believed that the drugs would actually float and could be picked up later. There is a story that on a couple of occasions a searching Nimrod was running short of fuel and actually landed, refuelled and found the drug runner again, such was the excellence of the Searchwater radar and the ability to drop DIFAR sonobuoys to help find the suspect.

According to the internet, the drug cartels were willing to spend very large amounts of money to get the drugs to market; on several occasions small submarines were actually built in an attempt to beat detection. Also on many occasions the drug barons used aircraft to smuggle the drugs and the USAF has a special balloon with an airborne radar under slung to it in the Florida Keys just to help detect low flying drugs aircraft; they also had a pair of F15s on standby at Homestead AFB and many Drug Enforcement aircraft ready to intercept any inbound boat or aircraft.

Besides trying to stop the drugs leaving the Caribbean, the Nimrod was occasionally used to catch the drug runners arriving in the British Isles after a 4,000-mile transit when the intelligence was good enough to know which area to search. From the small, very fast powerboats in the Caribbean, the drugs would be loaded into what was called a mother ship; this could be a tug, a sailboat or a small freighter. The reason for calling this vessel the mother ship was that on most occasions, the drugs would be off loaded into smaller 'daughter vessels' at the final destination. Almost anything that was seaworthy and would not draw attention to itself was used. These boats might only ever be used for one delivery and would usually have little value in relation to the millions of pounds of drugs being carried.

The advantage of the Nimrod was that it enabled a wide area to be searched at speed compared with piston-engined aircraft. If the identity, point of departure, and likely speed of the suspect was known then a large area search could be employed to locate the target; however, the aircraft had to be very careful not to alert the vessel. The drill was to try to identify the vessel from astern and if a likely suspect was found then the crew would need to avoid flying too close. The suspect would be trailed by the Nimrod above cloud and at night with the lights turned off. Obviously this could go on for days until it was close enough to the UK for a warship to send ratings on board or use some other method to assault the vessel. HM Customs or the police would also have some sort of presence as the arresting agency so that it was never necessary for the Nimrod to be mentioned, another reason why the public remained sublimely ignorant of the work the aircraft was doing.

Besides watching for drug shipments, apparently the Nimrods also played a part in detecting arms shipments to the IRA. Christopher Andrew's book *Defence of the Realm* mentions the success the Garda had on 29th September 1984 seizing the Irish trawler *Marita Ann* which was packed with weapons and ammunition. Allegedly a Nimrod, presumably from 42 Squadron then based in St Mawgan, observed arms being transferred to the trawler from an

HMS *Victorious*, no longer protected whilst at sea

American trawler which had crossed the Atlantic with its port of registration blanked out. There are many more stories that could be told but security prevents them appearing in print at this time. However, from the tales narrated above it can be seen what a great job the Nimrod did throughout the years without any publicity and little recognition.

5 NIMROD SEARCH AND RESCUE SORTIES

One of the primary jobs of the Nimrod was to provide search and rescue (SAR) for every sort of vessel from small yachts to large ships. The Nimrod was ideally suited to the task being able to drop rescue gear at long distances from the shores of the UK. It could fly 2,000 nautical miles into the Atlantic and way north to the Arctic Circle without air-to-air refuelling and even further if accompanied by a tanker. The aircraft was also important at closer distances by pinpointing the target so that helicopters could fly to their maximum rescue range without using critical fuel searching before rescuing. In addition under Operation Tapestry the Nimrods had the responsibility for protecting and monitoring the fishing fleet and the offshore oil rigs and pipe installations.

There were quite a few Russian intelligence-gathering ships disguised as trawlers in the area and so the Nimrods were not only checking for illegal fishing but also trying to identify the Soviet boats. In this chapter I have included a number of first-hand accounts of Nimrod search and rescues which demonstrate how effective the aircraft were in dealing with the whole range of emergencies from oil rig disasters to rescuing crews from small yachts.

While the Nimrod MR1/MR2 was in service there was always one aircraft available for search and rescue operations at one-hour standby 24/7 either at Kinloss or St Mawgan. The aircraft that was on standby would have the weapons bay fully loaded with two full SAR packages of Lindholme air sea rescue (ASR) gear and six further dinghy pairs; the ASR consisted of one ten-

Below: On search and rescue standby 24/7

man dinghy connected with two containers that had water, batteries, personal life buoys etc. The idea of the ASR was to drop the equipment up wind of the survivors with each individual part of the three items approximately 200 yards apart, joined by a floating line which, once in the water, would float down onto the survivors. Because of the low altitude of the drop, 200ft, the last container was still connected in the bomb bay when the first one hit the water.

In addition to the standby SAR aircraft there would often be another Nimrod airborne on a training mission which also carried a set of Lindholme gear. As well as using the aircraft sensors to find aircraft or ships in trouble, the Nimrod could also locate survivors in the water, with its capability to search areas of up to 20,000 square miles (52,000 km^2).

The main role for the aircraft, if the rescue location was within UK helicopter range, would be to act as the on-the-scene rescue coordinator to control all rescue ships, fixed-wing aircraft, and helicopters coming into the SAR area. Outside the helicopter rescue area, or even inside if necessary, the Nimrod would drop dinghies if it were appropriate.

PIPER ALPHA DISASTER, 6 JULY 1988

I am starting with this terrible event because it shows very dramatically how important it was to have the Nimrod on the spot coordinating all the rescue resources and reporting back to the rescue centres on the state of the emergency.

In July 1988 there was a major oil rig disaster at Piper Alpha, 120 miles off the north-east coast of Scotland. Sqn Ldr Garry Porter flying at 15,000 ft in XV228 was the first Nimrod in the area as they arrived at about 2am with the sky being illuminated by the burning rig. The challenge for the crew was to co-ordinate the rescue vessels, marine and airborne. Rescue helicopters from Lossiemouth and Sumburgh arrived about thirty minutes later and started taking survivors to the local hospitals. Most of the nearby rigs had helipads but only limited amounts

Below: Piper Alpha on fire

Piper Alpha after the fire

of fuel so decisions were required all the time on where the searching rescue helicopters could go if they needed to refuel, not an easy task with up to twelve helicopters to deal with. Nimrod crews were not air traffic controllers and in theory could not instruct the helicopters on what to do but could advise them; it was a delicate balancing act. As the night progressed the situation was complicated by the arrival of naval and commercial rescue boats. Sqn Ldr Porter and his crew were relieved by another Nimrod two hours after daybreak, and his flight had lasted eight hours, thirty-five minutes.

Joe Kennedy was the radio operator in the first crew to arrive on the scene and I cannot do better than to include his commentary on the disaster since it describes so clearly how complicated were the tasks being carried out by the various members of the crew:

"The phone downstairs rang again and someone answered. I lay there, ears cocked, expecting the call of 'Stand down' but instead the urgent shout 'Scramble' burst through the air. Immediately, everyone jumped out of bed and in a scuffle of arms and legs, pulled on flying clothing and dived downstairs to the SAR van which was already started. We all piled in and set off for the pan and XV228, our waiting Nimrod. I glanced at my watch; it was 2222. In a befuddled state of mind, I was trying to work out how a planned leisurely launch at about 2330 had turned into a scramble so quickly. We arrived at the pan within a minute and grabbed the plethora of heavy bags with confidential documents and planning material that were the hallmark of Nimrod operations, from the officer's wagon. I asked one of the officers what was happening and he said there was an oil rig in the North Sea with a small fire on the deck; we were being scrambled as a precaution.

"The groundcrew were buzzing round the jet preparing it for a quick start. SAR scrambles are emergencies and there was no time for the niceties of a standard planned flight, it was always a case of 'kick the tyres and light the fires', while still observing all safety procedures. Any Nimrod scramble was exciting and everyone played their part to get the jet airborne as soon as possible; the mandated timescale was to be in the air within one hour of receiving notification, but in reality, most crews managed anywhere between 15-30 mins depending on which runway at Kinloss was in use. We had a problem in aligning the navigation system and there was a delay. The inertial navigation system (INS) used gyros which required a finite period of time to spin up and become stable in order to fix their (and the jet's) position in space and time. This night, they took much longer than normal. The aircraft captain was in the tac nav's position controlling the whole mission and he decided that we should wait for the INS to align; failure to do so would have created an unacceptable workload not only for him but the whole crew, as the INS was pivotal to the Nimrod's mission brains, the central tactical system (CTS).

"I had jumped onto my position on the Searchwater radar and carried out rapid preflight checks. However, although the radar system itself was fine, it took its primary positional feeds from the CTS and so was next to useless without this facility. We waited while a nav instruments techie worked with the routine nav, Flt Lt Ali Barber, to troubleshoot and fix the problem. In the meantime, the radio operator was on the HF radio talking to the Rescue Co-ordination Centre (RCC) at Pitreavie Castle, north of Edinburgh. They gave him a Sitrep (situation report) of the latest SAR details which even at this stage were very sketchy. The aircraft's callsign was to be the standard Rescue 01. On intercom 'Radios' relayed the available news to the rest of the crew who were eagerly awaiting any sort of information with which they could start to plan the mission. By the end of his short and concise brief we knew that we were going to the Piper Alpha oil production platform about 120 miles NE of Aberdeen. The rig was on fire, the crew were evacuating and up to six military and civilian helicopters were en-route to the incident. As we continued to wait for the nav kit to come up, I pondered this information and began to realise that this was maybe not going to be a standard SAR event. The groundcrew chief plugged his headset in and quietly asked if we knew what the SAR shout was for; someone said it was a fire on a North Sea oil rig, the chief asked if we knew which one as his brother was out there, we told him the Piper Alpha, but by that time we were ready to start and we never did find out which platform he was on. After the nav problem was fixed, we rapidly started all four engines and carried out afterstart checks without further incident. We moved forward and taxied as fast as was allowed to make up for lost time. At the end of the runway, we received take-off clearance and with a roar from the power of four Rolls-Royce Spey engines, powered into the twilight of a summer's evening at 2255, just over thirty minutes from being called. None of us could begin to imagine the scene we were about to witness.

"As XV228 roared off the runway and climbed into the calm evening sky, various crewmembers started talking to all the agencies normally involved in SAR missions. Radios swivelled his seat 180 degrees from the take-off position to face rearwards at the cramped radio station with small desk, teletypewriters, and a bank of HF and V/UHF radio boxes. Immediately, he keyed the transmit switch and spoke to Edinburgh Rescue, the RCC at Pitreavie, advising them that Rescue 01 was airborne at 2255, fully serviceable and ETA on scene was 2325. He then transcribed this short message onto his paper radio log, standard practice for any Nimrod mission and kept as a legal record of all long-range communications coming into and out of the aircraft; a normal mission log would consist of three or four pages. As Radios used his own brand of short hand to contemporaneously record these messages, little did he realise that his log tonight would run into six times that amount and be the centrepiece of subsequent inquiries.

"While Radios spoke to the RCC, the AEO, George Woodhouse, was sitting at the tac nav's right shoulder, working the marine band FM radio with Aberdeen coastguard. At that time, the coastguard probably had the most up-to-date information on the incident, and George was kept busy compiling the details of all the rotary assets which were either en-route to Piper or were preparing to launch from the shore or from adjacent oil fields. Meanwhile, I selected the Searchwater radar to transmit and configured it to find the Lossiemouth helicopter, Rescue 137, which I knew was going to be on our track, albeit well below our transit altitude. I had no idea where Piper Alpha was in the vastness of the North Sea and where it fitted in with all the other oil fields and therefore broke into the busy intercom to request an electronic pointer from the tac nav so that I could concentrate my surface search in the required area. What nobody expected next was the P1 (Major Gary Barth, Canadian exchange officer) calmly advising the crew that he could see a large orange glow on track beyond the horizon. Our Nimrod was still over 80nm from the platform, and simultaneously the realisation struck everyone that this had developed well beyond a small deck fire. The atmosphere in Rescue 01 suddenly chilled as the implications of the new information became clear. This was going to be a very major incident.

"I identified the distinctive shaped eyebrow IFF 'squawk' from the Lossie Sea King R137 just ahead of us, and the pilots spoke to him to pass our flight information and to request an ETA on scene. No other helicopters had reached the Piper yet. As we got closer to the rig, the flight deck started giving a visual description of the scene unfolding in front of them, and it didn't make a reassuring picture; the captain had to break into the commentary to focus the crew on the task in hand and to get the aircraft 'cocked' for whatever we were required to do. Checks were read out, lookout positions manned and a quick radio 'box' brief was conducted so that the whole crew, but especially those with control over particular radios, were aware who had responsibility for what box and what net that box was covering. Specifically, the pilots had one V/UHF box for ATC, another to talk to surface vessels and rigs. The routine nav, Ali Barber, was responsible for co-ordinating helos and tasking them. George Woodhouse, the AEO, had perhaps the busiest circuit, talking to all the users of the FM Channel 16, which is the recognised maritime emergency channel, while Radios at the dedicated radio position, controlled both HF sets, one set exclusively to the RCC frequency and one as a 'floater' for weather broadcasts or long-range comms with our Maritime HQ at Northwood, Middlesex.

"No two SAR incidents are alike, although it was possible to apply a standard template to most Nimrod events; this incident was unlike any that the crew had experienced before in terms of the scale, complexity and initial chaos of the situation confronting Rescue 01 as we descended from a medium transit altitude to low level at the scene of the unfolding disaster. All crewmembers were working hard to make sense of the bedlam that manifested itself in the form of urgent calls on the FM, air-to-air net and between rig safety vessels. The initial explosion had occurred over ninety minutes prior to the time Rescue 01 arrived and the airwaves were full of uncoordinated reports and random screams and shouts. Total confusion reigned. On radar, I was heads in to my PPI screen, raising contact files on everything I could within the vicinity of the Piper Alpha and electronically copying those files through to the main CTS screen so that the tac nav, in overall command, could see the 'big' picture and control the incident using the best information available. His initial job was to correlate my radar files with information coming in from the radios and work out who was who.

"We arrived on scene at about 2330 and the captain directed that we fly by the burning rig to assess the situation for ourselves. On radar I had my window blind down, but as we approached the rig, it was as bright as day and I raised the blind to observe Piper Alpha for myself. I could not believe what I was seeing. We were all used to flying round the North Sea oil fields and seeing these massive steel structures rising from the water like some metal 'War of the Worlds' monsters, but tonight I was witnessing the complete destruction of one of them. The rig was engulfed in an angry red and orange fire from sea level to the top of its drilling tower and as I watched, an eruption of more gas-fuelled flames broke out under the main level towards the sea. At the same time, I could hear men screaming on the FM radio. I couldn't listen to the terror in those voices and deselected the radio from my panel so I could concentrate. As we flew past the Piper at about 500 feet and a mile distant, the senses were assailed by the ferocity of the fire and the smell and the smoke rupturing an otherwise peaceful North Sea summer evening. I wouldn't have believed it was possible, but you could feel the heat from the fire through the aircraft fuselage and at that point I think, the captain wisely decided to climb away from the scene in case of further explosions.

"On radar, I suddenly remembered the TEAC recording system and started loading bulky video tapes into the machine in order to capture the radar picture. In the initial confusion of the 'shout' this had not been the highest priority, but I assumed that any subsequent inquiries about the incident would want this information.

"Events moved on quickly now, the frequencies were being restored to order as everyone realised that the situation called for clarity of thought and accuracy of information. Rescue 137 arrived on scene and was directed initially to talk to the *Tharos*, a purpose-built fire fighting, rescue and accommodation semi-submersible which was adjacent to Piper. The radio chatter was constant on all nets and it was only by selecting and deselecting individual boxes and listening for a few minutes that anyone on Rescue 01 could assimilate information. On radar, I could hear the names *Tharos, Sandhaven,* and *Silver Pit* together with mention of various FRCs (fast rescue craft). At the time, I had no idea what any of these vessels were or where they were, they were just names used constantly on the radios, but I quickly realised they were all close by the Piper and all were heavily involved in the rescue.

"It's worth pointing out that by this stage of the incident, the only information we had been briefed from Aberdeen coastguard was that all personnel on Piper Alpha were evacuating. The mindset within Rescue 01 as we witnessed this catastrophe was that somewhere, either in lifeboats on the water or already on nearby vessels, the crew of Piper Alpha were safe. We couldn't begin to contemplate that they were anywhere near the inferno that raged in front of us. At this time also, we had no idea of the numbers of people involved, although that information had been requested as a matter of urgency. In short, we believed we were dealing with a situation where helicopters and fishing vessels would be able to search for and rescue those oil workers who must surely be in the vicinity of Piper Alpha. Before the helicopters arrived, it was even suggested that we should commence a visual search ourselves for lifeboats or survivors in the water, but the proximity to the burning rig and the fact that multiple helicopter assets would shortly be arriving quickly put paid to that plan.

"Radios on the RCC net, transmitted his initial Sitrep to Edinburgh Rescue and this was the first occasion that the outside world became aware of the scale of the disaster that had occurred in the North Sea. In 1988 this was before the internet or mass media capability had taken hold and little did we realise that the world's news organisations would be hanging on his every word.

"In pretty short order, three RAF Sea Kings and four civilian helicopters arrived at the scene and all required a tasking from Rescue 01 who they must have assumed was fully conversant with the situation. The truth was that no-one was on top of this incident, although as the designated on-scene commander, it was our responsibility to take control and effect the most efficient and expeditious rescue and recovery of the Piper people. The helicopters needed little direction other than a search sector, so the tac nav compiled a list of the available assets and divided up the search area around Piper up to two miles radius with a view to expand outwards as time progressed. Each helicopter was allocated a segment to search for survivors and I recall requesting unique IFF squawk codes to be assigned to each one to enable me to keep track of them on radar. It was important to emphasize that we were not trained ATC controllers and could take no responsibility for safe separation of the helos. Nevertheless I tried as best I could to monitor the progress of all the rotary traffic. Some of the military winch-capable aircraft were diverted from the search to conduct a transfer of injured survivors to the rescue facility on *Tharos* which had a good medical capability.

"I don't remember how long it took, but eventually, something akin to a calm workmanlike approach started to take hold of all assets and we began to get ahead of the game and take control of the situation. By now the helicopters were concerned about their fuel requirements and we then had to think about contacting nearby platforms to find out how much aviation fuel they had to give away. Additional to the seven helos which had responded initially, it became apparent to Radios on the HF that many other helicopters wanted to come out and help their oil colleagues. This was a noble gesture and under any other circumstance would have been welcomed; however, it was necessary to adopt a hardnosed pragmatic approach and Radios unilaterally held off the incoming rotary traffic and requested they return to shore until called in. This was a courageous and wise decision from our most inexperienced dry operator who recognised that, until the situation was clarified, we had sufficient helicopters in a very small area and adding more would simply compromise flight safety.

"Time passed in a blur and everyone on the Nimrod was working hard, either talking on a radio, or compiling details of nearby rigs, fuel, medical facilities, helicopter passenger capability, fuel requirements and a myriad of other information. Our own flight engineer was monitoring his systems performance and fuel burn to ensure we maximised our time over the scene. In short there was no-one spare to carry out any ancillary tasks such as making drinks or meals, and the normal hourly rotation of dry men on the radar went out of the window. This didn't seem to matter though as the whole crew were just intent on keeping on top of the situation and ensuring we did our job as professionally as possible. After what seemed a lifetime, we eventually managed to establish a routine whereby the captain would call for a brief from key players. At these points, all would finish the task they were doing and listen to briefs from other crewmen; if required they would make their own report. At the end of these two-minute mini briefs, the captain would summarise the current situation and detail his future intentions. This was the only way that command and control could be established in a chaotic, dynamic SAR incident. One of the defining moments of the night came just after midnight when the coastguard advised Rescue 01 that there were believed to be 220 persons onboard Piper Alpha. This was disheartening news as the reports of known survivors rescued had been in terms of ones and twos. One of the mini briefs recorded that the tally of survivors accounted for was less than forty. Everyone on board Rescue 01 realised at once the stark reality of this figure. Few people had been plucked from the water and the obvious inference was that many of Piper's crew remained on the rig. From our vantage point high over the scene it was clear by about 0030 that the fire had died down; at first we put this down to fire-fighting efforts, but radio traffic from *Tharos* indicated that most of the main structure of Piper Alpha had in fact fallen into the sea and there was little recognisable structure remaining other than the legs and a gas burn-off spar.

"The mood inside Rescue 01 became more and more subdued as weariness took hold and the reports from rescue vessels became less frequent. Helicopters were not reporting any rescue activity and the only chatter was to source fuel from adjacent rigs. By about 0300 the situation was stabilised and the major activity on Rescue 01 was on the HF radios. The world's media were clamouring for information and the RCC and coastguard were lining up interviews with the captain sitting in the tac nav seat. Those of us with an HF receive capability, ear-wigged as Garry Porter told the world clearly and concisely what had been happening overnight and who had been involved. It made for sombre listening and eventually I switched off to concentrate on my task of monitoring helicopter search patterns. Before we knew it, dawn was upon us and as the sun rose tentatively in the east, casting rays of hope across the still calm North Sea, we looked down from 20,000 ft and saw a jumble of vessels crowded round a stump of twisted and blackened metal; a disfigured structure which continued to spew out black smoke into the new day. Flames still poured high into the sky from one of the ruptured gas lines, but otherwise all was calm.

"At about 0600, it was almost time for Rescue 01 to depart and our relief aircraft was already on the radio looking for a handover brief. On radar I identified them coming out to us and listened as the familiar voices of a fellow 206 Sqn crew sounding fresh and eager got stronger as they neared our position. The handover they got was as comprehensive as we could make it, but they must have guessed from the tired and strained tones that the chance of further survivors was slim and that their main task would be comms relay. Then we powered up the engines and climbed away from the scene having completed all comms with the vessels we had got to know so well during the long night.

"Rescue 01 landed back at Kinloss at 0700 on Thursday morning, having been airborne for just over eight hours. Despite the fatigue, there was still plenty to do post flight. Principally, the AEO and captain had to compile the Form R, a standard SAR debrief message. Normally, this would be completed in minutes, but a major incident such as Piper Alpha required lots of detail as it would patently be used for the subsequent inquiry. George and Garry pored over their logs with the debriefing officer for ages. I handed all my safety equipment in and still had a large bag full of TEAC video tapes that I tried to hand into the cell dealing with such things. The chap on duty was obviously overwhelmed by the task of signing in so many tapes and couldn't understand the relevance of the data contained in them, so I took them back and placed them in my secure locker for safe keeping until someone required them for the inquiry which was certain to follow.

"The remainder of the crew were still on an adrenaline buzz although tiredness was creeping up and we milled around in ops waiting for some direction or a crew debrief. None came and eventually we all started sloping off to drive home to bed. Meanwhile the ops officer had told the crew execs, ie captain, P1 and AEO to freshen up as they would shortly be facing the major news organisations at a press conference which was being hastily convened. As the rest of us sneaked out of ops, I turned round to George, gave him a cheeky grin and mouthed "Unlucky!"

"I drove out of the camp gates as a normal day for the rest of Kinloss was just beginning. I was looking forward to jumping into my bed but then remembered, as I neared Forres, that my Scirocco GTI was booked in for its MOT that morning. I got home, changed, and drove down to my local garage to drop the car off. As I handed over the keys, the receptionist said what a terrible night that had been in the North Sea; I just nodded and muttered something about the tragedy of it, I couldn't face talking about Piper Alpha, I just wanted my bed. I walked back home through lovely woodland and park and listened as the birds sang their hearts out. The sun was shining bright, the morning warming up, it was another gorgeous day.

"Piper Alpha marked a watershed in UK offshore safety. It also marked a whole new approach to major SAR incidents involving Nimrods. In the days and weeks following the disaster, Sqn Ldr Porter and other crew members carried out a full debrief of the incident in order to ensure that lessons were learned. A formalised structure to any SAR incident was created and SAR checklists written to enable any crew to efficiently undertake any SAR mission no matter how routine or complex. The review enshrined the principle that everyone on the crew had a specific role to play and knew what that role was and his/her responsibilities. New simulator exercises were created and could be modified to build up the complexity of a scenario in order that crews could be trained from scratch. All Nimrod crews were mandated to undertake a dedicated SAR scenario in the simulator at least once every six months; additionally it was part of a new captain's workup package. The scenario replicated Piper in so far as no-one knew what was going to happen or where the incident was until the crew had been 'scrambled' and contacted Kinloss Ops or the RCC.

"Although the scenarios weren't specifically oil rig disasters, invariably they would involve a ship in distress drifting inside an oil field requiring mass evacuations, or more likely two or more inter-related incidents involving collisions at sea requiring the use of multiple surface and airborne rescue assets, dealing with survivors and the search for missing persons. They were always big exercises in co-ordination and were extremely challenging but incredibly satisfying when conducted well. In reality, the training paid off as Nimrod crews carried out many SAR missions, mostly routine 'top cover' sorties for helicopters, but a number of what could definitely be called large-scale events. At these times, crews were grateful for the quality of the training they had received; the effectiveness of the Nimrod aircraft in SAR incidents was well and truly recognised and any mention of Nimrod and SAR in the public domain is invariably accompanied by the words Piper Alpha.

"For 206 Sqn Crew 8, things moved on and we quickly got back into the routine of life on a maritime unit. There were no big discussions or counselling, we all just dealt with Piper Alpha in our own way. After a day's rest, we then had a crew training day at the radar station down the coast at RAF Buchan; the following week found us on a pre-planned detachment to NAS Valkenburg, a Dutch P3 base near Amsterdam. The following month I was mourning the loss of two former 206 Sqn colleagues who were killed in a Tornado mid-air collision over Cumbria. In December, I was part of a crew ferrying Kinloss personnel round the country on Xmas leave; as we flew back home we crossed high over the little known town of Lockerbie. A few hours later it became a very well known little town. For us life carried on; people moved on with postings and promotions and, within six months, the crew who had carried out the Piper Alpha SAR mission were split to the four winds.

"I've never forgotten Piper Alpha however, and even after twenty years, can still recall that first awe-inspiring sight of the inferno; despite that, the human cost of the tragedy has remained largely transparent to me – 165 crew of the oil rig died, as well as two men in a fast rescue craft. In July 2008, I was confronted with the reality of that human tragedy as, together with the then OC 42(R) Sqn and OC D Flt 202 Sqn at Lossiemouth, I attended services to mark the twentieth anniversary of the disaster in Aberdeen. At the main service of remembrance in the Kirk of St Nicholas, off Union Street, I finally came face to face with the friends and families of those who had lost their lives and felt humbled as the brother of one victim shook my hand for being there for him. He was eternally grateful that I had been at the scene of his brother's death and had a first-hand understanding of the disaster. Later, at a second service at the impressive Piper Alpha memorial and rose garden in Hazelhead Park, Aberdeen, I met other families and friends and was struck by their courage, humility and strength in dealing with the aftermath of the tragedy. I was in uniform and a gentleman took me to one side and thanked me profusely for my contribution to the SAR incident. I told him that it was very much a team effort and that actually our contribution on Rescue 01 was small in comparison to the helicopters and rescue vessels and those who had actually put their lives on the line. Nevertheless, he had heard the chaos and confusion on the radios when the incident had first occurred; once the Nimrod arrived, he said, calm and professionalism on the airwaves smoothed the situation and everyone knew that help had finally arrived. It was very gratifying to hear that, but I still felt very small in such a gathering of giants. However, when all is said and done, and despite the fact we could do nothing to prevent the fatalities on Piper Alpha, it was nice to know that the people who mattered were genuinely grateful for the contribution of Nimrod Rescue 01."

I have included the whole of Joe Kennedy's write up on Piper Alpha as it demonstrates so well the team work of a Nimrod crew. In the event a total of three Nimrods covered the disaster lasting twenty-four hours and at the peak the co-ordination task was supervising twenty-five rescue vessels and ten helicopters for which Porter got a Queens Commendation for Valuable

Above: Alexander Kielland rig in position; *Below left*: tilting and *bottom left*: upside down

Services in the Air. This tragedy when 167 lives were lost but sixty-one lives were saved demonstrates again what a wonderful job the Nimrod was capable of performing by being able to communicate with and control so many resources.

LOSS OF ALEXANDER L. KIELLAND 1980

Another disaster was the loss of the Alexander L. Kielland , a Norwegian semi-submersible drilling rig, that capsized whilst working in the Ekofisk oil field in March 1980 killing 123 people.

Six different Nimrods searched for survivors and took it in turn to provide a rescue co-ordination role, involving the control of eighty surface ships and twenty British and Norwegian helicopters; control became particularly important as the visibility deteriorated. The coordinating efforts of the aircraft helped to ensure that eighty-nine lives were saved.

DINGHY DROPPING

The Nimrod with its excellent search radar was supreme in locating survivors in liferafts and dropping dinghies and survival gear as necessary. Through the years the Nimrod rescued many yachtsmen, trawler and even ships' crews by this means. Chris Herbert sent me a list from the squadron histories of all the drops they made starting in 1973 with the freighter SS *Christa Thielemann* where all five crew were saved by a very accurate drop. In 1977 Mr Enda Coineen was saved trying to cross the Atlantic in a zodiac inflatable and in the same year two crew were rescued in the Mediterranean from a Cypriot freighter. In 1978 dinghies rescued a Dutch Bréguet Atlantique crew in the Atlantic.

In 1981 the Secretary of State John Nott was on board a Nimrod chasing a submarine when a trimaran capsized and the aircraft was diverted to the yacht and made a contact but had to return due to reaching PLE. Another Nimrod took over and dropped Lindholme gear which landed close enough for the crew to get into. However unbeknown to the crew the drop was faulty in that only one dinghy and the survival pack came out successfully. Luckily thirty minutes later they returned and discovered that the dinghy they had dropped had deflated and the guys were in serious trouble. They made another drop, again faulty, but this time the dinghy did not deflate. However though the crew got into the second dinghy they left their SARBE emergency beacon behind so the Nimrod crew did not know that all was well as they could not see any signs of life in the second dinghy. Luckily they had vectored a Fyffes banana boat to the dinghy and though the ship could not help to take on the crew because of the horrendous sea state they were able to tell the Nimrod crew that the crew were safely in the dinghy. They were finally winched to safety by a Sea King after it had refuelled in Eire on the way.

In January 1990 the *Irving Forest*, 8,000 tons, en route from Canada to Rouen with a load of wood pulp developed a list of 20 degrees due to water entering her ballast tanks. The weather was a force six-seven wind gusting forty knots but luckily the visibility was good. The sea was rough, height four-five metres and a heavy swell of about five metres. Next there was a complete electrical failure, containers were being lost overboard, the list increased to thirty-five degrees and the master sent out a mayday call. The accident report goes on:

Above and below: Irving Forest and dinghy

"The 2nd engineer had injured his back whilst working on the port generator, and was brought up to the boat deck on a stretcher, where all the crew were assembling wearing survival suits in preparation for abandoning ship. Prayers were said. Due to the heavy list, the lifeboats were unusable, and it was found impossible to launch the starboard inflatable liferaft. The port inflatable liferaft was launched with difficulty and brought round to the starboard quarter for boarding. In the meantime, the chief officer and the 2nd engineer's wife were swept overboard. By great good fortune, an RAF Nimrod aircraft arrived on scene at this moment, and was able to drop a Lindholme air sea rescue apparatus and two liferafts, one of which the chief officer and 2nd engineer's wife were able to reach and hook on to. Shortly after this, one of the seamen went overboard and managed to board this raft and assist the 2nd engineer's wife, who was exhausted, and the chief officer, who had injured his knee, to board the raft also. The raft drifted down towards BT NESTOR, which had just arrived, and the three survivors were taken on board."

The rest of the crew managed to get into the one remaining ship's liferaft and the *Nestor* managed to get them all on board. It was on occasions like this that the Nimrod was so essential and effective and the crew obviously did a great job in this rescue by dropping the gear in exactly the right place.

On 5 September 1998 the wooden trawler *Margaret and William II* with five crew went missing somewhere in the Western Approaches but fortunately the skipper of another trawler *Confide* noticed that the trawler had not returned to Newlyn as expected. He reported to the coastguard and a PAN message was broadcast soon after 0555. As no response was received a mayday relay message was sent out at 0935 and a Nimrod from 42 Squadron St Mawgan was scrambled to start a search from the trawler's last known position twenty-four hours earlier. At 1020 the Dutch tanker *Jacobus Broere* at anchor in Barry Roads received the mayday call; the master had already been advised by his crew when they anchored at 0650 that there was fresh paint on the bow of unknown origin and so he contacted the Swansea coastguard and advised them of a possible contact at about 1645 the previous day.

The Nimrod located an inflatable liferaft at 1343 and a helicopter from RNAS Culdrose consequently rescued three survivors who confirmed that the boat had been hit by a larger boat and had sunk immediately. The search continued for the remaining two crew members but was finally called off at 1950 hrs GMT with nothing further being found. It was estimated that the dinghy had drifted twenty-eight miles since the collision. The crew who had recently returned from Iraq after outstanding service were awarded the Sir Arthur Barratt Memorial Prize for 1991; the citation read " …in recognition of their outstanding skill and proficiency demonstrated, both at peace and war, throughout a very busy and often turbulent 1991."

Helicopter about to rescue survivors from *Margaret and William II* (Crown copyright)

I have included this rescue as it seems to be the perfect operation. The survivors were saved because everyone concerned played their part from the initiation of the alarm, the broadcast of the emergency messages, the tanker skipper immediately telling the coastguard, the Nimrod finding the dinghy and the helicopter rescuing the survivors. Per-

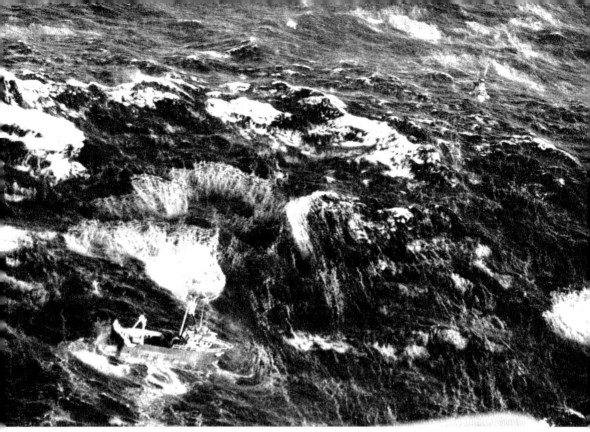

Above and below: Sonia Nancy. Note the size of the waves compared with that of the helicopter

haps it should be added that the weather was relatively kind ENE force 5.

Another use of dinghies occurred on 4 January 1998 when a Nimrod went to assist an Irish trawler, the *Sonia Nancy*, operating out of Spain with nine Spaniards and one Irishman. The boat was being towed by another trawler having had an engine failure when the tow line snapped and the boat started sinking 200 miles south west of the Scillies. The weather was dreadful with a wind of 60 knots, a huge sea state and a swell of 40 to 60ft. The situation was made even worse with extensive thunderstorm activity in the area. The Nimrod dropped two sets of dinghies and the trawler's crew managed to secure one of them. The aircraft was struck by lightning but the crew elected to provide safety cover until a second Nimrod came to relieve them. The crew captained by Flt Lt Kev Hughes got a special commendation for their exemplary perform-ance. The trawler's crew was rescued by a helicopter from Chivenor after having made two refuelling stops at Cork and Castledownbere.

On 5 March 2001 the German-registered trawler *Hansa* sank at 2310 in the Atlantic 240 miles west of Tiree in 15ft seas; there were fifteen Spanish nationals on board and one German. Nine members of the crew were airlifted by helicopter from a liferaft to Benbecula but seven were given up for dead due to the water temperature of 10°C . A Canadian Air Force Aurora was first on the scene and then relieved by a Nimrod, Captain Flt Lt Kev Hughes. Another Nimrod, Captain John Meston, arrived twelve hours after the trawler had sunk with the seas still very rough and all hope for survivors having been given up. Incredibly one of the crew, Mark Lister, spotted a figure in the water wearing an orange survival suit waving to the aircraft and, showing first class skill, the crew managed to drop two dinghies linked by 400 ft of rope upwind of the man, no mean feat. He managed to get hold of the rope, pull one of dinghies towards him and amazingly clamber in where he was rescued later by helicopter. The crew reported: 'What that guy did was superhuman and I think it was a tremendous will to survive that kept him going'. In fact he owed his life not only to the Nimrod crew but also to the fact that he was wearing an immersion suit which insulated him from the water temperature which was 27° below normal body temperature.

The final example given here was in 2005 in a yacht race from Le Havre to Salvador in Brazil. The 60 kt weather caused two French trimarans to capsize and dismasted a third. Dinghies were dropped and helicopters vectored to the stricken boats where the crews were saved. As mentioned, the Nimrod always played a double role, dropping dinghies if necessary and vectoring helicopters and rescue boats to the craft in difficulty.

THE FASTNET RACE 1979

The 1979 Fastnet Race is another splendid example of the role that the Nimrod carried out in helping to save lives when yachts got into distress. The race this particular year took place in terrible weather and will always be a special and sad memory for all concerned. The race as usual started from Cowes in the Isle of Wight and the course was round the Fastnet Rock off south-west Eire and then returning, finishing in Plymouth. I did the race once and it is about 605 nautical miles, a long way in a small boat. On this occasion we were living in Dartmouth and quite a few of the participants were from our yacht club, The Royal Dart, so I was taking a great interest in the progress of the race. I find it an amazing co-incidence that I am writing about it many years later.

At the start of the race the BBC radio shipping forecast at 13:55 predicted south-westerly

Below: Fastnet Race. Cowes-Fastnet Rock-Plymouth

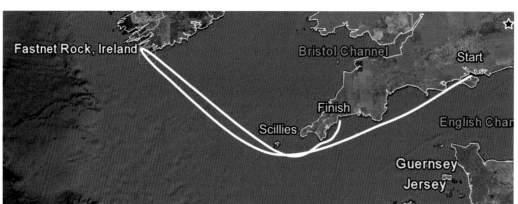

winds, force four to five increasing to force six to seven for a time. However after the start the winds were reported at force six, with gusts of force seven and then the forecast changed to predicting even stronger winds of force eight and later turning into a severe gale force nine and the new forecast was spot on. 306 yachts took part in the race and twenty-five boats were sunk or disabled and tragically fifteen lives were lost. The tally would have been much worse but for the wonderful work of the many boats, helicopters and Nimrods that took part in the search and rescue operation. Ian Marshall, then an AEOp, was in one of the Nimrods and I can't do better than include his verbatim account:

Top, below and bottom: Lifeboat and helicopter going to stricken yachts

"My crew, captained by Flt Lt Mike Graham, were tasked to fly to the south west approaches (SWAPPS) to search for some missing yachtsmen. We were not the regular crew on SAR standby who had been launched the previous day but we were the next crew on six-hour standby and launched on 16 Aug 79. I don't think any of the crew members knew much about the Fastnet race, nor do I think many of the UK public knew much either until it hit the evening news headlines for the next several nights.

"We arrived in the area to the west of Cornwall and east of south-west Eire at first light. The brief was that a yacht race had hit bad weather and several boats were in trouble. The Nimrod is fitted with beam windows, which are convex allowing the crew member to put his head out beyond the fuselage to get a good all-round view. These windows can also be opened at low altitude to allow the camera operator a clear view of the photo subject. There were yachts everywhere, some had capsized but were still floating, many had been knocked down and lost their mast, sails and rigging and there were some life rafts floating but without any survivors that we could see. Spotting an individual in the water from an aircraft at 200

ft and 220 knots is very difficult even if the survivor is wearing dayglo orange gear. Our mission was to locate each boat or piece of wreckage and home a Sea King helicopter onto the debris. The helicopter winch man would then be lowered and check if the boat or liferaft was manned and in need of assistance. Most survivors had stayed in their damaged yachts, the unlucky ones had decided to take to the liferafts in the middle of the night even though their boats continued to float. It was heartening to see so many sailors waving at us as we flew by."

In the ensuing drama, all seven of the crew from the yacht *Gringo* were saved because they were spotted by a Nimrod who radioed for a Sea King helicopter to come to the boat by giving it the position of the sinking yacht.

In spite of the weather 237 boats finished the course. Clearly it was the sudden and unexpected worsening of the weather that caused the tragedy and I was very impressed by the remarks of the responsible conservative minister John Nott who said: "It is a tragedy as many people have lost their lives. But man is going to go on pitting himself against the elements and ocean racing will carry on. There are always lessons to be learnt from every tragedy but I would not like people to feel that as a result of this disaster the Fastnet race will not continue."

MV *Victory* collision

MV *VICTORY* COLLISION 1982

The next account relates to a collision between MV *Victory* on 13 February 1982 with another vessel south of Eire. Ian Marshall again:

"My crew with Flt Lt Wallace as captain were all in bed in the officers' and sergeants' messes. There were specific rooms provided for the SAR crew who spent twenty-four hours on duty awaiting either the tannoy to order a scramble or to awake in the morning after a good night's sleep and face a fried breakfast. This time the hooter went off in the middle of the night for a scramble and all the crew went directly to the aircraft, lit the engines and took off as quickly as possible, well within the thirty minutes allowed from the signal to launch. Occasionally for an increased readiness state or an operational launch, some crew members would go to base operations en route to the aircraft to get a briefing, while the remainder of the crew prepared the aircraft.

"Tonight the AEO would be talking to operations on the VHF radio and provide the crew with the bare basics of what was required. We were to proceed to a position south west of Cornwall where a merchant ship had sent a mayday message. We arrived there approximately two hours later; it was still dark but dawn was approaching and while still at high level the radar picked up a couple of contacts in the vicinity of where we expected the incident to be. The crew started a descent to be at low level just where the radar echoes were coming from. We found the lights of two vessels, one very much larger than the other, the reason for which became very obvious when it became light. The survivors were pleading to be taken off the vessel but we explained that there was a warship to the south, with a helicopter but that it would not be there till first light; stay on board your ship was our suggestion. Unfortunately some of the crewmembers did not stay on board and elected to jump over the side. We did drop a couple of liferafts to help them but unfortunately to no avail.

"When it got light we could see the very large freighter MV *Manchester* had reversed onto the MV *Victory*, trying to provide some sort of protection from the waves. The *Victory* had broken in half, just forward of the bridge area but appeared to be floating quite well considering. We vectored in the Lynx helicopter using our radar to the ship and it began the process of winching the survivors across to the *Manchester*. In all the sixteen men who stayed with the ship throughout the night did survive. In the photograph, the Lynx helicopter can be seen very close to the stern of the *Victory*."

DISMASTING SOUTH PACIFIC 1998

Not every search and rescue operation was a dire emergency and this is a story of bad luck and good luck as a result of an almost incredible coincidence. On 3 February 1998 the Whitbread Yacht Race started from Southampton. There was an all-girl crew skippered by Tracy Edwards and forty-three days later in the South Pacific their boat *Royal Sun Alliance* was dismasted in a severe storm. However they managed to erect a jury mast and set sail for Puerto Montt in Chile over 2,300 nautical miles away. The boat speed was very slow at first, only three knots, but in fact they were not short of staple food and water as they had started with enough to get back to England. By pure chance there was a Nimrod taking part in the Santiago air show and on hearing of the yacht's predicament they made a flight to the yacht and dropped some very welcome supplies, sponsored by the *Daily Mail*. The captain of the aircraft was Wing Commander Sid Brown, but Group Captain Wils Metcalfe, Kinloss station commander, was one of the pilots on board and tells the story:

"We were en route to Fidae 98 at Santiago in Chile which is a bi-annual air show and the largest in South America. It is the equivalent of the Farnborough Air Show with trade days and public at the weekend. The Defence Export Sales Organisation (DESO) and BAE Systems funded the deployment of the Nimrod and two Tornado F3s with a VC10 for air-to-air refuelling and two C130s to carry the spares support. The Nimrod and F3s were to take part in both the flying and static displays whilst the VC10 was to be in the static display and also was tasked during the week to pay a visit to Buenos Aires as the first RAF aircraft to visit Argentina since the Falklands conflict. I discovered that there are videos of the Nimrod and F3 display at Fidae 98 on YouTube. (*still there Author*)

"We had routed via Lajes and Bermuda and following a night stop at Howard Air

South Pacific challenge for yacht and Nimrod

Force base in Panama, we were just about to start engines when I was called back to base ops to take a phone call. It was the personal staff officer (PSO) to the chief of the air staff (CAS). He informed me that a yacht crewed by eight British women had rolled over and been dismasted in a storm off the coast of Chile. CAS had been made aware of this at a social function the previous evening (I'm not sure if it was by a sponsor or the editor of the *Mail*). CAS was aware that a Nimrod was en route to Chile and had said that he would investigate if we could assist. The PSO then gave me the lat and long of the yacht's position and mindful that all the aircraft were about to start and taxi, I dashed back to our 'plane. The navs looked at the position and did not have any charts for the area but at that point an F3 had a start-up malfunction which allowed time for one nav to go back into ops and get some additional charts. During the long flight from Panama to Santiago the navs pointed out that the phrase 'off the coast of Chile' was somewhat misleading as it was actually well over 1,000 miles off the coast and even further from Santiago where we were heading. They considered various options such as deploying ourselves and the AAR VC10 to Puntas Arenas but the need for a diversion airfield for our return was going to be a challenge at that range. We decided to await developments when we landed in Santiago.

"We had a pleasant surprise when we landed and walked into the air show operations as the Chilean air force Wg Cdr in charge had been a student at RAF Staff College Bracknell when I had been on the directing staff. He spoke excellent English and was to prove to be a great help in overcoming difficulties. We made contact with the UK and discovered that Tracy and the yacht were no longer in danger, had carried out repairs and were making about 3 knots under a small jury rigged mast. There was thus no necessity for an urgent rescue operation but they would need to receive charts and some other bits if they were to make it safely to Chile.

"Over the next few days a plan came together. We did not have droppable containers with us: the Nimrod was carrying a standard rescue dinghy and supplies but this was inappropriate and was required for the return sortie. It was agreed between MOD and the *Mail* that two droppable containers and the safety equipment fitter to load them would be flown out, paid for by the *Mail*. A *Mail* reporter and photographer would come along on the sortie. We planned the sortie for the Friday of the week as this was a day on which the Nimrod was not flying in the air show, the VC10 was programmed to return from Buenos Aires on the Thursday afternoon and it would allow time for the containers and fitter to arrive from the UK. Importantly, by that time and with re-fuelling from the VC10 we could spend about an hour in the likely area, if Tracy main-

tained 3 knots. The reporter and photographer joined us at the hotel in the middle of the week. The containers also arrived and part of the drop was some beer and a special bottle of Macallan whisky.

Jury rig girls waving

"On the Thursday, the Nimrod landed after its display at Santiago International Airport. The air show was at Los Corrillos airfield but we needed to use the longer runway at the international airport to enable take-off with maximum fuel. The VC10 also landed there on return from Buenos Aires. After a rations faff we got airborne, followed by the VC10 some minutes later who caught us up for the RV. The first pilot, Squadron Leader Taylor Devlin did a superb, smooth AAR (as always) making first time contact and filling up. We transited to the area, made radio contact

with the yacht and radar found the contact where we expected.

"It was only when we de-scended that we discovered that the cloud was down almost to the surface so it was radar homings at minimum operating altitude to find the yacht which we only glimpsed briefly on each passage. We positioned the aircraft to drop the containers just downwind of the yacht with the navigator using the computer's weapons software for an accurate drop. We made a couple of practice runs and then a live drop. The *Mail* photographer had brought with him a small satellite type dish linked to a con-

View of Nimrod in driving rain

trol box and camera that enabled him to get video and audio from the yacht and trans-mit from us to the yacht. We circled the yacht at about 2,000 yds pointing the dish out of the beam window to maintain communications. Tracy was interviewed and a video of our drop and their opening the containers was uplinked – this was to prove an outstanding PR product. We departed the yacht with a song for the girls as we climbed away for an uneventful return flight back to Santiago and back into the air show."

The two cannisters and their contents – note Macallan whisky, beer, camera and instructions on containers

Usually when one reads about a drop the feeling is that it's all over and it's not often there is a matching commentary. However, the communication with the yacht had been first class so that the girls were very excited, waiting for the drop:

"When they were ten minutes away at 1640 GMT we were all in our places. Silence descended on the boat as we waited for Arienne (comms) to update us. When they were fifteen seconds away we all looked forward in the direction from which they would be coming. At ten seconds away we could hear them but as the visibility was so bad we could not see them. Suddenly they appeared from behind our tiny sails and out of the mist only 200 ft above the water and it seemed right next to us. Most of us screamed. The shock was amazing. The huge monster suddenly right there beside us in the middle of the Pacific.

"They dropped a smoke bomb first and we practised going over it, no problem. They dropped the first canister about 300 metres out in front and slightly downwind of us. Things went very smoothly until the last minute when we thought it would slide between the port hull and the net. Emma and Sam lay on their stomachs and reached down for the canister and grabbed it at the last moment. With the others hanging on to their legs we managed to manhandle it on board. The second canister unfortunately escaped the

Wg Cdr Sid Brown operating the tactical display

safety of between the hulls and bobbed down the starboard side of the boat. Sharon practically launched herself off the boat to grab it and I sat on her legs and held on to her safety harness, while Hannah managed to get the boat hook to it and we pulled it up. Complete success!"

The contents provided by the *Daily Mail* went down extremely well and as one would expect there was a digital camera to make certain everything was recorded. Wils continued:

"I flew home overnight Sunday evening (leaving the detachment) with British Airways to Gatwick as I had to attend a dinner on the Wed evening to celebrate the 90th Anniversary of the RAF's formation. When I landed at Gatwick the TV screens showing the ITN news were running the story almost continuously with the video from the yacht and the interview with Tracy and an excellent graphic display showing how the Nimrod had carried out the rescue and AAR footage from the Nimrod – I was most impressed. When I returned to RAF Kinloss, I was shown the coverage that the *Mail on Sunday* had included with its exclusive story on page one and all of page two. On

the Wednesday evening at the dinner at RAF Bentley Priory, I met the chief of the air staff, Air Chief Marshal Sir Richard Johns (he was one of my instructors when I was learning to fly) who congratulated us on the fantastic operation and subsequent publicity for the RAF. We then spoke to the Duke of Edinburgh who was the guest of honour (I was only there because he is the honorary air commodore of RAF Kinloss) and he was fascinated by the rescue and how we had refuelled and how the pictures had been exchanged between the aircraft and the yacht.

Thank you from the girls to 42 Squadron

"As a footnote: Some two weeks later, I received a phone call from an engineer at RAF Boscombe Down asking who had cleared the satellite dish and equipment for use in the Nimrod as he had no record of it. I told him that I had authorised it on a one off basis and that if he was not happy about that, he should ring the chief of the air staff whom I was sure would endorse my decision: I heard no more about it."

As an ex MOD test pilot I sympathise with Wils on the final Boscombe paragraph; I had a similar problem when I did the first automatic landing in the Vulcan and some engineer, who had been in the original concept, reported me to MOD(PE) because he thought he should have been consulted.

Incidentally the navigator on the mercy mission was Ian Hampton and he tells me that some months after the sortie he was rung up by an army officer in the port of Southampton where the yacht had been taken. "I've got two canisters here marked return to Kinloss. Are they yours and do you want them?"

MEDICAL EMERGENCY IN A RUSSIAN SUBMARINE FEBRUARY 1996

A surprising event occurred when the Nimrod did a great job helping the 'enemy'. Normally stories of chasing Russian submarines would be in the ASW section but this incident which is a joint account by Sqn Ldr Tim Yates and Flt Lt Jon Bowland of a sortie they had the pleasure of experiencing as members of the same crew on 29 February 1996, is slightly different.

"I was just stepping out of the van from the aircraft to hand over search and rescue duties when something strange struck me. The oncoming crew were all laughing with great gusto and remained seated in the coach. Even worse the groundcrew were sprinting out to the dispersal and commenced removing the engine air intake blanks. We had been scrambled and didn't even know it! The first nav could not believe it, he would have been on leave two minutes later.

"Resigned to our fate we roared off down the runway and I checked in with Kinloss Ops.

'This is Kinloss Ops, go and find a Russian submarine off the west coast of Scotland. One of his crew is seriously ill and arrange for him to be airlifted to hospital!'

"Yes, somewhere in the Atlantic was a Russian submarine with a sick sailor on board, and the chance for some lucky Nimrod crew to get some great intelligence photos, and get on the telly into the bargain. What could be simpler?

"As it turned out, lots of things. The submarine's request for assistance reached the Rescue Coordination Centre (RCC) via tortuous diplomatic channels, during which various bits of information were distorted or lost. The net result was that we got airborne with the task of co-ordinating sheer chaos. For a start RCC were promulgating three different positions, the most northerly of which was a box basically encompassing the entire west coast of Scotland. It was also unclear whether the submarine was on the surface or not. To cap it all, MoD had launched airborne virtually anything that could fly, and so the radios were jammed with confused helicopter pilots desperately seeking (no pun intended) a mission.

"Time is a great healer, and after an hour or so we had more or less got things under control. Two of the three helicopters had been sent back to the beach to refuel and await instructions, while the third searched the more unlikely positions to the south. Meanwhile the crew got on with a radar and visual search of the northern box, having decided that any submarine needing assistance would presumably co-operate by remaining on the surface. Not so!

"The next message from the RCC indicated that the submarine, a Victor, was probably submerged, and would surface at a position north of Stornoway at 1230z. At last, some solid information! (we thought). We arrived at the rendezvous at 1130z, arranged for the RN Sea King from Prestwick to move to Stornoway and refuel, and waited.

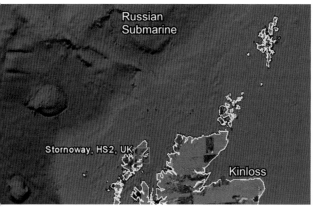

Location of Russian submarine with sick crewman

"And waited.

"And waited. 1230 came and went. In the absence of any other information we remained near the RV whilst trying everything else we could think of. A MAD mark raised hopes, but turned out to be false. HMS *Glasgow* arrived, fresh from the Joint Maritime Course (big exercise), with a Lynx and doctor on board. And then, over three hours late, radar picked up a contact. Radar homing, hearts in mouths, and there she was at last: a Victor III class submarine, Hull 661.

"Bugle 661 was quick to reply to my calls on the pre-briefed frequency, but inevitably the language barrier caused problems. The early exchanges went something like this:

"AEO: *'Bugle 661, this is Rescue 51, helicopter inbound to you with doctor on board, ETA your position 10 miles, casevac Stornoway, how copy.'*

"Bugle 661: *'Rescue 51, say again, please speak slowly.'*

"AEO (muttering 'bloody foreigners' to himself): *'Bugle 661, metal bird come from sky with medicine man, noise of thunder take comrade to good place, many buffalo.'*

"Bugle 661: *'Rescue 51, say again, please speak English.'*

"To cut a long story short, the Lynx from HMS *Glasgow* arrived bearing the ship's doctor (whose abiding impression of conditions on-board the Victor was the smell of cabbage), followed by the RN Sea King which casevaced the seaman to hospital in Stornoway. Before this process was completed, however, the valiant Crew 1 had reached PLE (out of gas) and we returned to base, leaving another Nimrod to escort the Sea King to land.

Helicopters doing rescue

"With a profound sense of a job well done, we prepared to celebrate. Alas, most of the crew caught the 6 o-clock news on the TV in ops, and found to our dismay, the entire operation being described as a shambles! In fairness, most criticism was levelled at the diplomats and not ourselves, but as usual the press had got hold of half a story, and secrecy denied anyone the chance to set the record straight. With their triumph turned to ashes, Crew 1 retired to the bar.

"There were some postscripts:

1. The seaman, Aleksandr Yerokhin, a nineteen-year-old turbine operative, had suffered an appendicitis. As far as we know, he made a good recovery, no doubt aided by the squadron print we sent him.

2. A letter from the then foreign affairs minister was sent four days later to his counterpart Malcolm Rifkind expressing the Russians' 'profound gratitude'.

3. Crew l's video footage and stills appeared on most TV reports and in the press the next day.

4. The personal twist on it was that the date was 29 Feb 1996, and Jane, my then-girlfriend now wife, had hatched a plot to propose to me that night. We were late back after the trip, and in such a foul mood, due to the negative press coverage we had had on the evening news, that she thought better of it! She had spent the day slaving over a recipe book and (not being a natural chef) on the phone to OC Catering Squadron for cooking tips. She was not willingly absent but as a junior engineering officer was on nights that week and, unable to wait any longer, had in fact gone to work leaving in the kitchen a beef Wellington and associated vegetables in the oven, and a bottle of champagne in the fridge. Returning from a gruelling night shift the following morning she found the whole lot had been consumed when a guy from another crew had turned up to announce his own engagement to girlfriend Annette and the pair of them having a 'lucky find' of food and champagne had celebrated their good fortune into the early hours!"

Above: Andy Redfearn's pencil drawing of the rescue
Left: The Russian submarine commander signing the picture

Because of the pressure on the crew while this rescue was taking place there was no actual photo of the event but Andy Redfearn of the crew produced a splendid pencil drawing after the event and he has given all the print proceeds of the picture to charity. Some of the prints were especially memorable as they were signed by the Russian submarine's captain and Air Marshal Sir Brian Burridge, Nimrod pilot and previously station commander Kinloss.

THE LOSS OF AIR INDIA 747

The next example I have chosen is the terrible disaster to befall the Air India 747 on 24 June 1985 when the aircraft was blown up by a bomb and dived into the water south of Eire out of control leaving no survivors. In this case the Nimrod was able to find the wreckage and confirm immediately that the aircraft must have hit the water, a very important point for the accident investigators. The Nimrod had the important task of liaising with the Rescue Coordination Centre and again vectoring the helicopters to the scene of the disaster, not that the helicopters could help in this case. Ian Marshall again:

"This SAR incident was slightly different for a couple of reasons. I was a dry specialist instructor on 236 OCU based at RAF St Mawgan and therefore did not have to do SAR standby, a duty normally carried out by the squadrons, but if the squadrons were busy and the OCU had been allocated an aircraft for training purposes, then the captain could elect to assist with an ongoing incident. In this case the OCU boss, Wg Cdr Gould, was the nominated captain. The Air India Boeing 747 had been missing since the previous day and according to air traffic control somewhere in the Atlantic south of Ireland, coming from the USA to the UK. We were allocated a large area to search at first light and there was a warship with a helicopter also in the area. It was assumed that there would be no floating wreckage that would provide a radar return and therefore the crew settled into a visual search at 500 ft, the optimum height for locating a survivor in the water. I think very quickly we started to locate bits of debris but nothing that we could say was definitely aircraft, our own speed made that sort of identification very difficult unless it was large pieces of wing or fuselage. Once the debris was located, we could mark it with a long-life smoke marker and home both the warship and the helicopter to the scene, while also reporting everything back to the Rescue Coordination Centre (RCC).

"Communications and relay of information between all units on the scene and the RCC were among the most important jobs that the Nimrod performed. Coordinating the search as scene of action commander (SAC) if there were multiple helicopters available and civilian ships could sometimes be the primary Nimrod task, as the other rescue units which flew lower and slower were better suited to the search.

"On 24 June it soon became obvious that there was a lot of wreckage and as the helicopter started to report, there were also a lot of bodies floating in the water; this was the first time that I had conducted a SAR search for a large civilian airliner and the death toll was vast. We continued to mark and report everything for the ship and helicopter to investigate until we reached our fuel limitation and had to head back to St Mawgan."

SOUTH ATLANTIC SEARCH 1987

A perfect example of the fantastic search capabilities of the Nimrod was in August 1987; I've chosen it because only the Nimrod could have carried out such an enormous search so quickly and with such accurate results. Without this aircraft there is now no other aircraft in the world which can combine large area searches with such speed and effectiveness. Two Cessna 210s were being ferried from Dakar in Senegal to Libreville in Gabon. Both aircraft had been fitted with long-range tanks giving an endurance of eighteen hours and a flight plan of twelve hours flying along the coast. They took off at 0810 hours on 8 August; one aircraft had a suspect inertial navigator and only one of the two had a radio but the forecast was good with a tail wind of 20 kt. However the wind changed to a 20 kt northerly head wind as it got dark, and above cloud they were blown out to sea, apparently without realising what was happening. The first inkling of a problem was when a DC8 of Affretair heard a Mayday call nearly fifteen hours after the take-off time of the Cessnas, 2300 hours Dakar time. Some hours later a South African Airways 747 heard another Mayday call saying that the aircraft had run out of fuel and was ditching. Shortly afterwards a personal locator beacon was heard by the 747 but

South Atlantic rescue

the aircraft at altitude could do nothing to help except report to air traffic control. Amazingly the control at Libreville did not initiate an overdue message and no local SAR action was launched. It was not until four days later that the Rescue Coordination Centre, heard of the problem and after extensive calculation based on the Mayday calls they worked out that there was an area of 1.3 million square miles to be searched.

The only aircraft capable of carrying out such a search was the Nimrod. Pete Rosie and his crew took off at midnight on 15 August, refuelled at Dakar, and went on to Ascension Island. There was a C130 tanker based on the island and after the first two search flights Rosie asked the 130 crew if they were prepared to refuel the Nimrod. The crew agreed and got authorisation from the UK. The next four sorties were flight refuelled and the search carried on almost non-stop with minimum sleep time for the crew and every time the search was broken off for refuelling a sonobuoy was dropped. Finally, wreckage and a body was spotted and even more incredibly, the Searchwater radar spotted a flask floating on the water. The Nimrod crew flew 92 hr 55 min in a ten-day period, and the aircraft burned 850,000 lb of fuel of which 240,000 came from the C130 tanker. The distance flown was over 30,000 miles and the area covered was twice the land mass of the UK.

Peter Rosie was given the Arthur Barrett award for his leadership and skill in carrying out this fantastic search ending in finding the wreckage but unfortunately the pilots could not be saved.

What puzzled me at first about these sorties was how the search ever got authorised, bearing in mind it was four days after the loss of the aircraft that the search started and the chances of either pilot being still alive must have been very small. Apparently the pilots were Australian, one of them well known, and the Australian High Commission in London asked for the search to take place through our foreign office. The Australian government must have been particularly keen for the pilots to be found for the search to have been of such a length.

MID-ATLANTIC RESCUE 10 MARCH 1987

The Nimrod crews of course never knew who they were rescuing, it was just sufficient to be doing a great job. However Wils Metcalfe told me about one of his crews when he was squadron commander:

> "We were scrambled to go to the aid of a light a/c which was transiting from Gander en route to Italy. The aircraft had lost the electrical supply to the fuel pump for its auxiliary fuel tank and therefore did not have enough fuel to make land (Ireland). The crew located the aircraft, vectored it towards a ship and talked the pilot through a ditching. He was picked up safely by the ship. Unknown to the crew, he was a rich and influential Italian with an aristocratic background. He subsequently flew another of his planes to RAF Kinloss to thank the crew personally and took them out for a meal. He invited them to visit him in Lucca, Italy and on the return leg from a Cyprus detachment the crew landed there. They hadn't realised how influential the rescued pilot was until, when they checked in at the Italian FIR boundary, they were welcomed to Italy and cleared direct to Lucca. Needless to say they were royally entertained in the city with a formal dinner and I think stayed in his huge mansion. I think that they were each presented with an Italian medal and one was awarded to the Squadron."

As an ex air force officer I'm puzzling how on earth they got permission to land at Lucca. Maybe Wils had some influence at group headquarters.

Mid-Atlantic rescue

SURPRISE YACHT RESCUE

The Nimrod did a lot of work keeping an eye on drug smugglers but of course it was not publicised and the navy and the customs got the credit when the boats were apprehended. However there was one case which was slightly unusual. There was a yacht taking on water off the coast of Aberdeen; the Nimrod found the yacht and vectored the helicopters to the boat so they could winch the crew off. The Nimrod crew felt very pleased with the job they had done but they were a bit surprised the following morning to read in the press that they had rescued drug smugglers. The crew had disappeared the moment they had been taken ashore and the coastguard found the reason why the boat was taking on water; it was overloaded with drugs inbound to the UK. The captain, Garrick Hill, had his name in the press when in this case he would have preferred no publicity.

LOSS OF THE MV *CHRISTINAKI*

Unfortunately not all calls for search and rescue are successful and below is the sad story of the loss of the MV *Christinaki* on the night of 3 February 1994. At 1600, the crew of MV *Christinaki* sent an emergency message that whilst carrying a cargo of scrap iron from Liverpool to Vera Cruz, the vessel had lost a cargo hatch and was beginning to take on water. The *Christinaki* had a crew of twenty-seven, mostly Greek and Filipino, sailors. The Aeronautical Rescue & Coordination Centre, ARCC (split between Pitreavie and Plymouth as Kinloss did not open until 1996) launched the Nimrod SAR crew – a crew on one-hour standby for a twenty-four-hour period that had begun at 0900 that morning – to the scene to assist. It was dark when they arrived – 240 miles to the south west of Ireland. The 'six-hour' standby crew were next on scene – still in the dark. Crew 3 from 206 Squadron, captained by Flt Lt 'Keefy' Edmunds, was the next to appear.

"We arrived, still in the dark, and set about a radar/PLB search; like the previous crews, we found nothing. As it got light, the scene of devastation became apparent; the weather was absolutely dreadful; as Keefy would put it to the BBC later, 'In twenty-odd years in the Air Force, man and boy, it's the worst weather I'd ever seen.' The radio altimeter was bouncing about +/- 100', the wind was 70 knots+ and the waves were enormous; the largest sea state that I had ever seen – SS10. Ultimately, only the members of the flight deck would not suffer from motion sickness during this sortie. We set about a visual search of the last known position of the ship; the scale of the tragedy soon became obvious; we spotted the remains of lifeboats – smashed to pieces; we found survival suits floating on the surface and the remains of a dinghy – we were unsure whether or not they held survivors so we set about dropping some of our search and rescue apparatus. The first dinghy pair that was dropped flew along the surface of the water at about 30 kts; there was no way that a survivor would have been able to get in.

"We continued to relay our intention to the ARCC and it was determined that we should pass some details of our sortie to the BBC for inclusion in a lunchtime bulletin; the captain informed the BBC that we were in the middle of a search and rescue – he would speak to them when we were complete! Our relief was delayed so we remained on task until the prudent limit of our endurance (PLE) before departing to Shannon Airport near Limerick in Eire. None of us had expected to land in Eire and there was a dearth of passports on board! So members of the British RAF landed in Eire without either documentation or civilian clothing – we were met by the Special Branch of An Garda Siochana and they were 'loaded for bear'. After 'Keefy' stole the hat from his 1st Nav, Flt Lt Martin Cannard, told his tale of derring-do to the BBC and sent them away with video footage of the scene, the crew were escorted to a hotel in Limerick. When the crew entered the hotel bar, it was like something from a cowboy film – silence whilst everyone turned to see the invaders. The situation changed when the BBC Six o'clock News was on TV; the visitors were no longer seen as invaders but as a SAR crew and rarely put their hands in their pockets again."

Sadly, the MV *Christinaki* went down with all hands.

FRENCH TRAWLER AT THE WEEKEND

My final choice is this strange story from Justin Morris:

"One dark Friday night in the nineties my crew and I were scrambled to the Bay of Biscay to search for a French fishing boat that a distress signal had been picked up from. The transit was a good hour and a half which was great for making the crew Honkers to keep them going for what could have been a long search. As it happened the beacon was still transmitting so it didn't take long to localise the emissions to a small area. We descended to low level to commence a visual search of that small area and it didn't take us long for the aircraft homer and navigation systems to narrow the spot to a very precise location. It was a fairly clear night and the moon's reflection was giving us enough light to see but the sea surface was quite smooth (unusually for the Biscay) which increased the reflections making the visual search quite difficult. The searchlight was struck for the next few passes over the datum and as ever, night turned to day. With the ambient light, the sea state and the 70 million candle power trying to evaporate the sea, the conditions for a visual search weren't good, the combination of light was just not right. We were convinced that we were in the right place however and someone suggested using the Very pistol, the same thing that has been used for decades to fire flares for reasons of distress. They didn't give off much light but we decided to give it a go. A short distance from the datum the engineer fired off a flare, red or green I can't recall, and we'd found our light source. The combination of the background light with our now stationary flare giving a slightly changing perspective on the scene was perfect for this job and what we suspected to be the case appeared to be true. We saw what we thought was the reflection from the upturned hull just below the water, but it was very difficult to say and only a couple of crew saw it, a tough call."

A strange story as one would think the French search and rescue facilities would be looking for a French fishing boat, even if it was a weekend.

CONCLUSION

I have chosen but a few of the countless stories of search and rescue sorties by Nimrod crews but sadly it is now no longer possible to search thousands of miles into the Atlantic up to 30°W and beyond if the need arises fulfilling our international responsibilities. The Nimrods used to patrol the North Sea roughly three times a week under Operation Tapestry protecting our trawlers and our oil rigs. Sadly without the Nimrod we can only provide search and rescue for short distances off shore, limited by the range of our helicopters.

Below: UK fixed wing search and rescue 2011-style

6 LAND BATTLES AND SPECIAL SORTIES

The Nimrod was born to monitor the almost limitless seas around the British Isles which it did extremely well improving year on year as the sensors were updated. However, inexorably the targets changed; the Falkland campaign came and went, the Cold War ended and then wars broke out in the Balkans and the Middle East. New camera technology and communication systems became available enabling the aircraft to support ground troops. The whole story cannot yet be told but there is no doubt that the aircraft did a vital job in Iraq and Afghanistan and the cancellation of the MRA4 leaves a military hole which is very difficult to fill.

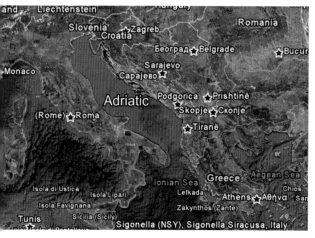

Monitoring the Adriatic

1993-1995 OPERATION MARITIME GUARD/SHARP GUARD IN THE BALKANS

During the Bosnian war Nimrods were based in Sigonella, Sicily searching for submarines and fast patrol boats (FPBs). They carried six live armed Stingray torpedoes and were also fitted with two BOZ pods, one on each pylon; these pods carried flares and chaff which could be fired automatically or manually if a threat to the aircraft was detected. A Sandpiper infrared camera was installed at this time but was soon superseded and improved with later technologies. A towed radar decoy, colloquially called a 'turd' was also fitted. It was streamed about 200ft behind the aircraft from the pod above the tailfin when the aircraft was on task.

The mission was to fly up and down the Bosnian coast to the west of Montenegro to make certain 'the coast was clear' for NATO naval forces. There were no real threats to the aircraft from the older Soviet-based SAM sites which had become ineffective.

OPERATION SHARP GUARD

In 1993 there was a multi-year joint naval blockade in the Adriatic Sea by NATO and the Western European Union on shipments to the former Yugoslavia. Twenty-two warships, from fourteen countries, and eight maritime patrol aircraft were involved in searching for and stopping blockade runners. It was suspended in June 1996, and was finally terminated in October of that year. Justin Morris has some recollections of the campaign:

"During Operation Sharp Guard, whilst my crew was deployed to Sigonella Italian air

Wescam camera and BOZ

force base in Sicily in August 1994, our mission was split between the maritime embargo/blockade and submarine hunting. The former Yugoslav Republic owned several diesel submarines and although they weren't new by any stretch of the imagination, small quiet submarines are always a huge worry to naval forces. We generally flew with full fuel loads for duration, as well as six Stingray torpedoes in the bomb bay. The Adriatic Sea would be our 'playground' and we'd normally work in support of a warship or submarine, of which there were many. At any time they could ask us to drop a Stingray on an 'intruder', regardless of whether or not we had actually detected it. Luckily for them, with all that metal out there, the submarine crews mostly decided to stay in port.

"During one daylight trip the summer sun was beating down on us on a wonderful morning and the prospect of another great flight over the sea beckoned. Everything went as per usual until the jet was lined up on the runway and the pilot 'opened the taps'. As the heavy aircraft accelerated slowly down the runway and reached 80 knots (when the rudder took authority over nosewheel steering), the microphone of one of the pilots opened up at an unusual time and those in the rear of the aircraft with their wits about them looked at each other wondering what he was going to say. The remark was brief, someone mentioned a speedo problem and we held our breath. Eye signals would have been exchanged on the flight deck and as we charged down the concrete a decision had to be made. 'ABORT, ABORT' came the shout – we were going nowhere. The indicated air speed indicators had been fluctuating enough to worry the pilots who couldn't be sure what speed they were travelling at, therefore cancelling the take-off was the only safe option. In this situation the procedure for the braking pilot was to apply maximum braking in case of unforeseen circumstances but this advice wasn't utilised. The co-pilot on that trip decided as he saw lots of runway left he'd moderate the braking to preserve the discs and pads, not an unreasonable idea really, although he took a good 'de-briefing' for it.

"The ground crew spent a fair amount of time doing investigative work and changing components to solve the problem, but to no end. The same happened the next day and also a few days after that. This final attempt to commit aviation was at a speed closer to the 'point of no return', a little faster still and a lot less comfortable. The braking advice was adhered to this time which was possibly the root of another problem but a rather dramatic couple of minutes followed. We came to a stop quicker than the previous two attempts which raised the prospect of hot brakes and the beam operators were asked to take a peek before the plane was stopped. Already there were signs of smoke so a warning was called for a possible evacuation. When a final stop was reached the smoke was billowing from the brakes and fearful of a fire, the crew unstrapped and made for the exit, which in this case was the front door, being the furthest from the undercarriage. The Nimrod escape plan didn't include air stairs or inflatable slides and in a timely evacuation, in this situation, someone would bring the spare slide (sheet of canvas) from the rear door to the front. Without this time available, the crew relied upon the trusty rope to descend to the concrete, a far from ideal scenario given the urgency. Most of the crew got out without event, albeit with much shouting, pushing and shoving until it was the turn of the AEO. He grabbed the rope on his way out and down but misjudged it a little and swung back into the fuselage with some momentum, impacting the lower door sill with his belly, a bruise which took some considerable time to go. He did a good job of cushioning the fall of the next few guys to the ground however!

"The threat of a brake fire and tyre explosion, followed by the fuel tanks catching and the torpedoes cooking off was quite enough to set the guys running. Imagining being caught in the blast was enough to set us off in the direction of the sea, five miles away. Once no explosions had been heard the next event was the arrival of the solitary Italian fire-fighter as the American fire trucks faced away from the airfield into the domestic site. They eventually turned up in their astronaut suits and breathing apparatus, to watch Mario squinting through the smoke, checking the Nimrod's brakes as he leaned over a tyre. His foil fire suit was rolled down to his waist (it was a hot day!) and he was smoking a cigarette. I guess the smoke had subsided a little but the heat was probably not subsiding and an explosion was still very possible.

"Eventually, after a deep rectification team was sent out from Kinloss, the reason was found to be down to the pitot-static tubes being full of sand and bumble bees! Another crew took it away a week later though as we'd become too anxious to get in it again."

As a test pilot reading this account I was a little surprised that it took so long to realise the pitot lines were blocked, but maybe I am showing unjustified hindsight!

MIDDLE EAST WARS

The wars in the Middle East can be divided into three:

The Gulf War (1990-91) was authorised by the United Nations and was fought in response to Saddam Hussein's invasion of Kuwait.
The Iraq War (2003–2010), was a military campaign which began with the invasion of Iraq by forces led by the United States and the United Kingdom followed by a seven-year occupation.

Afghanistan War (2001-) started as a result of the destruction of the Twin Towers in New York on 11 September 2001 and the USA's decision to seek out the terrorists.

The Nimrod was involved in all three wars, Operation Granby Gulf War 1, Operation Iraqi Freedom Gulf War 2 and Operation Enduring Freedom.

GULF WAR 1

OPERATION GRANBY

Besides carrying nuclear protection suits in the aircraft, receiving all sorts of injections and having anti-laser goggles, it was necessary before leaving the UK for Operation Granby for the Nimrod crews to have pre-war fighter affiliation training down to 500ft but it had to be done over the sea and to be successful it required good crew coordination. For example if the co-pilot saw the 'attacking' fighter first then the intercom might be:

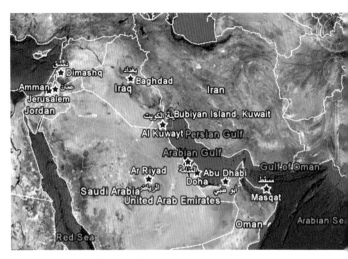

Operation Granby, Seeb in Oman

"Fighter! Right 2 o-clock, top-up, closing (top up meant he was in a position to get a missile off)! Now 3 o'clock coming to you Starboard Beam!"

"Starboard Beam visual! Fighter, 3 o'clock, Top-up, Closing! 4 o'clock, Top-up, Closing! 5 o'clock, Top-up, Closing. 6 o'clock, Top-up, Closing, over to you Port Beam!"

"Port Beam visual! Fighter, 6 o'clock, Top-up, Closing! 7 o'clock, Top-up, Closing! 8 o'clock – he's reversing his turn, now bottom-up, going away!"

And so it would go on, with the pilots trying to gauge when to put the Nimrod into a tight, rapid descending turn – or when to fire off a Sidewinder if it was so equipped – which they were, at times.

Apparently one moonlit night one of the navigators looked at the display from Sandpiper EO turret. He got immediate success:

"Pilots, Fighter, 6 o'clock, closing!"

The crew responded as per their pre-deployment training. The pilot flew the aircraft like a madman! And the navigator reported the desperate state of affairs. It didn't seem to matter whatever the pilot did, the navigator reported that it seemed impossible to shake off the chasing aircraft. Finally the pilot worked it out; the navigator was looking at the towed radar decoy from the top of the fin. Amazingly the crew still had a sense of humour after a demanding flight.

The Nimrods were used to support the naval forces when Iraq invaded Kuwait and attached is an anonymous account of a sortie, by an aircraft based in Seeb.

"We were tasked to work for the coalition naval forces in the northern Persian Gulf. It was early morning on about day 4/5 of the war. Previously the Iraqis had managed

Nimrod fighter affiliation with two Tornados. Note BOZ pods and i/r camera under wing

to fly four Mirages ostensibly on ASuW down the eastern seaboard and into Saudi airspace but were chased back. Additionally, there were early reports of a Saudi village being taken by Iraqi ground forces, so the intent to act aggressively against coalition forces had been demonstrated. Our task was to locate any Iraqi naval threats.

"On this particular sortie, we were tracking northwards towards Bubiyan Island, near the Iraq/Iran border and Kuwait City was to the west of us, maybe fifty miles away. It was a dark night, overcast with occasional thunderstorm clouds, the sea state was getting up to maybe six. We were variously between 6,000 & 8,000 ft according to changes in the detection ranges of our Searchwater looking for Iraqi missile-armed fast patrol boats (FPBs). We had already had a successful previous mission when the radar operator then had detected two FPBs. We had duly reported them and given radar vectors to US S3 MPAs who subsequently successfully attacked and sank the Iraqi units.

"That night, I was on ESM. I will never forget the Yellowgate ESM tactical display suddenly flashing with the Slotback radar symbol as fitted to the Mig-29.

"Now there was some doubt as to whether the Iraqis had Slotback-fitted Mig-29s, but what I do know for sure was that the audio was distinctly and utterly Russian. I also know, because the lead dry man had leapt from ESM to radar in one bound and looked hard at the radar screen: it was from the north, i.e. Iraqi-held territory, and having ascertained that there was no associated IFF squawk seen, there was a fast-moving airborne contact coming right towards us which needed immediate action.

"Back at ESM, shaking I have to admit, I reported '*Captain, ESM: Slotback, Hostile airborne radar fitted to Mig-29s, 12 o-clock, search-mode only, high confidence level*'.

"The Skipper's first reply was 'OK pilots, get us out of here' and then 'ESM, keep talking'.

"We dived southwards towards the nearest friendly warship – HMS *Cardiff* – at near maximum velocity to low-level – maybe 300ft – whilst the Skipper reported the ESM on the UHF frequency in use. I remember HMS *Cardiff* 'yelling' at us to 'move out of the way' because we were in her firing line. We decided against chaff as there was no lock-on and the friendly units would not have appreciated us destroying their air picture by cluttering it with chaff. Similarly we did not dump flares as that would have simply identified our position visually to the Mig.

"To appreciate the workload you need to think about what it meant to fly at 300ft in bad weather, at night, over a high sea state with warships and oil-installations flashing past and a Mig on your tail to get a sense of the atmosphere on-board! The idea was to electronically 'lose' ourselves in the sea-clutter. It certainly seemed to work!

"The radios were very busy. For a change the intercom was quiet! Just me, the Skipper and the P1.

"I kept reporting that the Slotback was still only in search-mode, i.e. still no lock-on and was infact starting to 'fade'.

"We swung around eventually for a quick look on radar – nothing. HMS *Cardiff* confirmed 'all clear'. So we simply climbed back up to our search height, turned north wards and started doing our job again.

"NB. A large number of Iraqi Mig pilots defected to Iran early in the conflict and it is my belief that this was one such defection who detected us – perhaps – and thought that he would have some fun before ending his war! There were also unsubstantiated rumours of Russian mercenary Mig pilots. Such a large number of defections to Iran caught the coalition by surprise and thereafter a specific MIGCAP was established to prevent them fleeing in that direction again.

"As a postscript, a US C-130 was attacked in the same vicinity. I believe that the two pilots died but twelve crew survived. They eventually baled out and made it to Kuwait City I think, where they 'temporarily borrowed' the most 'upmarket' cars that they could get their hands on. Iraqi soldiers simply waved the southbound vehicles past believing the occupants to be Sheiks or something!"

Some Nimrods of 42 Squadron were deployed to Seeb, Oman and operated in the Persian Gulf looking for Iraqi gunboats and warships. Nimrods of 236 OCU went to Cyprus and provided surveillance for defence units going through the Suez Canal. One was trialling a radar decoy system, reeled out and towed from the tail pod where the ARAR/ARAX aerials used to be,

Nimrod in Oman, AWACS in background

meant for the MRA4.

After two previous sorties during which they 'assisted' in the destruction of two Iraqi fast patrol boats (FPBs) and been chased by a Mig, they felt that everything happened in threes!

"Once again we were very far north, occupied Kuwait City was way to the south west and we were even north east of Iraqi-held Bubiyan Island, i.e. a high threat environment for a large MPA like the Nimrod! The tasking was the same: locate and help destroy any Iraqi naval units. As ever, the weather was filthy. Very, very active thunderstorms. (I often wonder now if the same weather system was what hit Andy Ryan's Bravo 20 patrol from his book of the same name).

"We had already detected a possible FPB, and a Lockheed S3 was being vectored by us for a visual ident. Radar reported 'hard-centred clouds' building rapidly all around, very harmful to aircraft and sure enough, the poor old Nimrod started banging and shaking. I have never since experienced anything like it, like something out of a storm-

Lockheed S3 Viking

chasing advert! That aircraft was literally flung around the night skies. The vibration was immense: fellow crewmen's heads were often a blur! Every member of the crew had donned their LSJs and some even positioned their Quickdons nearer. We really, really thought that we were going to have to ditch.

"I remember the air engineer hanging onto the acoustic seats whilst trying to check the airframe. He got as far as the hydraulic bay before going back to the flight deck where he reported 'Skipper, I think that we should head back'.

"The Skipper simply said 'This is what you get paid for, guys!' And so we continued vectoring the S3 which by now had confirmed a hostile FPB. I remember the captain warning our US surface playmate that we might have to ditch and were possibly suffering structural damage in the meantime. I also remember our US 'handler' telling us to fall back if required: he did not want to have to deal with an MPA ditching on his watch! It seemed like a lifetime on task that night. But the S3 got another kill courtesy of us staying put.

"On landing, the engineer reported back to some guy at Boscombe or Farnborough or somewhere like that who immediately grounded the airframe pending airframe investigation! The ground troops face the greatest hardships and hazards, but I would humbly suggest that even the crews of large MPAs work hard on occasion too!"

Stories of war are always horrifying and in these modern times the non-combatants are brought right up front thanks to the news broadcasters. Here a story is recounted where a very sad radio conversation was monitored:

"As aircrew, we are always taught to respond and log all distress communications. It is not always that simple.

"I remember being on task and suddenly hearing British accents breaking into the radio circuit. Obviously Tornado crews because of their oxygen-masked voices and distinctive callsigns. It was something like 'Saxon, Check-in!'

"Response: '1'

"'3'

"'5'

"'Saxon 2 & 4 Check-in'

"Nothing. Then 'Mayday Relay, Mayday Relay Saxon 2 & 4'. I cannot remember the exact callsigns or what was said, other than a fast conversation amongst the Tornado crews as to who saw who last and when. I think that there was discussion about seeing a Harrier GR4 fly behind a hill and then not reappear.

"Needless to say, nothing was logged or relayed as per our security training: the Tornado boys did it all themselves and besides, at that point we had picked up another FPB on radar.

"Another night, we heard a US pilot break into the circuit. He did not sound good. Again, a fighter guy, oxygen-masked voice, single seat. He was looking for vectors to his home carrier/airfield, but warned that he would have some difficulty following the vectors due to having lost the use of both his hands and legs.

"I do not know what happened to him."

One crew painted their aircraft XV244 calling it Battle Star. They then painted a cricket bat on the side for each sortie they did and a ship for each enemy ship they found and caused to be destroyed. In fact the Nimrod Force flew over 400 sorties in the first Iraq war.

Fourteen sorties and four ships accounted for

IRAQI WAR 2003

OPERATION SOUTHERN WATCH BECOMING IRAQI FREEDOM

As war became inevitable three Nimrod MR2s and four crews plus R1s were based in Saudi Arabia at Prince Sultan Air Base (PSAB) where the USAF aircraft were also based comprising AWACS, tankers plus SIGINT Rivet Joints and the Compass Call counter-communication Lockheed 130Hs; all these aircraft were classified as HVAA, high value airborne assets. The Nimrod R1s were doing their normal job sampling all communication and identifying all the various transmissions sources. The Nimrods had again been fitted with two BOZ pods with flares and chaff which could be fired automatically or manually if a threat was detected.

By this time five Nimrod MR2s had been fitted with the L-3 Communications Wescam

MX-15 electro-optical system, mounted in a pod on an underwing hard point, because it was realised that with this equipment the aircraft could better support the land forces. The system was a sophisticated day/night optical system, with a high magnification 4-step zoom lens. The aircraft could orbit overhead and act as a communications relay and, with the Wescam, identify potential targets and keep watch for enemy troops. At that time the Nimrods could not transmit images in real time over a datalink to ground stations, so intelligence reports had to be passed over voice radio nets. There was a soldier on the aircraft who had his own system for sending photos and information to the army. He would help to interpret what was being seen and then call his colleagues on the ground.

Boeing RC-135 SIGINT Rivet Joint – the Nimrod R1 replacement

Before the war started the Nimrod MR2s were patrolling just outside the Iraq border flying up to Jordan monitoring all the forts for military activity. Because of the number of aircraft operating in the area and the possibility of attack, the Nimrods relied on an AWACS aircraft with its capability of identifying hostile aircraft to keep a good look out. Ian Marshall told me of one flight when the AWACS had to withdraw for a bit and his aircraft had its own F16 formating on its wing for an hour before the AWACS returned.

The Nimrod MR2 did not have to use their ESM capability as the Nimrod R1s were much better equipped for this intelligence role. As the war got really close the R1s were used in a tactical role since, if they detected any fire control radars or voice commands being given to attack a specific target, they could warn all aircraft in the vicinity what was about to happen and, because of the aircraft's direction-finding capability, a rough area to watch.

When the war started in earnest the codename became Operation Freedom, UK Operation Telic. PSAB was incredibly crowded and because there was not enough fuel-storage capacity underground, fuel had to be stored in all the flight-refuelling tankers as well. A typical sortie is described:

"My one and only sortie in the war as captain was 24 March, which I think was the very first night. Some of our troops had crossed the border in a low level Hercules to be dropped somewhere behind enemy lines, then the Hercules would return back across the border. My mission was to provide some sort of SAR cover, monitor their progress through radio messages and watch the border forts for activity, picking a quiet spot for the Hercules to exit. This all went well but cloud cover was intruding in the area and I had to keep descending to keep visual with the ground using the camera. We were now well inside the danger height for SAMS and at one point we lit up the sky as our missile approach warning system (MAWS) detected a missile launch and automatically released lots of IR flares and chaff. Needless to say, this did make some of the crew members a bit jumpy. The Hercules came back across the border without incident and we returned to PSAB.

"If the politicians were to be believed, there were weapons of mass destruction all over the place which were to have been the Nimrod's primary mission, using the camera at high level looking for Scud missiles and their launchers. This never happened to my knowledge. My time in PSAB was limited – lack of aircraft parking space meant that one crew had to depart and because my crew was not air-to-air refuelling qualified and there were two crews from 206 Sqn who were, it was my crew who went home early. We did not miss out on much; with no weapons of mass destruction to hunt for, the Nimrod was used as a very expensive jailor. With our Wescam camera at high level, the Nimrod monitored a prisoner-of-war camp to make sure no one escaped, what a waste of an asset."

OPERATION TELIC AFTER THE WAR 2004-05

Though the direct fighting in Gulf War 2 was over very quickly the occupation lasted for seven years and the Nimrods were required to help the land forces. Ian Marshall describes graphically what it is was like during this time.

"Although the war finished in 03, according to our politicians, it seemed as if the Nimrod's role in the peace that followed was of much greater significance than during the war. My first 'peace' deployment was in April 04; crews usually went every six months for two months at a time. There were usually three aircraft and four crews available, based in Seeb, Oman and then redeployed to Basrah in Iraq. Seeb was treated as rest and recuperation from Basrah but there was still work to be done, either Operation Enduring Freedom if the aircraft was serviceable, usually supporting the Omani police in patrolling the Gulf of Oman looking for illegal immigrants, or checking shipping going through the Strait of Hormuz and conducting direct support missions for coalition warships in the Gulf of Oman, Arabian Sea and Straits, providing them with a surface picture. When a warship had to transit through the Strait of Hormuz (SOH), they tended to get jumpy following the explosion on the USS *Cole*. The Iranians used speedboats and jet skis to run contraband across the Strait and occasionally strayed too close to the transiting warships.

   "Usually there were two aircraft in Basrah both of which would be fitted with the Wescam IR/TV camera. Our tasking in Basrah was the support of two different units. In the south of the country the Multi-National Division South East (MND (SE)) were our customers but they would only get Nimrod support if we were not required in Baghdad.

   "The tasking from the local army HQ was fairly varied but could be mundane and boring. Many times we would monitor power lines for thieves stealing the aluminium and copper, we would watch waterways for illegal activity, we would help relay info to solders on the ground patrolling in Basrah city and we would do some self protection for Basrah airfield. On my first week there, we were mortared and rocketed every night, the firing positions were known and if we were airborne we would try and find them setting up the firing position. We never did locate them; they would use some sort of time delay fuse and be well clear of the area before we arrived.

   "One of the more interesting jobs for MND took place in 2004. The army in Al Amarah in the east of Iraq had been taking a beating for a long time. They were holed up in a house, running low on food and ammunition, surrounded by supporters of one of the breakaway Muslim clerics. The purpose of the operation was to drive a convoy of Warrior armoured cars, supported by some main battle tanks into the town to reach the besieged soldiers. Our mission was to watch for any hostile movement on the ground in response to the heavy armour moving into the town. On our two nights there, we also had the support of an AC 130 gunship. On the second evening there were more people on the streets and yet again the AC 130 was provided with targets to fire upon. During this period, one army driver of a Warrior was awarded the only living VC since the Falklands War for his bravery in Al Amarah around this time. It would appear from reading the book *Sniper One* by Dan Mills that the army in Al Amarah fired more ammunition in that one small town trying to keep the peace and desperately trying to defend themselves than was fired in the whole of the fighting war."

It is very clear from these accounts how important it was for the Nimrods to be present to help the army. Ian Marshall goes on to describe the way the aircraft carried out the ground support. The Wescam camera was clearly a formidable aid and apparently, according to *Sniper One*, could be used at quite high altitudes. In January 2005 they also had the unusual job of monitoring the delivery of ballot boxes to the counting centres. In Basrah the army was based in the Green Zone and the aircraft would patrol at night helping the troops on the ground looking for suspicious hostile activity. He goes on:

"Trying to follow a suspect car in Baghdad was not easy, they all appeared to be white to start with, the navigators would have very large-scale maps out, following every individual road and turning on our Wescam repeater and then using satellite photos to pinpoint individual buildings. On almost every night of May we would be overhead Baghdad with army soldiers on board the aircraft. The joke was, if we were ever shot down, stick as close to the soldiers as possible, they of course carried a full range of weapons onboard, where we had only a 9mm pistol and that was kept locked in an old ammo container."

Reading the account above it is clear that the Wescam camera was every bit as good as is claimed by the Canadian manufacturer (http://www.wescam.com). It is no wonder that Nimrods were very much requested and appreciated by the army for the fantastic support they were capable of giving.

Operation Oracle
Afghanistan

OPERATION ENDURING FREEDOM

UK NAME ORACLE

As technology improved the Nimrod Wescam, so information could be transmitted in real time to specially equipped personnel, often in Land Rovers, which was a real benefit for the ground troops. The need for such support rapidly became essential and when Nimrods stopped operating in Afghanistan it was a great loss for the army.

For Enduring Freedom the Nimrods were based at Thumrait in southern Oman instead of at Seeb, the main airport in

Afghanistan mountains

northern Oman. The USAF were also at Thumrait with their B1Bs which apparently were noisier than a Concorde taking off and which kept waking the Nimrod crews. There were three roles for the Nimrod. The first was exclusively for ground support of the troops and they had to use air-to-air refuelling because of the distances involved. The second role was to catch the fast small power boats with three outboard motors travelling at 50 knots carrying illegal immigrants; this problem had existed for several years but the Omanis were now worried that Al Qaeda would start using this route for escaping from Afghanistan. The Searchwater radar was able to detect the boats the moment they increased speed and stood out from the merchant shipping and tankers frequenting the route; the Omani police boats would then be vectored towards the places the boats were going to make their landfall.

The third role for the Nimrod was patrolling off the Iranian and Pakistani coast. This was a huge area search, sometimes monitoring Iranian naval exercises, sometimes watching the Indian and Pakistan navies squaring off at each other but mostly photographing every boat that looked suspicious or with a southbound track. Again, the thought being that Al Qaeda would try to escape the constant B1B and B52 bombing.

OTHER NIMROD OPERATIONS

When I started writing this book I thought it would be easy to classify the sorties into ASW and ASuW, search and rescue, Falklands campaign and land battles. However, I got a lot of responses which didn't come in to any of these categories and it seemed a shame not to include at least some of them in the book so the rest of this chapter is devoted to personal accounts of unusual occurrences which demonstrate the versatility of the Nimrod and its crews.

Nimrod in the Arctic Circle with the Northern Lights in the background

AIRCRAFT CARRIER *KUZNETZOV*, 29 DECEMBER 1995

The first one I've chosen happened when the Cold War was over and Russia's largest aircraft carrier came close to the UK. Here was the chance to get some pictures and the Russians were very happy to show off their ship and communicated with the Nimrod crew as they approached, sounding almost like air traffic control. Incidentally it was agreed between all the anti-submarine countries that reconnaissance aircraft would only make three runs photographing and that the aircraft would not come closer than a quarter of a mile. Here is the account of this particular trip by the camera operator.

RUSSIAN AIRCRAFT CARRIER *KUZNETZOV* AND FLANKER

"During the Christmas and New Year break our crew was tasked to fly from Kinloss on a surveillance mission to locate and photograph three Russian ships which included the *Kuznetzov* aircraft carrier. After de-icing our aircraft, XV 231, we eventually got airborne and, conscious of the short days experienced in the north, time may have been an issue to get quality photographs.

"The position given was way out from the pre-flight intelligence brief we had been given, but oh well perhaps they had been transmission silent for a while in order to start that 'cat and mouse' game we always played with the Soviets. Luckily for us Operations had decided to give the tasking to us rather than the oncoming SAR crew who normally got this sort of tasking. But all in all it was looking to be a very interesting and challenging flight.

"The *Kuznetzov* was a massive ship being the biggest in the Soviet navy – 900 feet long,displacement of 58,000 tons and top speed of 27 knots. It had sixteen Freestyle aircraft, twelve Flanker airborne fighters, four Helix helicopters, a mass of surface-to-air missiles (SAM), surface-to-surface (SSM), and sub-surface weapons. Not to mention the array of electronic equipment, long range, medium and close fire control, navigation radars, all that we could detect and use to home in on them. Or so we hoped.

"Airborne; all of us on tenterhooks with the thought of seeing this massive war machine, today was going to be the day we would see it: we had seen it in recce lessons, we had studied its performance, its electronics fit, we had seen its potential but today we would see it for real. ESM would be the way to detect it. Throughout the climb nothing from ESM, have we got the right software? Have we selected the right scan pattern? Are we searching for the right radars? Yes we were but still nothing. Well at least radar could not miss it, radar had the position and once in detection range on the longest range radar had it, he called a probable *Kuznetsov* on outline and size and position course and speed (PCS). WE HAD IT. We went direct to the radar contact.

"The ship loomed out of the gloom, a totally amazing sight of the vessel and its escorts. The AEO/captain called the ship on the FM radio channel 16 to get comms with it, to clear us in for the photo runs; by now ESM was calling the shots and all the radars were now illuminating us; our excellent ESM was now working like a one-armed paper hanger. But this is what he had trained for, for all those years.

"The camera team was set up and already taking shots from a distance. The carrier deck was clear apart from one aircraft, a lonely Flanker. Next pass the AEO got a receipt and comms with the vessel and requested to fly past it, the answer was short and sweet. 'Yes you can but be careful'. Those that could hear the radio looked at each other and chuckled, what did he mean? We would soon understand what he meant.

"As we approached we were aware that there was a Dutch P3 in the area doing a similar mission to ourselves. We were keen to get in and get some photos, and even spoke to the *Kuznetsov* to let them know our intentions. The standard procedure for photography was to start taking photos from the front of the ship as

Russian aircraft carrier
Kuznetzov

we flew past, then take sections along its beam and finish at the rear, and this was routinely practised on every sortie that included photography. Having taken photos of the Russian supporting oil tanker and destroyer both as part of the task, and to ensure the crew were carrying out procedures correctly, it became a waiting game.

"Eventually we were cleared in to fly past and take photos, with the warning of 'Be careful'. As we started our run in there was a call from the flight deck that they were launching an aircraft and that the camera should concentrate on that. This now became very non standard – starting taking photos from the middle of the ship and working in the opposite direction to the front as the aircraft went off the ski jump. Clearly there was a lot of excitement at what we had seen, but more importantly we had to ensure we did have them on film and to continue with the other two runs past the ship which we were allowed to do.

Flanker take-off from *Kuznetsov* (*Crown copyright*)

"The second run should have been as we ran across the front looking down the bow of the ship. The pilots positioned the aircraft and cleared for the window to be opened to start the photo run. Typically the camera jammed on the first shot, so as the camera operator, I shouted over my shoulder to the camera operator's mate for the spare camera. Careful because the window was open, we ensured that nothing would get sucked out during the swap and got back on with trying to get the best photos. We were almost past the bow, now with a 180mm lens on the camera, but something didn't make sense. I could take photos but couldn't see what I was taking. In the adrenalin-fuelled rush I hadn't noticed that the viewfinder cover had closed. In fact there is a photo looking straight down the bow of the ship that is a little high in the frame, because I had to just point and guess. While this was going on the pilots had called that a Flanker (Sukhoi Su-27) had just got airborne, was now in our 8 o' clock and moving round to our 7 o' clock, and asking if I could see it. At the same time the camera operator's mate recognised the camera problem and sorted that. I now knew I had to concentrate on photographing the closing aircraft.

"With the window open and both hands on the camera it is impossible to try and talk over the intercom and for the next few seconds everyone had to rely on the experience and expertise of each other. The pilots could no longer see the Flanker as it was too tight in behind. I could see it, but couldn't let anyone know. Fortunately I had an almost full roll of film, and probably better lens for the job although by accident. I just had to keep snapping as it came closer and closer filling more and more of the view finder. I could only see parts of the Flanker as it got so close, eventually flying past and in front of us. The pilots reportedly felt the jet wash as it cut in front of us and certainly left everyone on quite a high as to what we had just witnessed.

"The big question now was whether we got it on film, which we couldn't find out until we were back at base and the films had been processed. I did get a call from the captain the next day to say that they were very good and he was very pleased. I understood later from speaking to someone who worked in the photo section that they sent out 8,500 prints in the first batch such was the importance of the images. For instance, if one looks closely at the exhaust jet-pipes, visible is the differential thrust applied, illustrated by the differing size of the pipes, a new development in those days."

THE STAFF COLLEGE TRIP

The next one I have chosen shows how careful one must always be with visitors on an aircraft. Despite all the instructions and warnings there is always 'one in every crowd'.

"A simple sortie – just the ticket for a squadron commander – minimum crew to Valley in Anglesey, pick up fourteen Joint Service Staff College students, return to D807 (Moray Firth danger area) for thirty minutes of low level (anything more and they will be sick), disembark the students outside a Cold War HPS (hardened personnel shelter) and then an hour of circuits before joining the students at supper.

"The sortie went pretty well as planned until we got to D807. The weather was good, so we shut down No 1 (engine) and descended to low level for a photographic 'run of three' on the Beatrice energy platform – tightish turns on three engines at low level, an open window and a carefully briefed student handling the big F134 camera – it could only impress. After the first run and well into the first turn I heard the hush as the window closed and waited for the operator's report – too close, too far, just right etc. The hush was immediately broken by an apprehensive 'skipper from port beam – are the engines ok?' A quick glance by me and a rather more thorough one by the flight engineer elicited the response 'yes, why?' By way of an answer I got 'coming forward'.

"Within seconds I felt my right shoulder tapped as the lead wet shouted that one of our student passengers, unbriefed, had appeared from nowhere, pointed his own camera out of the window, literally, and lost it to the 160 kt airstream and quite possibly the No 2 engine. This was impressive, but not the event that we had planned. It was not the time for secrecy, the galley had not noticed a passing camera so I assumed the worst, restarted No 1, monitored No 2 closely, and returned to Kinloss and disembarked the students at the HPS. You would think that was the end of the sortie – but my log book suggests that we went off and did the circuits!

"The incident report needed careful wording to disguise the additional unauthorised photography and I got to supper a little late. At the end of an increasingly boisterous meal the president of the Mess Committee stole the show when he presented a certain visiting student with a mess bill that included an "Engine – Nimrod – replaced – £951,235.45" – no discount for the camera.

"In case you are wondering, there was no damage to the engine – I suspect that the camera went over the top of the wing."

"AND SCATTER MY ASHES IN THE SCAPA FLOW"

This next one is rather sad in a way, a story of doing one's best and the unexpected happens.

"For the most part, as squadron commander, I enjoyed sharing my philosophy on leadership with newly appointed captains. High among the key themes was the need for good communication. Thus I wanted to know, from the captain, of any crew incident, good or bad, especially bad, immediately. This would allow me, or us, to take the initiative in preparing defensive briefs – hearing first of an alleged 'bad news' incident direct from the station commander would have us on the back foot – and I would be a reluctant ally.

"Nonetheless I was a little surprised to have a navigator captain knock on my door within a week of his appointment. 'Excuse me boss – but you remember saying that you wanted to be the first to hear of any potential problem?' 'So soon! But of course – come in, tell me more.'

"It was a heart warming story of good intentions. An ex Royal Navy uncle of one of the crew SNCOs had asked that his ashes be scattered over Scapa Flow. What could be more appropriate than a Nimrod? The new captain felt that a suitable ceremony could be incorporated into a local area crew training sortie. He was well aware that once re-leased ashes have a mind of their own and stipulated suitable packing in a modified sonobuoy tube; he also suggested that the padre come along to conduct a brief service. So far so good; unfortunately the weather over Scapa Flow was down to the deck ruling out a visually aimed drop. Plan B was a timed run from the Kirkwall beacon on an ap-propriate heading – how long will the commitment take the captain asked of the padre? Oh just two minutes was the response. Two minutes at 2.5 miles a minute equates to 5 miles which takes us clear of land. Ok – on top NDB, now, now, now, start the service. The service reached 'dust to dust, ashes to ashes' in rather less than two minutes with the GPI (ground position indicator) showing the aircraft, in the captain's words, 'pos-sibly still over land'. Too late to interject he could only pray as the padre pulled the manual release to commit the ashes to a ballistic trajectory – ending where? A quick calculation of the forward throw of a sonobuoy tube suggested that the ashes could be safely in the Flow but on the other hand they might not. The captain concluded that he thought I would want to know.

"I could not suppress my laughter – the captain was surprised but much relieved. The follow-on action was to have the captain call the Orkney police, coastguard, RNLI etc with a description of the sonobuoy tube and its contents and hope to hear nothing more – oh and to tell ops that there was an inadvertent sonobuoy release off Orkney but we had already informed the appropriate agencies. Don't rush the incident report – if there is bad news we will know shortly – in which case you will have to claim an 'act of God' – or perhaps God's minion.

"As it happens the sonobuoy tube was found in an Orkney ditch by a postman who duly informed the police who got in touch with the captain. I don't know what hap-pened next. I never asked if there was a second attempt; if there was it passed off without further incident – as far as I know."

THE NORTH POLE

On 9 April 2004 two Nimrods conducted a fourteen-hour low-level operation at the North Pole, refuelling twice from VC10s of 101 Squadron. The mission was to support RN nuclear submarine HMS *Tireless* and USS *Hampton* which had both surfaced at the Pole. As can be seen both the crews met on the ice, including scientists travelling aboard both submarines to collect data and perform experiments. I must confess I am a bit puzzled why the RN submarine was not

Above: Nimrods liaising with a RN and a US submarine at the North Pole (*Crown copyright*)
Opposite page: The Nimrod navigation station at the North Pole (*Brian Cushion*)
Below: Postition recorded, *left.* Doug Torrance was there! (*Brian Cushion*)

flying the white ensign!

There was at least one earlier flight on 8 May 1988 when a Nimrod R1 flew to the North Pole out of Bodø. Fortunately Brian Cushion has let me have a photograph of the navigation station at the Pole taken on that flight and the position recorded is 89° 59.4' N 178° 31.1' W.

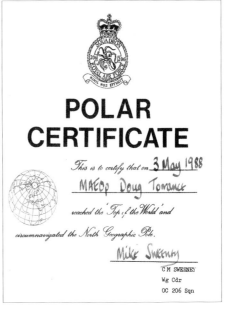

POLAR
CERTIFICATE

This is to certify that on 3 May 1988
MAEOp Doug Torrance
reached the 'Top of the World' and
circumnavigated the North Geographic Pole.

Mike Sweeney

C M SWEENEY
Wg Cdr
OC 206 Sqn

Nimrod R1 XW665 refuelling at Bodø on its way to the North Pole (*Brian Cushion*)

EXERCISE NEREUS, THE NORTH PACIFIC EXPERIMENT (NORPAX)

In 1977-78 the Scripps Institute of Oceanography, San Diego Ca., commenced a research project into the behaviour of ocean currents in the North Pacific. The project was being funded by the US Navy Office of Oceanographic Research. A key element of the research was the acquisition of water temperature data in the equatorial region south of Hawaii. The data gathering required sampling at 60nm intervals along a defined track with increased sampling at 30nm intervals over specified areas of particular interest. Whilst the project was civilian managed it possibly had a military application.

Scripps started by 'chartering' USN Reserve P3 units to carry out the task, but with disappointing results and this became known to the RAF liaison officer at San Diego who realised that this gave a great opportunity for the Nimrod and volunteered the services of the RAF.

Brian Cushion goes on:

"So it was that on 7 February 1979 we set off from St Mawgan in XV251, with Scripps paying, for NAS North Island, San Diego via CFB Greenwood, Nova Scotia. At North Island the aircraft was fitted with a palletised Litton 72 IN, as our Elliot platform was not deemed sufficiently accurate. We had a briefing at Scripps about NORPAX, North Pacific Experiment, and the sorties we were to fly. Although the briefing was accurate, the phrase 'cover story' sprung to mind! On 10 Feb we departed to NAS Barbers Point Hawaii, to be fitted with special recording equipment and to load the experimental bathy buoys (XBT). We were joined by a Scripps scientist who had briefed us and was to fly on the data-gathering sorties; he had previously flown on the Reserve P3 flights.

"On 16 February we departed Barbers Point for Tahiti, captained by Wg Cdr David Green, and carried out the briefed task without difficulty or incident. However, our navigator, Sqn Ldr Brian Sprosen, was looking questioningly at the marvellous Litton 72. The return leg was flown on 16 February, again without incident. However, on arrival back at Barbers Brian Sprosen conducted his own debrief, revealing why the results of the earlier sorties had been poor and making an offer of $50 for the Litton platform.

It had in fact been navigating erroneously wandering around the ocean whilst our old Elliot had behaved faultlessly. The recording equipment was removed at Barbers Point and we departed to NAS Moffet (San Francisco). After offloading the Litton we returned to St Mawgan via CFB Greenwood, arriving back on 21 February. There was a subsequent Nereus sortie flown by a Kinloss crew; IIRC Dave Angus of 120 Sqn ; and that completed the RAF involvement in Nereus."

As an enthusiastic amateur navigator I have tried to find out what the fault was with the Litton platform but so far I have failed.

LOW FLYING IN THE WASH

No pictures for this next one or the pilot would have been in trouble:

"George Morris's bombing practice on the range over the Wash in the MR2, with a 120 Squadron aircraft on the way back from a display symposium at Finningley. George decided it was a few years since he'd done the range on the Wash in fast jets so thought it would be worthwhile having a practice in an MR2 as it was cleared to drop 500lb bombs. He got cleared in by the range control and did first run at 300ft and fired a retro trying to hit part of a wreck. He didn't get very close so he went around for a second run, this time it was a port beams call and it was the beam operator if I remember rightly who conned on and got fairly close. The next thing that happened was that range control called up and requested confirmation of what type we were. George replies 'Nimrod', control says confirm size and when George replied 'Nimrod MR2 Heavy' range control screams 'clear range, and expedite immediately, avoid the local town' by which time George is about 600ft max power climbing right over the top of the town of Wainfleet, the source of frequent noise complaints. Somehow he still managed to talk himself out of deep trouble when we got back to Kinloss by blaming the range controller for letting us in."

SECOND-HAND SUBMARINES

Most countries which spend a lot of money on defence are always trying to sell their old equipment. I remember the Royal New Zealand Air Force bought the Andover Mk1 and Canada bought four Royal Naval diesel submarines at the end of the 1990s as they were being retired. The Canadians got a very good deal since they only cost £1 each but in return the UK got some low flying rights in the north of Canada.

On 5 October 2004, HMCS *Chicoutimi* (previously HMS *Upholder*) sailing from Faslane naval base, Scotland to Nova Scotia declared an emergency north west of Ireland following a fire onboard. The first Nimrod crew on the scene thought the boat 'was a goner'; it was rolling from side to side through 30⁰ each way due to the large swell and had virtually no power. Wikipedia continues the tale:

"The fire was caused by sea water entering through open hatches in rough seas. It soaked electrical insulation which had not been sufficiently waterproofed (since it conformed to an older specification than the three other submarines), starting a fire. The boat was rescued by Royal Navy frigates HMS *Montrose* and *Marlborough* on 6 October. Lt(N)

Chris Saunders died subsequently from the effects of smoke inhalation; due to the rough weather it had not been possible to airlift him and the other casualties to a hospital until two days later. *Chicoutimi* was later transported to Halifax for repair. A board of inquiry cleared the captain of any fault but the regulations permitting the submarine to run on the surface with open hatches were revised."

A Nimrod escorted the boat back to safe waters and it was mentioned in the local paper. However, Kinloss was told to keep quiet about the whole thing in case the Canadians changed their minds!

DEMONSTRATIONS TO TOP BRASS

I did many flying demonstrations in my career and it was amazing how often things went wrong, the aircraft went unserviceable, the weather was no good or the aircraft was overweight because too many people turned up for the flight. I feel sorry for Flt Lt Hughes who on 28 January 1974 was tasked with taking the Commander-in-Chief Near East Air Force, John Aiken from RAF Akrotiri to RAF Gibraltar, with a phase in the middle of the flight at low level showing the air marshal the Nimrod manoeuvring in its operational environment. Unfortunately, the low level phase went rather off plan when, south of Crete near the island of Gavdos when the aircraft was approaching the Soviet anchorage at Kythira, it suffered a multitude of lightning strikes, which set fire to the sound-proofing in the main cabin. The flight deck crew thought that the AEO's call on the intercom of 'fire in the fuselage' was a response to an exercise incident injected to test the crew by the air marshal, but soon realised that the call was for real when fumes reached the cockpit, not to mention the tone of the AEO's voice. The electronics team ripped sections of covering off and attacked the flames with fire extinguishers, just as the pilots prepared to head for Souda Bay air base. The flames were quickly extinguished, but an aircraft change was executed at Luqa before continuing to Gibraltar. The crew and the boss got more from that sortie than they had bargained for!

On another demonstration Barry Masefield, who now flies in Vulcan 558, spent some time as an AEO in the Nimrod MR1. He was in a Nimrod which was charged with bringing the First Sea Lord, Admiral Lewin, back from Keflavik. On the way back he expressed an interest in seeing the rotary sonobuoy dispenser operating. Barry goes on:

"As you recall, the linkage in the dispenser closes off a blanking plate when the lid of the dispenser is opened thereby preventing the aircraft suffering a rapid decompression when loading the sonobuoys. I explained this to the admiral and then demonstrated how we would load up a sonobuoy. He was leaning over the dispenser to observe the loading action when I opened the lid and unfortunately as he was leaning into the dispenser the linkage system failed thereby causing a sudden decompression. I watched in horror as he was being gently sucked down into the container and managed to haul him back to safety. Needless to say he was rather shocked and after saying thank you for the demonstration staggered back to the front of the aircraft and strapped himself into a seat next to the tac nav. Obviously there was no danger of him being sucked out of the aircraft but he wasn't to know that and just sat there contemplating what he possibly thought were his final moments as the first sea lord. After we landed and he said goodbye to the crew it was quite evident that he was not impressed with me because he shook hands with all the crew except me."

LOW FLYING A NIMROD R1

For obvious reasons it has not been possible to relate stories about 51 Squadron and the Nimrod R1s. Their routine flying was probably less exciting and demanding than in the MR1 since the role was generally listening to everyone else, not carrying out search and rescue or chasing a submarine. When Colin Pomeroy left 203 Squadron in January 1976 he joined 51 Squadron, then at RAF Wyton, flying the Nimrod R1, which was highly unusual unless you were a qualified flying instructor, the first ex-maritime Nimrod pilot to do so except for the Squadron QFI. Interestingly Colin felt that being in 1 Group and not 18 Group the crew were treated with far more respect and the crews' efforts were more appreciated. Perhaps more importantly they even got Lone Ranger allowances on detachment. On occasions he went to Teheran while the Shah was still there and he remarked that it was a wonderful experience with everyone being so friendly, which doesn't surprise me as I too used to stage through there delivering aircraft and it was always a delightful night stop.

Colin enjoyed his two years away from 'Coastal' but apparently he was always a maritime aviator at heart.

> "I always enjoyed trips back out to Malta, which we used as a base for sorties off the North African coast. Recovering to Luqa one day, with Flt Lt Chris Bond in the right-hand seat (we were all first pilots and flew trip-and-trip about in the left-hand seat) I let down to 500 feet some miles away from the island and meandered back through the Comino Channel enjoying the scenery – just as I had always done. It was only when Chris enquired of me 'Are we authorised for low flying?' that I realised that, at least temporarily, my old searching days in the Nimrod MR was a thing of the past!"

HONG KONG WHEN IT WAS EXCITING

I spent three months in the Philippines selling the Avro 748 to Philippine Airlines in 1967. While I was there I went to Hong Kong several times sitting in the jump seat of a 737 looking at the famous checker board when landing at Kai Tak on runway 13. I always wanted to have a go myself but all I could manage was a Trident on runway 31 a year or so later as I could not find an excuse to take our demonstration aircraft there. I am therefore very jealous of Terry Earl:

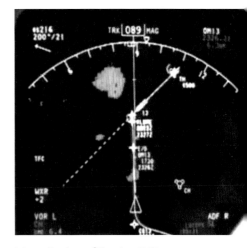

Map display of Boeing 747

> "While on detachment to Singapore my crew was fortunate enough to be allocated the first Nimrod trip into Hong Kong towards the end of 1971, but there was a problem. I had no experience of landing at Kai Tak and there was a long-standing RAF rule that a pilot should not do so unless he had been there before to be shown the local procedures. However, previous maritime operations from Singapore had been conducted under the command of Far East Air Force Headquarters (which no longer existed) and Coastal Command Air Staff Instructions (which might have contained guidance on the matter) no longer existed following the formation of Strike Command. If we were to follow traditional guidance I and my co-pilot would

have to hitch a ride on a passing RAF transport aircraft, as Tengah was used as a staging post for Transport Command flights to HK. But this would mean that one crew would then be unavailable for operations for several days whilst its pilots were away, an arrange-

Chequer Board

ment which both my CO and I thought to be operationally unacceptable. However, rather than refer this matter to higher authority, I suggested an alternative solution based on the fact that I knew that there was an official RAF film which provided comprehensive guidance on the approach and landing procedures at Kai Tak, and a copy of this film was available at Tengah. So I convinced my squadron commander that if my crew studied the approach charts and watched the film a couple of times we could obviate the need to visit Hong

Approaching the Kai Tak checker board

Kong in advance and thus maintain the integrity of the detachment. In the detachment report we would highlight this neat solution and hopefully establish a beneficial precedent for future detachments.

"Having agreed this course of action we departed Tengah on 17 March, conducted a surveillance task en route and in less than five hours were established on radar vectors for the ILS approach to Runway 31 at Kai Tak. This was of course a major disappointment as it meant that we would fly the straight-in approach over the sea and not expe-

Above left: Turning finals and (*right*) Made it!

rience the chequer-board approach with its late turn onto final for Runway 13. But when we were some four miles from touchdown, passing the northern tip of Hong Kong Island out to our left, the controller called us with the instruction, 'clear for harbour circuit to land Runway 13'. Before I could stop him the co-pilot blurted out on intercom, 'this wasn't on the film!' and I could immediately sense the rest of the crew stiffening and tightening their seat-belts. But as I did so I realised what this call actually

Nimrod in Sepang, Malaysia

meant – nothing less than the best way to experience a landing at Kai Tak! Turning left to over-fly the harbour provided a wonderful view of Hong Kong Island and with the runway now out on our right-hand side I began looking for the famous chequer-board painted on the hill to help guide us onto final approach for Runway 13. Once I had this in view it was a straight-forward matter to line up with the runway at about 600 feet on final, with the roof-tops and TV aerials of Kowloon city close below us.

"I confess I was feeling rather proud of myself as we taxied back from the seaward end of the runway towards our parking area, but as we did so we passed a row of 747s seemingly towering above our Nimrod. And it struck me that if they could carry passengers in and out of Kai Tak on a regular basis then it was hard to see what the problem was for us. However, and unsurprisingly perhaps, our lords and masters took a different view and greeted the recommendation in our report with unfeigned horror, immediately issuing orders to prevent such lunatic behaviour occurring in the future."

Nowadays there is a world class airport at Chek Lap Kok and the skill required to land has been considerably reduced but Terry Earl and many others will take delight in remembering how it used to be.

CONCLUSION

The varied stories above show that the Nimrod did many different things and their crews were always resourceful. Whatever the task the aircraft would take off and invariably could make a contribution because it had so many tools that the crew seemed to be able to deal with any problems which arose.

7 THE FALKLANDS CAMPAIGN

Memorial in Port Stanley to those killed in the Falklands campaign

The Atlantic Ocean

On 1 April 1982 the Argentinians landed troops on the Falkland Islands and the decision was taken to recapture the islands a day or so later by the UK Government under Mrs Thatcher.

It was obvious right from the start that Nimrod aircraft would be needed for reconnaissance and potential search and rescue duties but the distances involved were far greater than the Nimrod could fly with standard fuel loading. The only feasible military base anywhere near the Falklands was Ascension Island, owned by the UK but operated militarily by the United States. It was 3,528 nautical miles great circle distance from St Mawgan where the Nimrods operated in Cornwall to Ascension Island and a further 3,376 nautical miles from there to Port Stanley in the Falklands. In fact the distance to Ascension was actually greater since the aircraft would need to fly over water to avoid having to get overflight permission from non-combatant countries. The only solution therefore to enable Nimrods to operate in the South Atlantic and the Falklands was to fit them with flight-refuelling equipment.

FLIGHT-REFUELLING INSTALLATION

John Scott-Wilson, chief designer at British Aerospace's Manchester facility, had been asked by MOD shortly after the outbreak of hostilities how long it would take to design, fit and clear flight refuelling on the Nimrod. Normally to do such a large and important modification in peacetime would take at least a year, not counting the time it would take to get the modification cleared and released to the RAF for service use. Brilliantly, he estimated a month which was a key decision. On 14 April he received instructions to proceed and he immediately moved the whole design team with their drawing boards to the aircraft at Woodford in the 'New Assembly' sheds where the aircraft were being modified. Each part of the total modification, as it was designed, was fitted onto the aircraft on the basis of the designers and John Scott-Wilson giving verbal instructions for their fitment; only when there had been a successful trial installation were the official drawings made out. Incidentally, as I write this I am reminded that I recently read in *Flight International* that Boeing, clearly mistakenly, thought they had achieved a 'world first' on the 787 programme by relocating the design team down onto the production line beside the aircraft!

Clearly the most important piece of hardware for the modification was the flight-refuelling probe and there were none immediately available which should have 'scuppered' the whole project. However, by chance Avros had, a month or two previously, paid MOD(PE) £7,500 for Vulcan XA603 so that it could be on static display on their airfield at Woodford. Fortuitously Charles Masefield who was still chief test pilot had just collected the aircraft on 12 March from Waddington. An instant decision was taken to rob the probe of XA603 and use it on the test Nimrod XV229 and a special invoice was made out to MOD 'for supplying flight refuelling probe on test Nimrod £7,500'.

The actual installation of the fuel piping from the drogue to the aircraft's fuel system was a challenge. The only quick solution was to fix a metal pipe to the aircraft end of the probe and lead it through the upper crew escape hatch which was then rendered inoperable. The metal pipe was then split behind the captain's seat and two standard fuel bowser hoses were fixed to the cabin floor with the equivalent of jubilee clips. The pipes were taken down the whole length of the cabin behind the operators' seats and through the cabin floor where two flare chutes had been removed. The pipes were then taken forward and joined to the aircraft's normal refuelling system.

Besides the availability of the probe there had been another fortunate happening to enable the Nimrod to be able to refuel. In 1980 the MOD had asked Avros to investigate whether a Nimrod could formate in the refuelling position close up under a Victor K2. Charles Masefield and Robbie Robinson, shortly to take over as chief test pilot from Charles, had done the trial and found that though the aircraft could be made to formate nicely with the windscreen close up behind the Victor, every time any aileron was applied the nose would yaw away from the correct position because on the Comet 4 there was a modification, fitted for general flying and directional stability, which applied rudder on application of aileron. Clearly this modification wasn't required on the Nimrod and needed to be removed before the air-to-air refuelling tests started. The actual flight testing is described in Robbie Robinson's book *Avro One* when the modification instead of being removed was reversed by mistake which made matters worse! On 28 April only fourteen days after the go-ahead was given, test pilot Johnny Cruse and Flt Lt Tony Banfield made successful dry contacts with a Victor tanker.

In fact a further aerodynamic modification was required as it was realised straightaway that the directional stability of the aircraft had been impaired by the fitting of the probe and that something would have to be done immediately to ensure that the aircraft would be able to connect easily with a tanker's drogue and take on fuel. This was fixed 'overnight' by bolting on a wooden 'keel' under the rear fuselage in place of the standard tail 'bumper'. In addition to this the Nimrod R1 mod, which added vertical avionics antennae to the top and bottom surfaces of each tailplane, was also fitted in the expectation that these aerials would provide some additional fin area. Of course for this modification on the MR2s the R1 antennae were purely aerodynamic with no electrical connections. These, plus the 'keel', fixed the problem totally.

On 30 April Johnny Cruse and Tony Banfield made the first wet contacts with a Victor tanker and on 1 May, Nimrod XV 238 was delivered with the flight refuelling modification complete. On 2 May wet contacts were made at night and on 3 May the aircraft was cleared for wet contacts, taking on fuel as required so that nineteen days after the start of the project, the Nimrod had full flight-refuelling clearance.

Above left to right: Nimrod flight-refuelling training sequence as seen from the Victor (*Andy Collins*)

During the trials it was found that the pilots were unable to achieve repeated connections with the probe. This problem was diagnosed as being due to the probe being full of fuel and causing hydraulic locking at the probe head. The problem was overcome by drilling a small vent hole 3/32nds of an inch in diameter in the probe blanking plate to allow the pressure to be relieved. However, later in the trial it was reported that fuel was running back along the top of the fuselage and entering the APU bay so that fuel contamination was discovered in the APU bay at the next ground APU start. Luckily this vent hole was not needed when fuel was being transferred and was removed prior to the aircraft receiving the full refuelling clearance.

It is worth mentioning that in order for this release to be achieved so quickly there was a senior MOD civil servant resident at Woodford while all the work was going on who was not afraid to make decisions; in fact the final flight-refuelling release was transmitted from the Woodford test pilot's telex machine in their operations room. The speed at which this modification was installed was a tribute to all concerned, a truly remarkable achievement. However it was a 'wartime' modification and some test work on the impact of flight refuelling on the aircraft and the existing fuel system understandably was not carried out, which will be discussed later in the next chapter.

Below: Ascension Island and Wideawake runway

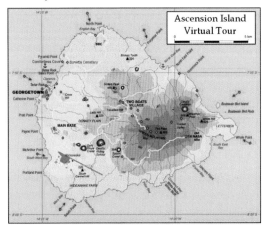

Once the clearance for air-to-air refuelling had been given, eighteen pilots were instructed and checked out in the next few days so that they would be able to carry out Nimrod refuelling operations as required. Aircraft were modified at Woodford and at Kinloss using probes recovered from Vulcans going out of service. In a very few days there were Nimrods with refuelling probes at Ascension Island so the patrols gradually lengthened in range until the aircraft were flying down to the Falkland Islands and beyond. The aircraft theoretically could fly for twenty-four hours with flight refuelling, the limit being the amount of engine oil available; however there were other considerations such as crew fatigue which had to be taken into account.

ASCENSION ISLAND

In fact the first Nimrods to fly to Ascension were Nimrod MR1s from 42 Squadron under the command of Wg Cdr Dave Baugh (XV244 Crew 1, captained by Flt Lt Smith and XV258 Crew 4, led by Flt Lt Norris) arriving 6 April and forming the first permanent detachment. Because they didn't have flight refuelling the aircraft had to refuel at Gibraltar. On arrival at Ascension Dave Baugh immediately commandeered the only air-conditioned briefing rooms which actually belonged to the US Navy but had been used by Nimrod crews in the past.

First look (*David Emmerson*)

On 7 April, Flt Lt Turnbull and Crew 8 aboard XV258 carried out a six-hour search for Argentine surface vessels and submarines, and also acted as a communications link between the submerged RN nuclear submarines, which were leading the British armed forces to the Falklands, and Group Headquarters at Northwood. The initial sorties were all fifty nautical miles on either side of the intended track of the Task Force making its way to the Falklands and as far ahead as possible. Occasional mail-drop sorties were also flown as well as SAR sorties providing top cover for Victor tankers.

The first MR2 to arrive at Wideawake airfield on Ascension was the non-probe-equipped XV230 on 13 April, and four days later XV255 joined it from Kinloss. The first MR2 mission was flown by XV230 on 15 April which dropped the secret orders for Operation Paraquat (the retaking of South Geor-

Approaching the runway at Wideawake airfield (*David Emmerson*)

gia) to HMS *Antrim*. The first Nimrod fitted with flight refuelling to reach Wideawake Field on Ascension Island was MR2 XV227 on 7 May, twenty-three days after Avros had been given permission to fit flight refuelling to the aircraft, almost unbelievable. From then on there were between two and five Nimrods based at Ascension. XV227 made its first operational flight on 9 May of 12 hours 45 minutes duration, covering 2,750 miles with a 206 Squadron crew, supported by three Victor tankers; the purpose of this mission was to provide anti-submarine cover for the British Fleet.

Wg Cdr David Emmerson went out on 21 April to command the detachment. Prior to

Above: Nimrod being refuelled by a Victor (*David Emmerson*)
Opposite: Refuelling views from the Nimrod and Victor

arrival he had been clearing the new Stingray torpedo on the range at Machrihanish, Scotland. As a result, the Nimrods at Ascension had the Stingray and Mk44 torpedoes plus 1,000 lb bombs. Terry Earl was involved with the training for dropping the bombs:

"All crews that deployed to Ascension were trained to drop a visually aimed stick of four 1,000 lb bombs. The drop height was 500 feet at an indicated airspeed of 250 knots, which immediately raised the uncomfortable question of what might the proposed targets be – if there were even basic air defences to be penetrated this could well prove to be a one-way trip! Nimrod pilots had been accustomed to judging visually the release point for various ordnance from the bomb bay, such as torpedoes and SAR equipment, but such drops were normally made from not above 300 feet and at around 210 knots. So it was decided that the extra height and speed justified an aiming device in the cockpit. Boscombe Down were tasked to come up with something suitable and on 4 May 1982 I flew down to have the prototype version fitted for a trial on Wainfleet Range. We were informed that this would be a TLAR sight, and when we asked what this stood for we were told – 'That Looks About Right'….! In fact what we saw on arrival was not much better, appearing to be a small rectangle of perspex with a piece from a wire coat-hangar attached. This contraption was mounted on the coaming in front of the first pilot and allowed him to assess a depression angle by aligning the metal bar with a particular angle marked on the perspex plate. The required angle to indicate the correct release point would be calculated and called by the navigator based on the ground speed as the aircraft approached the target. All the pilot had to do was to wait until the bar appeared super-imposed on that angle as indicated on the perspex plate and at that moment press the release button – all rather Heath Robinson but simple, effective and easy to use. Over the next three days I conducted training with six pilots using 25 kg practice bombs with the radar buoy in D807 as an aiming point. This was

followed by dropping some inert 1,000 lb bombs on the Rosehearty Range. All this proved the validity of the concept and crews due to deploy to Ascension were trained firstly using practice bombs to get used to the sight, and then taken to Garvie Island to do one live drop with a full stick of bombs.

"As best as I can see from my log book only six crews made live drops although a couple more may have completed the practice bombing phase. As I recall I was the only one doing the training so I suspect that this somewhat dubious idea of Nimrod 'lay-down' bombing was nipped in the bud at a reasonably early stage."

The aircraft had a full set of survival gear and dinghies and so their bomb-bay load varied depending on the type of mission, since there were five different types. There was the normal look out for submarines and enemy shipping giving support for the Royal Navy. In addition there was a daily sweep around Ascension Island itself to make certain the Argentinians were not planning to attack the island. Then the aircraft was used to sweep ahead of the deploying fleet for enemy warships though there was a gap as the fleet neared the Falklands until the Nimrod could be flight refuelled. There was the need to provide one aircraft on SAR standby at all times but though it was launched on a few occasions to answer emergency calls, there was never an active SAR incident. The fourth type of mission was supporting Harrier deliveries to the carriers and the Vulcan Black Buck sorties actually attacking the runway and facilities at Port Stanley. Finally there were the very important long-range reconnaissance

Bomb-aiming sight

sorties down to the Falklands and Argentina.

A typical SAR role was supporting the Vulcans on their departure and return from the Black Buck missions. For example, on the return from Black Buck the Nimrod would time its take-off to meet up with the Vulcan at its refuelling point on the way home and would get a top up of fuel from one of the 'intermediate' Victors returning from refuelling the final Victor which was going to 'feed' the Black Buck Vulcan. Using the Searchwater the aircraft could see both the Vulcan and the Victor up to 400 miles apart and vector the two aircraft to meet up. As the aircraft got closer the Victor and Vulcan would use their air-to-air Tacan for the final link up. Meanwhile the Nimrod would fly close by in case there were any problems. David Emmerson did SAR for Black Buck 1,2 and 6 (see log book opposite) and in fact the only problem that occurred was the always dreaded one on Black Buck 6 when the tip of the refuelling probe came off the Vulcan.

On 31 May a Vulcan returning to Wideawake after launching two Shrike missiles at the Port Stanley radar had a damaged probe while refuelling from a Victor off the Brazilian coast. The captain, Sqn Ldr Neil McDougal, realised the only place he could land was at Rio de Janeiro in Brazil 400 miles away. After jettisoning the two Shrikes he had left he went down to 10,000 ft to depressurise the aircraft and then the confidential documents were thrown out of the entrance door. The door could not be closed again for some reason so it was impossible to climb up to economise on fuel. The aircraft had a slightly difficult time explaining to Brazilian air traffic control the type of aircraft it was but permission was granted to land at Galeão International Airport which was just as well as there was only 3,000 lb of fuel remaining, insufficient for another circuit. While all the negotiation was taking place Emmerson in the Nimrod just outside Brazilian airspace was giving navigation advice to the crew who had lost a lot of charts when the documents were jettisoned. The Nimrod also tried to pass messages to Group Headquarters at Northwood but it proved very difficult using the only equipment available, single sideband HF. The story goes that the Vulcan was only released very quickly because it was parked in the place allocated to the Pope's aircraft which was due a few days later!

The long-range reconnaissance missions were tracking from north of the Falklands towards the coast of Argentina and then turning north looking for shipping, submarines and listening to all radio transmissions. The aircraft flew at low level to keep beneath the reach of the Argentinian radar. In fact Spanish-speaking specialists flew on these missions carrying extra listening equipment to monitor all the Argentinian activity, army, navy and air force. The flights were long ones requiring at least two refuellings. David Emmerson's longest and record-breaking trip was on 15 May, 19 hours 35 minutes; the aircraft flew 8,300 miles down to a point 150 miles north of Port Stanley, then west until only sixty miles from the coast of Argentina keeping below radar cover, turning to fly north east, parallel to the coastline; its Searchwater radar was used to survey a strip 400 miles wide and 1,000 miles long, confirming that all Argentine warships were still fully blockaded in port by the threat of British nuclear-powered submarines.

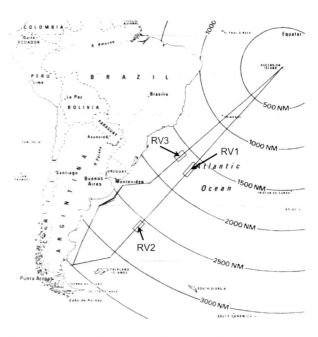

Nimrod reconnaissance sortie – note three refuelling location rectangles
(*David Emmerson*)

It was a fine day and the aircraft was vulnerable to attack from fighters during some segments of that flight, but it returned safely to Wideawake Field at Ascension. The mission required three air-to-air refuellings by Victor tankers; the refuelling spots were obviously planned with great care and the three refuelling spots for the really long flights are shown on the map as rectangles on the planned tracks. I notice from Emmerson's log book that his next flight was nearly as long on 20 May, 18 hours 50 minutes. He notes 'Perhaps the most interesting of these sorties was on the night prior to the landing by British troops when, to our surprise, we found we could still see the lights on Port Stanley blazing fiercely despite the war activities.'

It is worth remarking that the Falklands War took place before the availability of satellites for navigation. The Nimrod MR2 system had one inertial navigation system, INS, with a significant drift rate, so that the longer the sortie the more inaccurate was the aircraft's position.

Below: Wing Commander David Emmerson's log book

For an aircraft flying over land this was not too serious as it was possible to update the navigation system from known ground positions but for a maritime aircraft the lack of precise knowledge of position was a definite handicap, and of course with the introduction of flight refuelling and the increased sortie length the lack of an accurate position became even more of an embarrassment. As usual the crews made the best of the situation and in fact one of the upgrades to the Nimrod during the Falklands was an improvement to the accuracy of the INS.

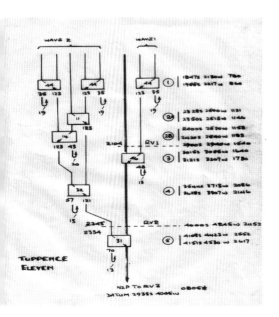

Above: Victor refuelling plan for a double-refuelling sortie (*David Emmerson*)

These long trips needed a lot of careful planning as it was not possible for one Victor by itself to deliver to the Nimrod the required amount of fuel. To understand the magnitude of the problem it must be realised that for a Victor tanker to be able to deliver the necessary fuel at long ranges, it had to be refuelled itself by other Victor tankers on the way to the rendezvous point. There were many variations of how the Victors operated and the diagram is a typical Victor refuelling planning chart for supporting the Nimrod outbound on one of its long sorties. The solid line is the Nimrod and where it refuelled.

A pair of Victors in Wave 1 took off after the Nimrod and caught it up; on the way one of the pair give 44,000 lb of fuel to the other Victor completely filling it and then returned home with 35,000 lb of fuel landing with 19,000 lb – see return arrow. The refuelled Victor then gave 46,000 lb to the Nimrod and returned home landing with only 13,000lb of fuel, obviously relying on the perfect flying weather on Ascension. Five Victors in Wave 2 took off after Wave 1 and this time two of the five were refuelled so that three were left to carry on. The fifth Victor later topped up both Victors that had been refuelled and returned home. One of the two Victors left then refuelled the other to just short of full tanks, 121,000 lb instead of 123,000 lb, and returned home. Finally the last Victor gave 31,000 lb of fuel to the Nimrod and returned home with 70,000 lb left so that it only had 13,000 lb again at Ascension. The figures on the right of the chart are the latitudes and longitudes of the expected refuelling points. On the return home only a pair of Victors were required to meet the Nimrod at RV3. I'm grateful to David Emmerson for explaining the charts to me and one can well understand his comment: 'my most vivid lasting memory is listening to the radio communication during the first Vulcan Black Buck sortie when the Victor tanker crews totally reorganised the complex refuelling programme as unserviceabilities and other potential disasters occurred. An incredible performance and one so complex that it would have confused any eavesdropper.'

The Victor refuelling diagram is shown to give some idea of the detailed planning required for each sortie. It is an enormous tribute to the reliability of both the Nimrod and the Victors that no aircraft had to ditch in the unforgiving Atlantic. In fact it was the Victor crews that were the unsung heroes of the airborne side of the Falklands War; they flew ceaselessly night and day supporting the Nimrods and the Vulcans and their crews must have been exhausted. Without the Victors the airborne part of the Falklands War could not have taken place. It was a truly amazing feat of planning, logistics and human determination.

Paul Warrener describes a long-range sortie:

"After briefing in our own 'Nimrod Operations' the crew were taken to 'Victor Ops' in an old US-style school bus – judging by the age of the vehicle it could have taken Ronald Regan to school. Victor Operation was a tented affair much like the set up of the 4077th

MASH in the iconic TV series, air conditioned, the vents could be rolled up to adjust the level of comfort. The crew exec's attended the tanker brief and the rest of the Nimrod crew went on to conduct the preflight check on the aircraft.

"The brief was much like a WWII Bomber Command briefing, with the crews sat at tables and a screen at the front with the duty overhead projector. The routes for that were shown, with each progression to the next rendezvous point, the tankers turning back for Ascension and then the Nimrod track continued. This was followed by sharp intakes of breath from the Victor

AHC Victor K2, the work horse of the Falklands

crews when they saw how far south into the Argentinian fighter cover we were to venture. As well as the AAR brief we also received an additional intelligence brief.

"The same bus picked up the crew and took them to the waiting and prepared Nimrod aircraft. To say that the groundcrew fussed over the aircraft would be an understatement. Meticulous preparation had taken place and not one item was allowed to be unserviceable or to go unchecked. The Nimrod Force had always had tremendous groundcrew, but the detachment at Ascension produced the best of the best. I remember as we taxied out not one of the groundcrew left the dispersal area, and they were still there as we rolled down the runway. At Kinloss they would have hurried off to their crew room or next task.

"Once airborne the dry team who handled the surface-surveillance sensors, radar and the 'ARAR/ARAX' electronic support measures equipment (ESM) effectively worked a defence watch system with hourly rotating watches. The crew therefore went to 'action stations' at 35 degrees south. By that point we were all wearing the green regular issue immersions suits, which were considered necessary due to the hostile South Atlantic weather conditions. Due to the heat on the ground it would have been intolerable to wear them from take-off, but the high level transit allowed the aircraft to cool enough for them to be comfortable.

"The ARAR/ARAX was our early warning system as it detected any radar signal which swept over the aircraft within the S, C and X-band part of the electronic spectrum. The detector head was in the distinctive canoe atop the tailplane.

"After 35 degrees south the dry team members stayed on their equipment, the radar operators rotated watches when able, but as the lead of the dry team the crew AEO had suggested I stay on the ESM as I was capable of instant radar recognition. The rest of the crew who were not being used on the search sensors would man any available window.

"As we were heading south we detected two aircraft on the ESM which we would normally have expected to see in the Norwegian Sea. We were a little surprised to find them operating in the South Atlantic. Two TU-95 'Bear Deltas' were identified through their 'big bulge' radars. The 'Bears' were operating out of Luanda and collecting data on the RN forces involved. There was also a Russian naval auxiliary of the Primorye

Victor crews preparing for flights (*David Emmerson*)

Class loitering off Ascension Island throughout most of the campaign. The Primorye was a modern signals and communications intercept vessel monitoring the UK forces at Ascension.

"Later in the flight we detected an Argentinian Boeing 707. The RN Task Force ships during their transit south had already been under surveillance from the 707 and on 21 April a pair of Sea Harriers of 800 Naval Air Squadron had closed to visual range on one.

"At the time of the ESM detection the spectrum was fairly quiet, the intercept was initially classified as a 'Possible' 707

radar, with a hint of 'Probable' a few minutes later. The Nimrod maintained heading until I detected a hint of a bearing change, which also gave some indication of the transmitting aircraft range. Throughout the monitoring of the ESM intercept I continued a commentary on the bearing and also reported the clock code for the crew manning the beam and other windows.

"The lookouts on the starboard side were straining to detect the 707 aircraft but it was the flight deck who saw him first. It was at a similar level to us and passing right to left. The first pilot pushed the throttles open and the crew were pushed back into their seats as the engines responded, and we turned to port to intercept – albeit unarmed. It

Squadron commander's transport (*David Emmerson*)

was a lost cause. Perhaps with an earlier visual pick up we may have stood a chance to get closer. The 707 was certainly going faster than the Nimrod and in a straight race would probably have left us standing.

"Another factor in the chase was our fuel, we could not afford to 'pour on the coals' for long. Fuel when you only had a little island with one runway a few thousand miles away was a precious commodity.

"Had we had Sidewinders the fleet would have been a little less worried and the Nimrod would have added another feather to its cap. I later found out the Air Staff signed off the order to fit Sidewinders not long after that day."

Aircrew concertina accommodation

Groundcrew accommodation (*David Emmerson*)

Conditions on Wideawake airfield were very cramped. The aircrew sleeping arrangements were sorted out by the arrival of a USAF C5 with twelve concertina-type sleeping quarters which when expanded yielded instant made-up bedding and accommodation but the groundcrew were not so lucky and had tenting of a sort. Emmerson found transport a problem but managed to buy a Mini from a local for $400 and the groundcrew did a fantastic job making it Wideawake worthy with spares purchased in Gibraltar and delivered by transiting Nimrods. So far David's invoice has not been accepted by the MOD, maybe because he did not say how he disposed of the vehicle!

The airfield at Ascension was incredibly crowded and every space was allocated with more Victors than any other aircraft. Ian Marshall flew three times on Nimrod sorties and his account confirms the space limitation at Wideawake and how they were only able to position at Ascension after the Vulcan had landed in Brazil.

"All this time, things in the South Atlantic were hotting up, we as a crew began to wonder if we should head straight there, being half way there already. (*Author: they were in the USA*). We had been out of the country for a couple of weeks and really did not know what was going on back home.

"On our return we transited through Lajes in the Azores and met up with some crews from 42 Sqn. They were tracking a USSR Charlie class submarine that was in the trail

Crowded Wideawake airfield with Victors, Vulcans and a VC10 (*David Emmerson*)

behind the Task Force. After Maggie gave the order that all unidentified subs anywhere in the South Atlantic were to be sunk, the Charlie backed off north of the equator. Can you imagine the UK issuing a proclamation like that now and anybody listening to it?

"Our crew got home to Kinloss, did a test drop of the new Stingray torpedoes in the Minches, to get urgent clearance for their release to service. We then had our pilots trained for air-to-air refuelling and fighter affiliation, and this was the time when we got four Sidewinders hung under the wings and the bomb bay filled with 500 pounders. I think the pilots went and bombed the s.t out of Garvie Island using a plastic bomb site fitted on the cockpit combing.

"On 24 May my crew departed south for Ascension. We did two flights, which were to protect Ascension from a presumed threat from Argentinian special forces and a known freighter that was to drop them in the area; our 500 pounders were to bomb the ship if we ever found it.

"My crew then took one Nimrod up to Gibraltar; Wideawake airfield was lacking in space because of all the Victor tankers and the arrival of a couple of Vulcans for the Black Buck missions. After spending a week hanging around Gib, the Black Buck 6 Vulcan with the damaged probe diverted into Brazil and suddenly there was space for our aircraft to park, so we returned to Ascension on 3 June. We then did many standby nights, for each long-range trip south there was another crew and aircraft ready to go. Once the first aircraft made the second refuel zone, the standby crew would stand down. The one advantage of this was that the next day, we would always have a big beach BBQ of the unused rations.

"My only long-range sortie ended up being the closest to a Nimrod in theatre. After take-off we lost one of four hydraulic systems but continued south to the first and second refuel points but after the second refuel we lost another hydraulic system and were now running on the yellow pump which relied on one 28 volt electric motor. Unfortunately, Ascension was a long way north and we had to fly for several hours on this system with no back-up. We then had to rely on the emergency red system to get the landing gear and flaps down, to operate the brakes and the nosewheel steering and this pump was only cleared for one hour's use. Fortunately we landed safely and on opening the hatch at the back of the aircraft, out flowed gallons of hydraulic fluid."

Marshall's story of the hydraulic failure seems all right if you read it quickly. But in fact it must have been a very worrying if not alarming experience flying all those hours across the featureless and unforgiving ocean wondering if the fault that caused the first two hydraulic systems to fail was going to cause the third and last one to go. The flight is a good example of very significant events which hardly ever got mentioned.

While all this was going on Avros again showed the speed at which modifications could be done in a wartime environment. On 14 May there was a feasibility study followed by an Instruction to Proceed to fit Sidewinders to the Nimrod. Luckily the aircraft had been designed to carry two SS12 surface-to-air missiles from pylons underneath the wings but the requirement was never taken up though the wiring was in place. Two pylons were quickly made and fitted and twelve days later Robbie Robinson and Flt Lt Tony Banfield flew down in XV229 to Boscombe Down and had two Sidewinders fitted to each pylon.

The next day they checked that the Sidewinders acquired their targets satisfactorily, apparently according to Robbie in his book by using some unsuspecting civil aircraft. That being

done they landed, the Sidewinders were made live and they flew up to the range near Ailsa Craig in Scotland and shot down a Jindivik unmanned aircraft. The next day on 28 May the modification was released to service. Meanwhile XV232 had flown back from Ascension to Woodford and on 31 May the modification was fitted at Woodford. The aircraft returned to Wideawake on 5 June and became the first Nimrod cleared for operations with the Sidewinder. In the end, the Sidewinders (intended mostly to counter Argentine Boeing 707 sea patrols) were not used during the conflict, possibly because a picture appeared in the UK press of the aircraft at Woodford with the four missiles in place which probably discouraged the 707 crews.

Nimrod with Sidewinders on board (*Derek Ferguson*)

Early in the war, 13 April, it was decided to fit the Harpoon missile to the Nimrod to be carried in the bomb bay and Avros received an ITP on 7 May. The first flight took place on 9 June and the first live firing at Boscombe Down on 11 June. A release to service was given on 12

June and the first modified aircraft was delivered on 24 June: later aircraft were modified at Kinloss. Though Nimrods could also be loaded with Stingray torpedoes in the bomb bay the war ended on 14 June so neither of these new capabilities were ever tested in anger.

Up to now no mention has been made of the Nimrod R1 but Lawrence Freedman in his book *The Official History of the Falklands War* does discuss how the Chilean government co-operated to some extent with the UK because of their long-standing dispute with Argentina over access to the Beagle Channel at the southern tip of South America.

The Chileans were not too keen for the Nimrod to operate from bases in the south of Chile, they preferred to offer San Felix in the Desventuradas Islands, the Unfortunate Islands. The distance to the Falklands from San

Below: San Felix – Concepcion – Falklands

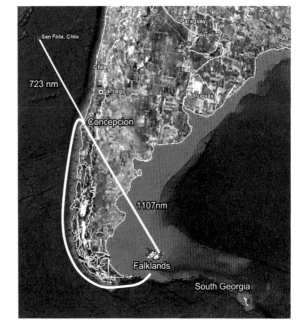

Felix was 1,839 nautical miles overflying Comodoro Rivadavia but by flying south from the island the distances to key military airfields and ports could be dramatically reduced. The UK
Chilean ambassador warned the UK government that in the long term it would be counter pro-
ductive politically for the Nimrods actually to penetrate Argentinian airspace.

The Chilean government were keen to purchase two Canberra PR9s and the deal was that
the Nimrods could transit Chilean airspace and land in an emergency. There is some doubt as
to when the PR9s actually arrived in Chile but it was almost certainly after the Falklands War
had ended. Freedman's book hints that the Nimrod R1s carried out more sorties than have been
officially described. However there is no doubt that at least one Nimrod, probably R1, XW664,
supported by a VC10 tanker was at San Felix but there may have been other Nimrod R1s as
well. One sortie which he described without saying which type of Nimrod, took place on 9
May followed by others on 15 and 17 May. These involved refuelling at the Chilean air force
base at Concepcion at night and then flying into the South Atlantic. Admiral Woodward wanted
more sorties but the Chileans by this time were very nervous and the aircraft was withdrawn.

There was a total of 111 Nimrod MR2 sorties carried out during the nine-week campaign and
for each extended-range sortie it needed twelve Victor Mk 2s. The last Falklands mission was
flown from Ascension by XV234 on 17 August, which then returned to Kinloss two days later via
Gibraltar. It was operated by No 201 Squadron Crew 1, commanded by Flt Lt Moncaster.

The Falklands War demonstrated how brilliantly the armed forces and industry could react
in an emergency. The availability of the Nimrod and the Victor was a godsend thanks to the far
sightedness of the Ministry of Defence and the various governments authorising the expenditure
on these aircraft. On a personal note I was working in the United States while the war was
taking place and I found some satisfaction in that the Vulcan, the Nimrod and the Victor tanker
were all aircraft that we had built and tested while I was at Avros.

As I write this amazing story one can appreciate not only the fortitude of the ground troops
and the sailors on the very exposed RN ships, but also, on the Royal Air Force side, the skill
and flexibility of all the crews, ground and airborne, that supported their aircraft in difficult
and sometimes inhospitable circumstances carrying out missions that seemed virtually impossible but which made the retaking of the Falklands a certainty.

POST WAR

Immediately after the war ended, the MOD decided they wanted to show that the Nimrod could
operate from the short airfield at Port Stanley, however the runway length during the Falklands
War was only 4,000 ft. Royal Engineers increased the length to 6,000 ft as well as the manoeuvring
areas using solid airfield matting which apparently was bought from the United States for £52m.
MoD asked Woodford test pilots the best way to do short landings and not surprisingly they recommended the way I always used to land at the Farnborough Air Show by selecting reverse thrust
just before touch down; however, peace had returned by this time and so Boscombe Down felt
the method wasn't prudent. So instead the pilots had to land very exactly at the minimum landing
speed for the aircraft's weight and use the brakes, a more demanding option. With 6,000 ft available landing at Port Stanley was relatively straightforward but the winds could be very strong,
gusty with a cross wind component, so care was always needed; in fact one aircraft did damage its
tyres and undercarriage one day while landing. To complete the Nimrod Mk2 story at Port Stanley,
on 18/19 November 1983 a Nimrod flew non-stop from the Falklands to RAF Kinloss – a total
of 7,066 nautical miles – and then just over a year later another Nimrod did the round trip from

Kinloss in 38 hours and 30 minutes.

Andy Collins was based at Port Stanley for a month. On arrival the crew were understandably very popular with the locals but then he detected that perhaps the Royal Navy had reservations about them. Maybe it was because before landing but after two refuellings, one after Ascension and another from a locally based C130 tanker, they were asked to look for and identify shipping in the Falkland Island Protection Zone (FIPZ); in virtually no time at all their Searchwater radar had

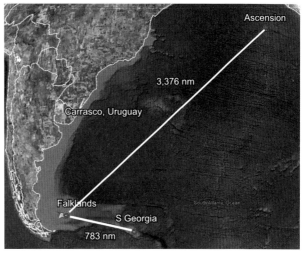

Falklands, South Georgia, Carrasco, Uruguay

found all the shipping and with identification; apparently this task would have taken the navy several days which probably put some noses out of joint.

For landing the aircraft had to be at 130,000 lb, 10,000 lb above the normal maximum landing weight because their alternate airfield was 1,013 nautical miles away in Carrasco, Uruguay. Because of the wind the cross wind limit was raised from 25kts to 30 kts. Andy told me that he didn't select reverse thrust in the air as we used to but he didn't wait very long after touch down before applying it! As his log book shows he did one trip to South Georgia 783 nautical miles away; unfortunately the cloud base was very low so having got there they were unable to see anything. The southern tip of the islands are not far north of the 60⁰ protection latitude for the Antarctic which is the internationally agreed latitude preventing military aircraft from going further south.

Their final trip was directly back to Brize Norton with the Rt Honorable Michael Heseltine

Below: South Georgia and VC10 3 September 1995, taken from a Nimrod

Andy Collins's log book

on board plus the inevitable TV crew. They refuelled as usual from the local C130, then at Ascension and finally over Gibraltar. For this trip Andy was in the co-pilot's seat but on the final refuel the captain allowed Heseltine to sit in the right-hand seat, presumably to have his picture taken, yet again. 17hr 15min later they landed and presumably the pictures were available very shortly afterwards.

Terry Earl also had occasion to go down to Port Stanley about ten months later than Andy.

"We departed on 23 November and refuelled from a VC10 tanker over the South-West Approaches before continuing to Ascension Island where we landed after a flight of eleven hours. The following day we flew on to Port Stanley, refuelling on the way from an Ascension-based Victor tanker and landing after nine hours and five minutes, holding diversion fuel for Montevideo some 1,000 miles to the north. The next day we briefed on local procedures and then flew a surveillance sortie around the Falkland Islands Protection Zone, taking on a total of 41,000 lb of fuel in two contacts with the locally-based C-130 tanker during the sortie; this allowed us to remain airborne for almost nine hours whilst still carrying sufficient fuel for a diversion to Montevideo should there be an incident on the airfield at Port Stanley.

"The plan was that we would continue with a double sortie the following day but unfortunately fate took a hand. Aiming for an early touch down on the landing from the first sortie we kicked up some stones from the very edge of the threshold where the aluminium planking began, and when we came to shut down in dispersal the crew chief noticed some damage to the flaps. As a result we had to cancel the second sortie while our groundcrew made a thorough inspection, after which it was established that the damage was only superficial and could be patched up with 'speed tape'."

Terry also had the opportunity to take the Governor of the Falkland Islands, Sir Rex Hunt on a flying visit down to the South Sandwich Islands and South Georgia since there was a requirement for him to visit them at least once a year. The military commissioner, General Sir Peter de la Billière accompanied them. Unfortunately, as with Andy's trip, the weather was not kind and they didn't see very much.

"Sir Rex flew the aircraft for a while – in fact it turned out that he had been a Spitfire pilot in the RAF during the latter part of the Second World War. After refuelling from a C-130 on the outbound leg to give us sufficient fuel for the round trip, we arrived over the South Sandwich Islands to find very few breaks in the low cloud which covered the area. Thus we only had occasional glimpses over what appeared to be most inhospitable terrain, but Sir Rex was satisfied and we returned to Port Stanley after seven hours airborne. Once we had completed our post-flight procedures, Sir Rex asked if any of us would be interested in joining him for the evening service at the cathedral – which was probably the only one in the world with a corrugated-iron roof! A few of us accepted the invitation and it was agreed that we would join Sir Rex at Government House beforehand, where we were rewarded with a visit to the study where he had taken refuge when Argentinian soldiers had approached during the invasion in 1982. Bullet marks around the walls provided clear evidence that this had not been a social visit and Sir Rex remained most grateful to the small contingent of Royal Marines who had protected him on that fateful day.

"Sadly this was our last full day in Port Stanley and the next day we started on our way back home. After making a pass over the town in formation with two F4s and then taking on 18,000lb of fuel we continued on to Ascension Island landing there after almost six and a half hours. The following day we completed the deployment with a ten-hour transit back to Kinloss, taking on 28,000lb of fuel from a Victor tanker en route. Apart from the problem with the flaps this had been a most successful ten-day detachment with XV228 performing flawlessly during a total of fifty-four hours flying."

SEQUELS TO THE FALKLANDS CAMPAIGN

The British government felt that Stanley airfield was not the best option for a large, permanent base and decided to construct a new RAF station and make it the centrepiece of the islands' considerably strengthened defences. This was intended to deter any future Argentine attempts to take the islands by force. Mount Pleasant, to the west of Stanley, was chosen as the site for the new station. The airfield was opened by Prince Andrew in 1985 since he had served in the Falklands campaign. It became fully operational in 1986. The main airfield 10/28 is 8,500 ft long with a short runway 05/23 of 5,000 ft in length to cater for high winds. The £52 million pounds worth of airfield matting at Port Stanley was then taken up and shipped to the UK as war reserves!

Drew Steel was a Nimrod crew member operating from Mount Pleasant:

"I was deployed to Mount Pleasant airport during the second half of March 1988 as part of Exercise Fire Focus – the island reinforcement exercise. Over the first few days, we flew 'standard' maritime patrol-type sorties, with various tasks and targets, but soon after our presence became obvious, the army brigadier who was Commander British Forces Falkland Islands (COMBFFI) summoned the captain and asked if we could

Wideawake airfield, Ascension Island 1988 (*Drew Steel*)

carry out a series of photo-recce tasks for him, aimed at assessing the islands' defences as viewed from the air. This included medium-level vertical photography of the airfield itself, but he was also keen to understand how well concealed his Rapier sites and gun positions were, as well as wondering about the visibility of various minefields and ex-minefields. Our captain didn't hesitate to agree to attempt this novel tasking. It may be very unfair of me to suggest this, but I suspect that, as an ex-F4 pilot, but still young and 'vigorous', he may have sensed the opportunity for some 'unconventional' flying!

"The aircraft carried a fixed vertical camera (can't recall if the nomenclature was F-135 or F-139), so nothing unusual with the vertical shots, but oblique photography was conducted from one or other of the beam lookout windows, using a hand-held camera. On the basis that COMBFFI wanted an attack aircraft's view of the Rapier sites etc., our task became high-speed, low-level oblique photography, barrelling in from seaward direct towards the 'facility' in question so that Biggles could get a good look at it; followed by a quick jink left or right to let the beam camera operator get it in the frame and photograph it. They had to be quick but the whole thing appears to have achieved the multiple aims of being great fun, and of giving COMBBFI what he wanted.

"The task extended over the days to modify the approach directions and so on, and also to exercise the air defence system by trying to sneak in avoiding detection by the Mt Kent radar. Although we never quite managed that, we did have fun trying, and we did get to exercise the F4 crews on quick reaction alert – much to the delight of our ex-F4 captain. The added bonus for us was that, instead of eight or nine hours maritime patrol sorties, these averaged out at about four or five hours – part-time working !

"I've tagged on a photo taken whilst taxying out, or in, at Wideawake airfield on Ascension – famously mispronounced by a well-travelled pilot, on R/T, as "Widy-a-waky" when he free-called the tower – he was used to strange foreign pronunciations!"

ANOTHER FALKLANDS TRIP

The UK keeps four fighter aircraft as a matter of routine at MPA. The aircraft have been accompanied by Nimrods in case of problems en route, dubbed 'SAR trail'. In April 1995 two Nimrods and three tankers, VC10, Tristar and C130, were accompanying four Tornados. The first leg was to Dakar for a night stop and then on to Ascension Island for another night stop. One Nimrod remained at Ascension and the rest of the aircraft set course for the Falklands. After the first lot of refuelling one of the Tornados had a hydraulic problem and the whole 'trail' diverted to Brazil. They were met by two Brazilian F5s and escorted to Rio de Janeiro's international airport at

Galeão. Three days later the trail set course for MPA and the tankers plus Nimrod were ready for return. There was a further two days delay before the returning trail set course for Ascension.

Frigate-bird strike on tank 4A

Meanwhile the Nimrod at Ascension Island did a local flight while waiting for the returning aircraft and as bad luck would have it they had a bird strike when a large frigate-bird hit 4A pod tank. Due to the damage the aircraft was declared unserviceable to fly the distance back to Kinloss and the aircrew and groundcrew returned to the UK as passengers on a Tristar. The aircraft remained at Ascension Island until a repair team was sent from the Aircraft Maintenance Flight at Kinloss to replace the damaged pod tank.

This story clearly demonstrates what a lot of planning and resource goes in to what at first seems a simple operation. Still I heard on good account that on this trip the crews suffered their unexpected stay in Brazil with their usual fortitude.

While Mount Pleasant is a really useful facility on the Falklands Island, one cannot help having a slight feeling of unease wondering what would happen now if the Argentinians decided that they should retake their Malvinas Islands. Not having Nimrod aircraft to watch for submarines and naval vessels leaves a huge hole in the ability of the UK to defend the islands, not to mention a gap in the safety provision accompanying fighters on the exchange flights.

8 NIMROD ACCIDENTS

Every aircraft type in the world has or will have accidents. However carefully airframes and engines are designed, constructed and then certificated by the regulatory authorities, something unexpected always occurs. Having said that, the accident rates measured by flying hours are improving all the time, certainly on commercial aircraft. In the case of the Nimrod the design was based on the Comet 4C and so it proved to be a very reliable aircraft. As an ex-test pilot and one time regulator I believe that it is always important to review all accidents and incidents that have occurred on a type to see if there is any pattern of failures that should have been or needs to be addressed.

Altogether the aircraft flew over 500,000 hours and had five accidents that resulted in losses of the airframe; it also had an incident which was relevant to the final accident. This last accident is commented on in more detail because the findings started an investigation which ultimately led to the early retirement of the whole Nimrod fleet.

However, before discussing accidents which resulted in the loss of the aircraft Bill Speight, air engineer, who probably flew more hours on the Nimrod, over 12,000, than anyone else makes the point that accidents occur during maintenance as well as in the air and unfortunately some did occur to the Nimrod Squadron servicing engineers while maintaining the aircraft.

There was a corporal who lost his life being sucked into an engine while it was running on test at full power. There was a sergeant air frame fitter who was paralysed when his head was caught in the air brakes and there was an armourer who was killed when an explosive sonar underwater sound (SUS) exploded:

> "It happened during Operation Backscratch which was the calibration of the newly laid SOSUS chains in the Atlantic. We were tasked to drop explosive SUSs at regular intervals at predetermined positions and on predetermined tracks. The SUSs were dropped internally through a hole made available by the removal of one of the launchers. A pressure plate was removed from the floor when the aircraft was depressurised and the SUS was dropped by one of the rear crew on a call from the tac nav.
>
> "The explosive SUS had a drag plate fitted which was removed by the airstream and this armed the device. A preset hydrostatic trigger then fired the device at the selected depth. On this day the crew noticed that the drag plate had moved and the arming pin was nearly removed from the arming device so they carefully placed the SUS in an ammunition box for return to the armoury.
>
> "Unbeknown to anyone the hydrostatic unit had already operated for some reason so when the armourer tried to push the drag plate locking pin back into the arming pin he slipped and the pin came out. The device exploded in his face fatally injuring him. It was thought that the hydrostatic trigger had also been affected by the aircraft pressurisation. The armourer should not have tried to reset the drag plate as the correct procedure was to destroy the device by a controlled explosion. The device contained about 2 ounces of TNT."

Besides servicing misfortunes there were flying events which might well have ended in disaster but didn't. One particular incident was the case popularly known as 'the 80-ton glider'.

I have mentioned before that crew drills were the reason that the Nimrod worked, with separate acoustics, radar and ESM all feeding in to the tactical navigator. But pilot drills were also very important; an MR1 was on patrol at night at 12,000 ft and the two outboard engines had been stopped to give optimum time on cruise. The co-pilot was flying the aircraft and the captain was talking to the tactical navigator. The air engineer was trying to re-attach some piping lying on the floor.

There was a loud bang and No 2 engine surged. The exhaust gas temperature suddenly went off the clock and the co-pilot decided he had better shut the engine down quickly. He reached down and shut the second high pressure cock from the left, unfortunately forgetting that the No 1 engine high pressure cock was already closed. No 2 engine then No 1 failed completely so that with the good engine having been stopped by the co-pilot the aircraft became a heavyweight glider.

The next thing that happened was that the lights went out so the air engineer thought there had been a total generator failure which was absolutely correct but, of course, not due to an electrical fault and he started going through his drills. The co-pilot, not sure what was going on, luckily continued to fly the aircraft and started to descend to keep the airspeed up.

The captain appeared at high speed to find out what was happening while the engineer was swearing at the co-pilot asking what the 'fxxxxxx xxxk' was going on. The captain sized up the situation straightaway and did windmill relights on the outboard engines knowing that those engines had to be good as they had been shut down. By the time the aircraft reached 5,000 ft the aircraft was no longer a glider and a rather subdued crew returned to Kinloss.

In those days crew drills had not been perfected, human error was not recognised, discipline had to be maintained and somebody had to be court martialled. The legal department first thought of having a go at the engineer for swearing at an officer but on second thoughts went for the co-pilot. Quoting Bill Speight in *Flight Safety Magazine*:

> "Throughout my long association with the RAF the legal branch has not been one of the most successful elements and this court martial was definitely not one of their finest hours. An incident during the hearing probably destroyed any hope of anyone taking it seriously. The air engineer was called to the stand and on cross examination by the prosecution got himself into a bit of a Tiz Waz. He was under the impression that the judge advocate, who was dressed in his entire regalia including his legal wig, was like the judge one sees in a legal court. When asked by the prosecutor to whom he was addressing his remarks, the air engineer replied:
>
> "'That gentleman over there.'
> "'What gentleman?' shouted the frustrated prosecutor.
> "'The one wearing the sheep skin headset' replied the beleaguered engineer."

Apparently this brought the whole court into hysterics and the case was dismissed shortly afterwards, not because of the air engineer, but because there were no procedures in place to guard against human error. After that standard operating procedures ensured that no engine could be shut down without confirmation by another crewmember.

NIMROD MR2 XV 256, 17 NOVEMBER 1980
BIRD STRIKE AT ROSEISLE FOREST, NEAR KINLOSS

On 17 November 1980, Nimrod MR2 XV256 crashed near RAF Kinloss after three engines failed following multiple bird strikes. Both pilots were killed but the eighteen remaining crew survived. The aircraft took off at 0730 just as it was getting light. This was the final sortie of their conversion from the Nimrod MR1 to the Nimrod MR2. Because it was the last one there were five 'checking' crew plus an additional air engineer on board the aircraft.

The surface wind was 070 degrees at 02 kts, with 8 kms visibility in rain and a main cloud base of 3,000 ft. The take-off run and initial rotation was normal but shortly after unstick at an estimated height of 20 ft the aircraft flew through a dense flock of Canada Geese flying in arrowhead formation between overnight roosting and daily feeding grounds. The aircraft suffered numerous bird strikes resulting in No1 engine surging violently and then suffering a catastrophic internal failure. The low pressure compressors on the Nos 2 and 3 engines were also damaged and, although they continued to run, they produced little thrust. Effectively the fully laden aircraft was being powered by only the No 4 engine which itself may have been damaged. There was insufficient power for the aircraft to climb and despite the efforts of the pilots some twenty-seven seconds after take-off, the aircraft came down on the relatively soft tree-tops of a forest of young pine trees 1,300 yards from the end of the runway and was quickly engulfed in flames.

The accident investigation report established that the cause was a multiple bird strike which occurred at a critical stage of the flight. The aircraft suffered such a severe loss of thrust that maintenance of height and flying speed quickly became impossible. It was the captain's skill in keeping the stricken aircraft airborne long enough to make a very smooth and controlled crash at minimum speed into the tree-tops that undoubtedly saved the lives of the rear crewmembers. After the accident seventy-seven dead Canada Geese were found on or near the runway. It is not known how many others were ingested by the aircraft engines.

This accident is the sort that airports, airlines and aircrew are always dreading. The risk is particularly high in coastal areas where there are large flocks of sea birds and where bird-scaring measures are required at all times. Nothing is known of the standing instructions existing at the time nor the bird-scaring measures in place but dawn and dusk are always particularly dangerous times for the appearance of flocks of birds.

NIMROD MR2 XV 257, 3 JUNE 1984
FIRE ON BOARD AT ST MAWGAN, CORNWALL

On 3 June 1984, Nimrod MR2 XV257 stationed at RAF St Mawgan suffered extensive damage when a reconnaissance flare ignited in the bomb bay during flight. The aircraft successfully returned to base; there were no casualties.

The aircraft had taken off on an exercise search and rescue (SAR) sortie from its base at RAF St Mawgan. It was carrying in the bomb bay, as part of the SAR equipment, a normal load of 5 inch reconnaissance flares. In accordance with normal practice, the first navigator switched the flare's release units to live shortly after take-off. Some thirty seconds later a cockpit indicator warned the crew of a fire in the bomb bay. The captain immediately instructed the co-pilot to fly the aircraft back to base while he transmitted a mayday call and informed the rest of the crew.

During the return flight ground witnesses saw the Nimrod trailing smoke, with several burning flares, a parachute and other objects falling from the aircraft but it landed safely. Although the fire services quickly extinguished the intense fire, the aircraft was extensively damaged. The accident investigation found that a reconnaissance flare became detached from its carrier and subsequently ignited in the bomb bay. It was not possible to determine how it came to be released. The prompt action of the pilots resulted in all the thirteen crew surviving.

The damaged aircraft was temporarily repaired by BAe on site at RAF St Mawgan, and flown back to Woodford by BAe test pilots without a rear pannier and weapons bay doors. Subsequently, after much negotiation with MOD(PE) to instigate a full production standard repair, the aircraft was deemed not required for service, and was cut up on the Woodford airfield.

NIMROD R1 XW 666, 16 MAY 1995
ENGINE FIRE NEAR LOSSIEMOUTH

On 16 May 1995, XW666, a Nimrod R1 from RAF Waddington ditched in the Moray Firth 4.5 miles (7.2 km) from Lossiemouth after an uncontained fire occurred in the No 4 engine bay following a mechanical failure. The incident occurred during a post-servicing test flight from RAF Kinloss. The MOD inquiry identified a number of technical issues as the cause. There were no casualties. The aircraft was one of three Nimrod reconnaissance variants and had just undergone a major servicing at the Nimrod Major Servicing Unit (NMSU), RAF Kinloss by RAF maintenance personnel.

The aircraft departed on a routine post-servicing air test. After approximately thirty-five minutes of flight, following a test of the aircraft's anti-icing system, the No 4 engine fire warning illuminated. Whilst the crew were carrying out the fire drill, the No 3 engine fire warning also illuminated. A rear crew member confirmed that the aircraft was on fire and advised the captain

Below: Successful ditching of XW666

that panels were falling away from the starboard wing. After two explosions, the captain feared for the structural integrity of the aircraft and decided to ditch before he lost control authority. There was a failure of the normal hydraulic system which operated the flaps and the captain decided to ditch without the aid of flaps since he feared that trying to lower flaps with the emergency system would result in an asymmetric operation and loss of flight control. He completed a controlled ditching into the Moray Firth with the aircraft bouncing twice onto the sea before settling. The fuselage broke into two and the aircraft subsequently sank. Parts were salvaged and the cockpit section is now on display at AeroVenture South Yorkshire Aircraft Museum in Doncaster.

With the assistance of the Department of Transport's Air Accident Investigation Branch, the inquiry established that despite the correct application of maintenance procedures, the DC electrical loom attached to No 4 engine had sustained mechanical damage, although it could not be positively determined how or when. Arcing occurred when the engine anti-icing system was switched on and this led to the initiation of the air-starter system. With the No 4 engine already running at idle as part of the overall air test there was no load on the starter turbine, which quickly ran up to high speed. The nut holding the starter turbine disk in place failed, allowing the disk to move back on its shaft and out of its protective housing. It then struck the engine bypass casing and the No 2 fuel tank, puncturing both. The resultant fuel leak was ignited either by electrical arcing within the faulty DC loom or by the heat of the engine. The fire spread rapidly to the wing area and forward to the engine-intake area.

Successful ditching of a jet aircraft is a very rare event and the pilots did a superb job in getting it down without it breaking up uncontrollably, thus saving the lives of all seven crew. In my opinion the decision of the captain not to lower the flaps was a really first class one which prevented a disaster since the Board of Inquiry acknowledged that the flaps might have extended asymmetrically due to fire damage. The accident is of the type that cannot be foreseen despite all the correct maintenance procedures and the survival of the occupants in such an emergency depends completely on the skill of the crew.

NIMROD MR2 XV 239, 2 SEPTEMBER 1995
CRASH AT TORONTO AIR SHOW, CANADA

The Nimrod display aircraft and crew had deployed to Canada on 23 August 1995 for displays at the Canadian Forces Base Shearwater and the Canadian International Air Show (CIAS) at Toronto. In excellent weather, with a light on-shore wind, the aircraft took off on time for its display. Upon completion of the safety checks, it ran in for the standard Nimrod display sequence which featured two orbits and two dumb-bell turns. The latter manoeuvres each involved a turn away from the display line, a climb to not above 1,000 ft, followed by a turn in the opposite direction and descent, to fly back parallel with the display line. Having completed the two orbits, the first dumb-bell turn was completed uneventfully. After a slow flypast with undercarriage down, the aircraft entered its final manoeuvre, the second dumb-bell turn. It was seen to turn away approximately 75° to starboard under full power before the flaps were retracted to 20° and the undercarriage raised. The nose was then pitched up into a climbing attitude of 24°. As the aircraft passed 950 ft, engine power was reduced to almost flight idle, following which the speed reduced rapidly to 122 knots, below the 150 knots recommended and taught for that stage of the display. The aircraft was rolled to 70° of port bank, shortly afterwards reducing to 45°, and the nose lowered to 5° below the horizon. During this turn the airspeed increased slightly and the G-loading increased to 1.6G. However, the combination of the low airspeed and the G-loading led the aircraft to stall, whereupon the port wing dropped to 85° of bank and the nose dropped to 18° below the horizon. Full starboard aileron and full engine power were applied in an attempt to recover the aircraft but, by this stage, there was insufficient height to recover and the aircraft hit the water.

The inquiry determined that the captain made an error of judgement in modifying one of the display manoeuvres to the extent that he stalled the aircraft at a height and attitude from which recovery was impossible. The inquiry considered that contributory factors could have included deficiencies in the flight deck crew's training and in the method of supervision which could have allowed the captain to develop an unsafe technique without a full appreciation of the consequences.

This accident is typical of accidents that occur at flying displays. The pilot is always under great pressure to do his/her very best demonstrating to the crowd. The aircraft is invariably flying in a way which is outside its normal operating conditions and it only needs the slightest change from the planned display manoeuvres for things to happen which are irrecoverable when so close to the ground. I have recorded elsewhere in this book where I made a mistake demonstrating the Nimrod at the SBAC show at Farnborough but unlike the accident described above, I was lucky and able to recover the situation.

NIMROD MR2 XV 227, 23 NOVEMBER 2004

This aircraft suffered a duct failure when hot air at 420°C escaped from the pipe and damaged aileron and flap control cables, melted hydraulic pipe fastenings, damaged the front face of number 7 tank and did other damage including to fuel seals. There was a recommendation from the Unit Inquiry to fit a hot air detection and warning system but the system was not fitted because the MR2s were scheduled to go out of service in 2012 and be replaced by the MRA4. The aircraft had to be written off as a result of the damage. The inquiry recognised the serious nature of the fault which could easily have caused the aircraft to crash.

The Unit Inquiry made the point that:

"It is important to note that there are other ducts of similar construction used within the engine bleed air systems. As the conditions that caused the extensive corrosion in the ruptured duct will be present throughout the rest of the system, it must be considered that other ducts will be subject to the effects of corrosion. Therefore the inquiry believes that all other ducts should be subject to investigation for signs of corrosion damage. However, the possible implications of a failure in some other sections of the bleed air system are mitigated by the presence of hot air leak warning systems. There is no hot air leak warning system for the ruptured duct or the cross-bleed air duct as it passes through the bomb bay.

"Lifeing Policy. BAE's investigation shows that the ruptured duct was manufactured in 1980 but no records exist as to when this duct was fitted to the aircraft. The lack of a lifeing policy allowed the corrosion within the duct to go undetected until failure occurred. The lack of a lifeing policy was a contributory factor.

Recommendations

"The inquiry recommends that:

"A maintenance policy is investigated for the ruptured duct and all similar ducts.

"A lifeing policy is introduced for the ruptured duct and all similar ducts.

"The ruptured duct is replaced with new manufactured items as soon as possible.

"A hot air leak warning system be introduced for the ruptured duct and cross-air bleed ducts.

"The extent of the hot air leak warning system be reviewed to ensure that all possible duct failures are covered."

This accident was a clear warning that if the life of the aircraft was going to be extended it would be necessary at the very least to inspect thoroughly the ducting of all the aircraft.

XV 230, 2 SEPTEMBER 2006

CRASH NEAR KANDAHAR, AFGHANISTAN

The aircraft was on an operational mission over Helmand Province in southern Afghanistan in support of NATO and Afghani ground forces when it suffered a catastrophic mid-air fire after air-to-air refuelling, resulting in the loss of the aircraft and all fourteen crewmembers. It took off from its operational base at 0913 and two hours later, after the completion of refuelling from a Tristar aircraft, there were two simultaneous crew warnings of a fire in the bomb bay and a smoke/hydraulic mist warning in the elevator bay[1]. A minute later the aircraft depressurised and the camera operator reported flames coming from the rear of the starboard engines. The crew immediately commenced emergency drills and transmitted a mayday call whilst diverting to Kandahar airfield. In spite of all the crew's efforts the fire could not be controlled and a Harrier aircraft reported seeing it exploding at about 3,000 ft above the ground. The aircraft came down in open fields close to the village of Farhellah, in an area called Chalaghor in the Panjwaye District of Kandahar, Afghanistan.

The crash site was in a known area of Taliban activity. The initial priority was to recover the crew's bodies, personal effects and classified documentation. Local nationals started invading the area but RAF regiment personnel were able to prevent the crash site being overrun for twenty-one hours. Fortunately, a detailed photographic record of some key parts of the wreckage was made by the officer commanding 904 EAW2 which proved invaluable in the accident analysis.

There was an RAF Board of Inquiry and later an Independent Review by a barrister, Charles Haddon-Cave QC, into the broader issues surrounding the loss of the aircraft. The RAF Board of Inquiry 'decided it did not have the evidence to determine the likely source of the fuel leak'. The combustion analysis into how the fire spread throughout the airframe was in favour of a spillage onto the floor of the No 7 dry bay. The Independent Review came to the conclusion that there was an escape of fuel during air-to-air refuelling due to an overflow from the blow-off valve on No 1 tank causing the fuel to track back along the fuselage and the lower wing surface, and then be ingested into the airframe onto the floor of the No 7 dry bay. Another possibility was that there could have been a leak from a fuel pipe or coupling or, thirdly, there could have been a fuel leak due to a hot air escape from the cross-feed duct. The source of ignition was thought to be due to an exposed hot element of the cross-feed duct/supplementary cooling pack (SCP) coming into contact with fuel. The basis for this conclusion was as a result of an analysis of the air-to-air refuelling system.

As mentioned earlier, flight refuelling was fitted to the Nimrod in great haste for the Falklands campaign in 1982, Mod 700, which was a great tribute to all concerned. Understandably, no tests were ever done at that time to find out where the fuel from the tank blow-off valves would

---

[1.] Note that the supplementary cooling pack tripped off 2 minutes 10 seconds before bomb bay warning

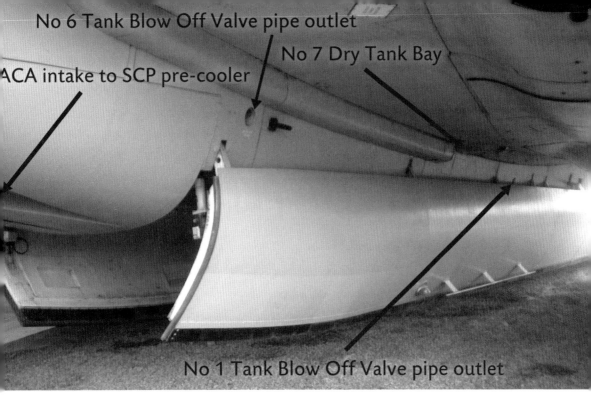

No 6 Tank Blow Off Valve pipe outlet

No 7 Dry Tank Bay

ACA intake to SCP pre-cooler

No 1 Tank Blow Off Valve pipe outlet

Underside Nimrod starboard bomb bay

go but the Haddon-Cave inquiry pointed out that in the mid 1980s work was done on the Nimrod AEW in connection with air-to-air refuelling which showed that there were risks associated with fuel being ejected from the blow-off valves and tracking back along the fuselage. The BAe report stated:

> '[T]here may be some cause for concern with regard to the wetted surfaces caused by a discharge of fuel and it is suggested that tests are made in flight using a coloured dye to study the behaviour of liquid in relation to the various ports and intakes, particularly the tail-pack pre-cooler in the bottom of the rear fairing. If the liquid is found to enter this intake, it may be necessary either to switch off the tail pack before commencing an air-to-air refuel, or to carry out a modification on the blow-off valve outlets of tanks 1 and 6 to prevent the fuel running down the skin.'

The tail-pack pre-cooler referred to in the report above is the pre-cooler for the supplementary cooling pack situated just behind the bomb bay bulkhead and is fed from air coming from a large NACA-type air inlet; BAe were concerned because it is understood that the pre-cooler would have been at a similar temperature to the unlagged cross-feed duct judged to be the ignition source recognised by the Independent Review. Presumably it is for this reason that the BAe report above suggested switching off the tail pack and therefore the SCP before air-to-air refuelling since there was concern that any fuel mixed with the forced flow cooling air, getting in contact with the metal fins of the matrix, would create a fiercely hot fire.

The Independent Review published in October 2009 felt that there were three risks:

(a) the risks associated with fuel being ejected from the blow-off valves during flight and tracking back into the fuselage;

(b) the risks associated with an overflow of fuel into the vent system and fuel leaking from the No 1 tank vent system around the aircraft; and

(c) the higher flow rates and the potential for pressure spikes associated with air-to-air refu-elling compared with ground refuelling.

The problem of course for the investigating team was that no test work had ever been done to ascertain where the blow-off fuel would go nor could any relevant part of the wreckage be found. Interestingly, the investigation team did not ask for any test work to be done using dyed fluid to support their assumption that the fuel had gone into No 7 tank dry bay. The blow-off fuel must have started tracking along the outside fuselage skin and there was clear evidence from earlier and later flights that blow-off fuel went into the bomb bay and therefore presumably along the outside of the bomb-bay skin at the same time towards the NACA intake.

Clearly there seems to be no argument that the fire was caused by the ignition of an excessive discharge of fuel from the blow-off valve of No 1 tank but the actual location of where the fire started can never be known; the choices are either the fuel penetrating the skin of the aircraft and getting into No 7 tank dry bay in sufficient quantities to cause a fire or fuel running down the fuselage into and outside the bomb bay and then straight into the NACA inlet of the SCP intercooler; strangely though the inquiry found the BAe report indicating the danger, this source of ignition did not seem to have been considered by the accident investigators. Considering the SCP tripped off well before the bomb bay warning a probable sequence of events might have been the fuel catching fire in the intercooler causing the SCP to trip; a fire in this area would then have heated the bomb bay rear bulkhead causing the bomb bay warning to occur.

If the initial fire was caused by fuel going into the SCP intercooler then the arrangement of the pipes and ducting in the No 7 dry bay, though undesirable, was not nearly as critical and relevant to this particular accident. The criticism of the design in the review, perhaps unneces-sarily, led the way to the premature grounding of the whole Nimrod fleet due to doubts on the fuel-piping system. Furthermore, it is now apparent from this accident that had the SCP been switched off during the flight refuelling the accident would not have happened. What was not properly considered by the Independent Review was why the accident had not occurred earlier since satisfactory refuelling had been taking place for twenty-four years; one explanation is that there was a distinct probability that the SCP for refuelling at the time did not reflect adequately refuelling to full tanks bearing in mind the very high refuelling rate obtainable from the Tristar compared with other tankers.

Looking back it is clear that the introduction of the cross-feed duct in order to support engine starting of the Spey engines as part of the initial Nimrod design would not be permitted in ac-cordance with present-day design standards. In the MR1 this duct only got hot during engine starting and when operating with engines deliberately shut down. With the introduction of the MR2 the supplementary cooling pack was fitted to cool the cabin and this pack was fed by hot air from the engines so the cross-feed duct was hot whenever the SCP was running. It was con-sidered by the Independent Review that this modification was definitely not to a sufficiently high safety standard and it lays the blame for the accident primarily on British Aerospace but, as has been said above, the SCP duct design, good or bad, may well not have been the cause of the fire, particularly as the cross-feed duct would have cooled down the moment the SCP tripped off.

As a test pilot I cannot understand why there were no tests carried out to determine where the blow-off fuel went before the full flight-refuelling modification was carried out. Had the tests been done the instructions to the crews not to use the SCP pack while refuelling might have been issued much earlier. Furthermore why the inquiry did not investigate where the blow-off fuel from Nos 1 and 6 tanks actually went in order to substantiate the cause of the accident is in my view inexplicable. Finally, I find it amazing that BAe were not invited to take part in either the RAF Board of Inquiry or the Haddon-Cave Review when the risk of having the SCP operating during refuelling and the dangerous proximity of the NACA intake with the matrix intercooler would have been explained.

NIMROD MR2 XV235, 5 NOVEMBER 2007
FUEL LEAK WHILE AIR-TO-AIR REFUELLING

The aircraft was involved in a mid-air incident over Afghanistan when the crew noticed a fuel leak during air-to-air refuelling. After transmitting a mayday call the crew landed the aircraft successfully. Significantly there was fuel in the bomb bay which suggests that, as before, there had been a large blow-off of fuel from No 1 tank. The incident came only a month before the issue of the report of a Board of Inquiry into the 2 September 2006 fatal accident to XV230 in probably similar circumstances. However showing hindsight, undesirable though the situation was, the aircraft would almost certainly not have been in danger because apparently, after the accident to XV230, an instruction had gone out not to use the SCP when flight refuelling so the SCP intercooler behind the bomb bay would have been cool as would have been the cross-feed duct. However, the RAF very wisely subsequently suspended air-to-air refuelling operations for the Nimrod since the real problem was the fuel blowing off from No 1 tank, though again it is strange that no tests were requested to find where the blow-off fuel actually went.

SUMMARY OF ALL NIMROD ACCIDENTS

The Nimrod design was based on the Comet 4 and had a very good safety record with no pattern of similar accidents. Though the introduction of the cross-feed ducting in to the basic Comet design would not be permitted using today's safety standards, it did not in fact cause any accidents though one duct did fail which resulted in the aircraft being written off after landing. The Nimrod proved to be a very safe and reliable aircraft.

However, problems occurred during flight refuelling due to the operation of the fuel blow-off valves; apparently fuel had been found frequently in the bomb bay, the significance of which had not been appreciated. It is clear that had there been some flight testing carried out prior to the production flight-refuelling modification, MOD 715, instructions would have been given not to have the SCP running during flight refuelling and action would also have been taken to alter the blow-off situation for No 1 tank.

9 NIMROD AEW

This chapter is a saga of a project that went wrong. It is not possible to be certain twenty-five years later about what actually happened and all the parties concerned had different views on what was the cause. All we can be sure about is that the project was a financial disaster for the country and reflected adversely on its engineering skills.

Boeing AWACS in NATO colours

Shackleton AEW (*AHC*)

While I was chief test pilot at Avros at Woodford in the early 1970s, the need to have a land-based airborne early warning system (AEW) was becoming apparent. However, much earlier, soon after the Second World War, it was very clear that the navies of the world needed radar to detect aircraft as early as possible coming in to attack their ships because the ships' radars did not have the necessary range; the Royal Navy tackled the problem by using ship-borne Fairey Gannet aircraft equipped with American radar called AN/APS 20 which was probably the first to have the capability of recognising moving targets and indicating these targets to the radar operator. However, to try to defeat these early warning radars, intruding aircraft adopted a very low level attack technique and this caused a gradual shift in the United Kingdom from naval aircraft to airfield-based air force aircraft to provide a better early warning capability with greater range and effectiveness.

The United States had started to develop an airborne early warning aircraft called AWACS which was a modified Boeing 707 with a large 360° circular scanning radar mounted on top of the fuselage. British Aerospace and GEC decided that a modified Nimrod would be able to offer the same capability but it would not be possible to have a 360° radar antenna like the Boeing aircraft; instead it would have two 180° scanning radar antennae housed in special radomes, one in the front of the aircraft and one in the tail with the concept given the name FASS, fore and aft scanning system. As an interim solution it was decided to equip the venerable Avro Shackleton Mk 2 with the same radar which the Gannet had used and in fact these aircraft did stalwart service from 1972 until 1989, though the Boeing AWACS aircraft didn't finally arrive in the Royal Air Force until 1991.

The government pondered whether to choose the Boeing solution which was being developed or have an indigenous UK proposal with all the benefit that that would bring in developing local expertise and furthering local employment. The matter was becoming urgent as at that time Europe was exposed to the threat of low level attacks from the East and NATO was heavily involved. Finally in 1977 the government decided that there should be a UK solution and that therefore the Nimrod AEW should go ahead. However, it should be noted that unlike the original successful Nimrod MR1 programme, British Aerospace was not the prime contractor. It was contracted to build the airframe but Marconi Elliott, a division of the then all powerful GEC company, was to manage all the electronics and integrate all the sensors, the whole system going under the name of MSA, mission system avionics. The plan was to have eleven aircraft, three for development, which later could be made operational, and eight production aircraft. The radar which was proposed by Marconi Elliott was a design that had been conceived by the Royal Signals and Radar Establishment (RSRE) at Malvern and therefore clearly had the backing of part of the Ministry of Defence.

The decision to choose the Nimrod rather than the Boeing AWACS was made largely to keep the project in the UK with the obvious technical and manufacturing benefits that would result, but it was seen by some as a high risk decision because the AWACS aircraft, according to Boeing, was already a proven system, airframe and radar. A possible mid-Atlantic solution might have been to have used the Nimrod with American radar and electronics but political pressure encouraged the government to go all the way and make the AEW aircraft entirely UK designed and built using the GEC FASS radar solution.

It was clear to us at the time at Woodford that the chosen method of controlling the project by the Ministry of Defence was unsatisfactory in that there were two reporting lines to the MOD Procurement Executive, MOD(PE), the organisation responsible for specifying the aircraft and then overseeing the development. There was the normal aircraft reporting line to the director of aircraft projects but in addition the specification and the contracted performance of the electronic systems lay with the director of air weapons and electronic systems. There was no aircraft AEW prime contractor and there was no single director in MOD(PE) responsible for the total AEW project. As a very small example I remember criticising the rather complicated crew intercommunication system on the aircraft when I saw it and being told that it was nothing to do with BAe as Marconi Elliott were responsible, something which was clearly unacceptable.

With the project launched, BAe and Marconi Systems proceeded with defining the airframe, the required electronics, the systems required to power the electronics and the crew layout – to name just a few of the critical decisions required to meet the very demanding specification. Initially, the shape of the radomes on the Nimrod caused some debate since it was hoped to have identically shaped radomes fore and aft but the shape of the front radome was determined by the need to avoid rain erosion and minimise damage in the event of a bird strike while at the rear of the aircraft the radome had to be profiled to ensure adequate ground clearance for take-off and touch down.

On 28 June 1977 I made the initial flight in a Comet 4C (XW626) which had been converted to carry the nose radar unit. The initial flights went well and the aircraft did some radar trials from Woodford. By the beginning of 1979 these trials were over and RAE at Bedford wanted the aircraft for other work. We had not bothered to do a full aerodynamic check on the aircraft since we were flying in a very conservative flight envelope, but in order for the aircraft to be released for a normal flight envelope Avros were charged in doing some, albeit limited, handling checks. Test pilot Robbie Robinson drew the short straw and was briefed to check whether rudder assistance was required when rolling the aircraft. He describes in his book *Avro One* how he discovered that when rolling with full aileron the sideslip suddenly built up and was uncontrollable even with full opposite rudder so that achieved sideslip was beyond the permitted limit. Luckily no damage was done and the RAE accepted the aircraft with some quite severe flight envelope limitations.

Comet 2 with AEW radome (*AHC*)

It was not until 16 July 1980 that the full FASS-enabled aircraft with a radome fore and aft did its initial flight, flown by my successor Charles Masefield as chief test pilot. Fortuitously, the addition of the radomes actually improved the aircraft's directional handling, particularly as there were no destabilising effects from opening the bomb doors since they were not required and had been removed. The main initial problem was that there was vibration right from the moment of rotation which felt just like pre-stall buffet. Charles told me that on

Below: Nimrod AEW (*AHC*)

the first flight he thought it *was* pre-stall buffet and that he had rotated the aircraft too early but to his relief but not to that of the aerodynamicists, the faster he went the more pronounced was the buffet. The rear radome had tufts stuck all over it so that the airflow could be examined and from a formating Hunter it was discovered that there was a total flow breakdown from the widest part of the radome. It was very important to stop the buffet because the vibration in the rear fuselage was completely unacceptable not only for the radar but also for the crew bouncing up and down in their seats. Charles in fact then had the unenviable task of having to demonstrate the aircraft at the Farnborough Air Show at the beginning of September with the aircraft buffeting all the time which was very disconcerting, particularly when he was applying g manoeuvring the aircraft in front of a crowd.

Back from the SBAC show a succession of test flights took place trying to isolate the problem and it was discovered that removing the cooling air intake under the fin made matters worse which gave the team confidence that the addition of vortex generators could solve the problem. The chosen solution was to try pairs of vortex generators three inches high and four inches long placed at various positions on the radome. Finally a position was found which energised the flow behind the vortex generators and the final fix was to have pairs of these vortex generators right round the circumference of the radome.

There were two other less serious problems which needed fixing. Firstly, unlike the Comet 4, the AEW Nimrod was only slightly unstable longitudinally approaching the limiting mach number; however there was a very crude mach trimmer on the Comet which gave a rather unpleasant nose-up trim change as the maximum mach number was approached to deter the pilot from going any faster. Not only was this device not needed but it was actually unacceptable because of the magnitude of the nose-up trim change. Luckily the buffet on the AEW Nimrod increased steadily approaching the maximum mach number so it was agreed by Boscombe that the mach trim device could be removed. The second problem that occurred when flying the aircraft to its maximum speed was that the flow broke down at the radome/fuselage join and this disturbed flow went into the inner engines' intakes which caused serious overheating. Luck-

Below: Nimrod AEW being refuelled from Vulcan XV571

ily, judiciously placed vortex generators again cured the problem. All these problems were fixed on the first aircraft so that by the time the next two arrived, seven and twelve months later, there was no hold up for Marconi Elliott to develop the mission system avionics.

The aircraft carried out some flight refuelling since the operational mission required it to remain airborne for long periods. Presumably it was as a result of this work that the report referred to in the Haddon-Cave Inquiry was written saying that more testing was required to ascertain where the blow-off fuel from No 1 tank was going.

The mission system avionics of an AEW aircraft needed more than an active radar to find enemy aircraft and control friendly ones. It was necessary to be able to listen to transmissions and identify them. Consequently, the AEW had special ESM antennae fitted to the wingtips. The ESM passive listening and detection system was especially important on the AEW to enable the mission system avionics to detect, identify and track electronic transmissions from ground, airborne and maritime sources. Using the ESM system, the mission operators could determine radar and weapon-system types. In addition the aircraft had to be able to identify prearranged codes with an IFF receiver, identification friend or foe. Furthermore, because the aircraft had to able to navigate very accurately it was necessary to fit inertial navigators, the best solution available at that time.

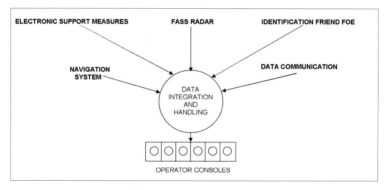

Mission system avionics

The function of the AEW aircraft was not only to see the incoming aircraft but also to control friendly aircraft that might be required to attack hostile ones. The initial Air Staff Requirement (ASR) wanted the Nimrod to be able to track 400 aircraft which was probably an unrealistically high expectation bearing in mind the technology available at the time. However this meant that there had to be sufficient crew on the aircraft not only to operate the sensors but also to act as fighter controllers for all the friendly aircraft; the plan was to have four operators with radar displays, one communications operator and one for the ESM. The requirement to be able to track 400 aircraft was later reduced but apparently even lower figures proved to be very demanding.

When the complete mission avionics started flying in a Nimrod in 1981 it was crewed by the Marconi Elliott system designers and operators. The first most urgent computing requirement was to compute the direction and magnitude of 'moving target' returns to the Nimrod radar scanner and to plot the returns on the screen. However, overland there were far too many spurious returns and as a matter of urgency something had to be done to filter all the unwanted returns from the screen so that only 'targets of interest' flying below the Nimrod were shown and unwanted returns being displayed from ground vehicles and other spurious echoes were prevented. This filtering, 'target delineation', was the core problem and was never really sorted out.

There were two fundamental problems that prevented Marconi Elliott from making the AEW system work effectively. The first related to the antenna design; when a radar transmits a pulse of power at a given frequency it is vital for as much of that power to be transmitted straight ahead and as little as possible to be sent out on either side of the main beam into the 'side lobes'. This requirement is needed because radar returns are only wanted from the main beam. If there is a significant amount of power transmitted from the side lobes then radar returns will be received from unwanted sources in the direction of the side lobes. Marconi Elliott realised that the aerial they were using suffered interference from the side lobes and that the number of unwanted returns resulting from these side lobes caused major overloading problems within the data-processing system. It is worthy of note that the original aerial design was replaced toward the end of the programme but with only a minor improvement.

It is significant from a time-scale viewpoint that the NATO AEW force, to be equipped with eighteen Boeing AWACS aircraft, was being formed in 1981 just as the first MSA Nimrod was being delivered. The first AWACS aircraft was delivered in 1982 and as the RAF had a team in the NATO force they were aware of the airborne early warning performance of both aircraft.

Towards the end of 1984 the first production AEW was delivered to Waddington and a Joint Trials Unit was formed with the RAF operators working with Marconi Elliott. The moment this occurred the RAF could see the magnitude of the problems. Following is a description of some of the problems existing in the middle of the AEW development.

As mentioned the radar did not seem capable of operating over the land because it was 'seeing' all sorts of spurious targets. Though there was an improvement when the antenna was changed it still was not possible to operate over the land without a lot of 'noise' or clutter appearing which moved across the screen at around 50 kt. Apparently the initial radar design included a device called a 'notch filter' but it was never fitted; it has been suggested that if this device had been installed the problem could at least have been mitigated if not cured; where this suggestion came from is not known, maybe from RSRE since they were very keen to see their design succeed but unfortunately no such filter appeared.

Because of the FASS arrangement of the antennae, the wave guides had to run up and down the fuselage close to the engines and Marconi blamed the engines for producing electromagnetic interference which increased the 'noise' on the screen. Apparently it was impossible to shield the wave guides without introducing an excessive amount of weight and the Nimrod with the two radomes, multi-crew positions and supporting electronics was already undesirably heavy.

The AEW radar performance on the Nimrod was apparently way short of the Westinghouse radar, probably due to the AWACS having very small side lobes because of the large size and type of the antenna. Of course there would have been one very good advantage of the FASS design compared with AWACS in that the aircraft fuselage did not block the radar signal and thus create a blind spot directly underneath the aircraft. It should be added that the FASS concept worked well in that there was no problem matching the returns from the two antennae to make a virtual 360° sweep contrary to some information reported on the internet.

The result of all these problems meant that the MSA processors were swamped by radar returns making the identification of genuine tracks very difficult; often these false extra returns completely overloaded the computer. Indeed without IFF there was no way the operator could tell which tracks were true or false and the ability to continuously track a genuine target was questionable. Consequently, it was difficult for the operator to have any genuine confidence in the quality of the air picture they were responsible for compiling.

This unsatisfactory situation was compounded by the design and functionality of the mission

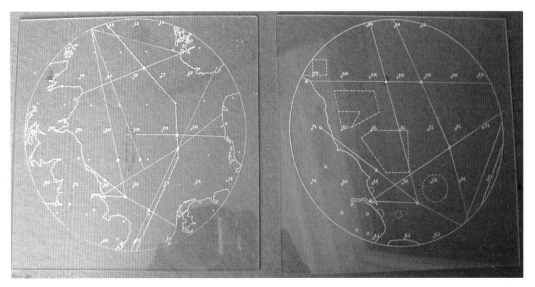
Mapping overlays required for AEW radar displays

operator consoles. Each console had a radar tactical display, on which all the tracks were shown, and a computer interface tabular display where track information and system management information were available. The operation of the console was by a sequence of hierarchical button presses and it could take over seventy button presses to find the answer for just one of the many tasks an operator had to perform; if a mistake was made the operator had to start all over again though a 'back one stage' option was eventually produced which helped a bit.

So far no mention has been made of the computer which seems to have been totally inadequate for its task. It was short of computing speed as well as of computing capacity and it had inadequate storage. The lack of performance was compounded by having its work load increased unacceptably by the need to compute so many ghost tracks and this overload made the computer stop operating, or 'crash'. The computer could take between fifteen to twenty minutes to reboot and it was said that more time was spent on the flight rebooting the system with coastline and airspace data than operating the equipment. Apparently the computer was not able to generate a basic map display with airspace data and the operator had to place a pre-engraved perspex screen over the display and then the display had to be 'slewed' to match the map. As can be imagined, changing scales on the display must have been a nightmare in shuffling perspex screens.

As well as the radar and computing problems outlined above there was another serious problem in that apparently the amount of heat generated from the equipment was not being cooled adequately. In theory the equipment was to be cooled by a heat exchanger using a silicon coolant, the heat being taken away by aircraft fuel which had been cooled by contact with the aircraft skin; it is not clear whether the design was faulty or whether the equipment was producing too much heat. The problem was compounded by the fact that the silicon coolant leaked and was extremely slippery; great care was needed therefore when moving in the aircraft, particularly leaving at the end of the flight.

It is difficult to get an unbiased view of the state of the mission system avionics just before cancellation. The RAF crewmembers in the trial force would have been quite happy to have had the Nimrod AEW if it could be made to work but of course they were aware of the superior performance of the AWACS aircraft. The system clearly worked up to a point but the problem of spurious returns from the ground and road traffic never went away. There was no doubt that the programme was slipping to the right and was costing a lot of money. Then, while the testing

UK AWACS

was still proceeding, Boeing AWACS gave not only demonstrations in the UK and France but also there was a measured test against the AEW Nimrod which demonstrated a marked superiority. Understandably after this test it was announced that the MOD was to renegotiate the contract and thus invitations to tender were issued to other contenders; the AWACS had become a competitor to the Nimrod AEW and, unlike the Nimrod, the AWACS was fully developed and therefore a lower risk proposal. While this bidding process was proceeding the BBC, very well briefed, started attacking GEC and its management in its programme Panorama on the pretext of informative interviews; furthermore there was an apparently authorised article in *The Listener* slamming the project. Very shortly after this the AEW programme was cancelled and the AWACS was ordered.

When talking to the people involved, however, I found that the situation was not as clear cut as has been inferred. Certainly the test pilots I spoke to who had been flying the aircraft had got the impression that the development was proceeding steadily. However, Robbie Robinson in his book *Avro One* describes clearly the pre-planned cancellation visit of the then Secretary of State for Defence, George Younger, and hearing the RAF officer in the back of the aircraft criticising the system to the defence secretary.

In my view the situation was not helped by the fact that BAe was not the prime contractor and these days a project of this magnitude has to be controlled not only technically and financially but also in the media. BAe was on a fixed-price contract for the airframes which it produced on time and ahead of the availability of the electronics. Marconi Elliott on the other hand was on a cost-plus contract. Furthermore GEC never let BAe technicians handle and see the operation of the mission system avionics. Had BAe been the prime contractor then perhaps they could have switched to a United States manufacturer of the mission system avionics but they would have had to have made sure that the replacement radar obtained with its computer did not suffer from the problems Marconi Systems had, barely acceptable over water and incapable of dealing with ground returns. Boeing apparently had no such problem and clearly used the media to good effect whereas GEC and BAe were reluctant to criticise the government.

However it is strange that after the attack on the AEW programme by the media GEC did not contest what was being said which inevitably led people to believe that the electronics was as bad as the BBC and *The Listener* had claimed. Perhaps had BAe been the prime contractor on a fixed-price contract with a firm specification they could have switched the manufacturer of the whole mission system avionics or of a component that was inadequate. As it was the UK lost a wonderful chance to produce an effective weapons system. Hundreds of millions of pounds were poured into the project and wasted and then more millions had to be spent overseas to give the country the much needed AEW capability.

The cancellation resulted in the destruction of eleven Nimrods. Five of the aircraft had been fitted out with MSA and operated by Hawker Siddeley and GEC Avionics. Two were delivered to RAF Waddington and the rest were at Woodford fully equipped. In some ways the cancellation had some similarities to the later cancellation of the MRA4; the money had been spent and the squadron and the crews had been trained but in the case of the AEW, despite the protestations of Marconi Systems, the AEW system not only did not work but was thought to be incapable of ever working, unlike the MRA4 avionics which was working well. Unfortunately therefore the UK spent the money twice, once on the AEW and again on the RAF AWACS which went into service some years later. However, at least the country was spared the ignominious sight of a TSR2 mass-destruction routine as happened later to the MRA4. Unfortunately the Nimrod AEW was yet another example of the UK's inability to manage defence projects effectively.

10 NIMROD MRA4

It was 19 October 2010 and I was giving the annual Fresson lecture at Elgin, Morayshire, close by RAF Kinloss in Scotland where the crews were all waiting eagerly for the latest variant of the Nimrod reconnaissance aircraft, the MRA4, to be delivered. As luck would have it, that day was also the day that the incoming Coalition Government had chosen for its first defence review since coming to power.

Nimrod MRA4

The previous government had left an unsustainable budget deficit and the coalition was faced with having to make enormous cuts in the UK defence budget. However, few of us involved in the Town Hall that night, let alone all the squadron aircrew and groundcrew who had been trained to operate the aircraft on the most modern simulator imaginable, had expected to hear the news that the MRA4, arguably the best reconnaissance aircraft in the world, was to be scrapped forthwith leaving the country bereft of any realistic reconnaissance capability, either on land or at sea. The decision seemed incredible and almost irresponsible, knowing full well that in the near future the country would be forced to buy a United States-built aircraft at a price just as great as the money they claimed they were saving and possibly fitted with some inferior equipment. Furthermore, the decision would make thousands of UK workers unemployed, not just in the Royal Air Force but also at the aircraft manufacturers and at all their suppliers. It could be argued cogently, therefore, that an incoming government did not take advantage of alternative budget options to adjust its defence spending and concentrate on its primary task of providing a proper defence of the UK.

This chapter explains the history of the project, the vastly improved crew layout using the latest technology, why the aircraft was a world beater and why, when the money had already been spent, the government was convinced that it should be cancelled. The specification for the aircraft was detailed and reflected the changing roles that were needed for a United Kingdom reconnaissance aircraft in the 21st Century with the end of the active cold war against Russia and her Warsaw Pact allies. Maritime reconnaissance, search and rescue, and submarine tracking would still be required but in addition there was the need to be able to help land forces using the long-range optical sensors already discussed. Furthermore, there was the ever-present need to listen to electronic transmissions, record their characteristics and identify them from wherever they came, ELINT or electronic intelligence.

The Spey-engined Nimrod MR2s could remain airborne for ten hours without flight refuelling but the engines were old and inefficient by modern standards and it seemed sensible to increase the range and endurance of the new aircraft by fitting the latest technology engines thus reducing the need for frequent flight refuelling. The design team looked at a Honeywell engine that would have fitted into the space vacated by the Spey but because of the desire to use European technology and the need for a very long endurance, the only engine suitable from both a technical and political viewpoint was the Rolls-Royce BR710 with 15,500 lb thrust replacing the Spey's 12,140 lb. Unfortunately, the new engine could not fit in the space vacated by the Spey so though the basic Comet/Nimrod fuselage could be retained the inner wing had to be completely redesigned with an increase of 23% total wing area. It was the size of this task and the difficulty of mating old and new technology that BAe underestimated, causing the programme to slip and the costs to rise.

To keep the MRA4 at the very edge of reconnaissance technology it was necessary to have the best sensors and the best computer systems available to receive and manipulate the data. Consequently, BAe collaborated with Boeing to develop the Boeing TMS 2000 tactical command system with fibre-optic cables to connect the sensors to the computers and using the military standard 1553B databus for data transmission. The tactical control situation could be displayed on seven high resolution multi-tasking displays and the crew layout was therefore significantly different from the MR2.

Below: Nimrod MRA4 crew layout

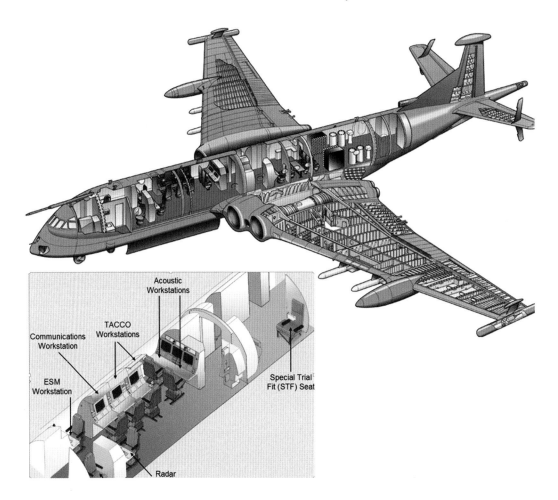

FLIGHT DECK

The flight deck was state of the art, developed from the Airbus 300/330/340, the only real differences from the civil aircraft being the weapons control panels, the bomb doors selector and the tactical situation display. This modified Airbus technology allowed two pilot-operation without the flight engineer and routine navigator who were employed in the MR2. Losing the flight engineer took some getting used to, given that nearly all of the aircraft systems previously set up post engine start and pre take off were replaced by computer automation. All the main systems familiar to any large-aircraft operator were carefully and safely controlled by four utility systems management computers; this was achieved by having considerable redundancy throughout the aircraft systems. Very little pilot input was required and the two pilots were therefore able to concentrate on the job of flying the aircraft and monitoring the autopilot. This autopilot had proved very reliable during flight-test, and was constantly being modified to cope with the finesse and safety requirements of flying a large, high-performance aircraft down to 200 feet over the sea in a tactical, perhaps threat-laden environment. Below 1000 feet, at least one pilot was required to 'follow through' on the control column and auto-throttle, in case either were to trip out, although this was rare.

FLIGHT INSTRUMENTS

The high level of automation coupled with the user-friendly tactical situation display (TSD), enabled very comprehensive situation awareness to be achieved by the flight deck crew. The TSD could display any map overlay loaded pre-flight by the mission support system and fed from the tactical command system; crews could easily pre-note the MSS operator's pre-flight with any map overlay required, and the TCS had a large catalogue to choose from, allowing for a large degree of flexibility. Married in with this, the pilots could quickly select a huge amount of information fed from the aircraft sensors, including the Link, weather radar, and the plethora of information fed into the TCS. Navigation became the flight deck responsibility; in this respect

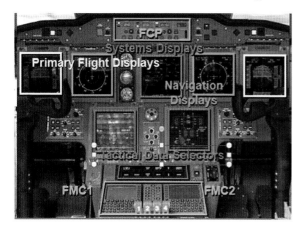

too MRA4 differed from MR2. Rapid flight planning pre-flight, and, if required, during flight was very straightforward using the twin flight management computers, navigation displays and TSD.

The pilots' job on MRA4 differed greatly from that on MR2. Raw piloting skills were similar, however, the aircraft was very 'pilot-friendly' to fly given the stability augmentation system (a fly-by-wire system), but the two pilots had to shoulder responsibility for the 'engineering' and 'navigation' roles too; as stated above, these were hugely eased by the MRA4's automatic management of the aircraft systems; apparently it was enjoyable to fly and was very responsive to the controls. The pilots were always aware of the excess of power available from the fantastic engines too!

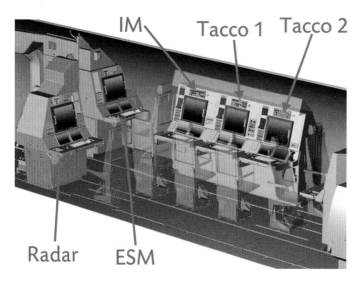

TACTICAL AREA

The MRA4 mission system comprised a mission hard disk (plus another for instantaneous redundancy) which controlled the network-based architecture that fed all the workstations. Apart from the acoustic information, everything was fully integrated and included provision for alternative consoles for crewmembers in case of malfunction. The only difference with the acoustics was that other consoles couldn't display the acoustic data, though it was expected that this feature would be incorporated later. The TCS (tactical command system) was the 'hub' of the machine, the 'server' in computer terms.

The heart of the tactical operation comprised the three seats on the starboard side of the system called the tac rail. Information was said to 'flow' up and down the tac rail with each operator having a great deal of similar functionality, meaning a number of the jobs could be shared depending on the work load and experience of the individual crewmembers.

TAC RAIL

The MRA4 tac rail consisted of three crew. Their role was to control all the sensors and the weapons system to make the aircraft an effective operating platform. In the centre sat the tacco 1, previously known as the tac nav, who was the main driving force of the aircraft and on other maritime fleets would be known as the mission commander. This meant using all the inputs given to him/her from the sensors to decide where to position the aircraft and what to do with it. The control panel for the weapons was also positioned with the tacco 1 although some of these controls were replicated on the flight deck.

To the tacco 1's right sat the tacco 2. Although the role of the tacco 1 in a number of ways was similar to the MR2 tac nav the tacco 2's role differed greatly from the MR2 route nav. Instead of carrying out the traditional navigation duties this position was predominantly about supporting the tacco 1. The tacco 2 still had to have a good awareness of fuel, airspace etc but this was now done in conjunction with the flight deck and was mainly concentrated during the on-task period. Instead the tacco 2 was now in charge of ensuring that the correct buoys were loaded, helping the tacco 1 with the control of the aircraft if required and controlling the EOSDS camera. The latter was previously a job done by the acoustics team.

The third member of the tac rail sat to the tacco 1's left, the information manager, IM.

INFORMATION MANAGER

The information manager was a brand new role for the MRA4 compared with the MR2. The task comprised radio operator/part AEO/part route nav/part lead dry weapons system operator. The duties of the IM included: communication suite manager, data link manager, assisting with the compilation/maintenance of the tactical picture and including track data fusion. The IM managed five secure V/UHF radios; two secure HF radios; SHF SATCOM; DF equipment to aid aircrew rescue using their locator-beacons; the Link 11 tactical data link (TDL) system (over either UHF or HF); and the joint tactical information distribution system (JTIDS) Link 16 TDL system. In addition to these duties he was responsible to the tacco for the maintenance of the tactical picture and to ensure that all digital intelligence data transmitted from the aircraft was accurate and released in a timely manner. Because of the responsibility and nature of the role only

operators who had shown an above-average capability matched with significant experience from the MR2 fleet were selected. The step up in equipment capability from the MR2 saw an increase from one secure voice capable (UHF) radio and three data capable radios (one UHF, two HF) to eight secure voice and data capable radios (five V/UHF, two HF, one SHF). In addition to this the MRA4 was able to transmit digital pictures (either photos or system screen shots) over UHF line of sight or SHF satellite comms (SATCOM) increasing enormously the intelligence applications of the platform. With the addition of the tactical data link systems the MRA4 was able to handle up to 1000 combined digital contacts. Although not initially cleared to do so, the platform was capable of operating both data links simultaneously in a data forwarding role, which could have significantly stretched the range of the Link 16 picture. Overall the MRA4's communications suite offered a quantum leap forward in capability over the MR2 and other existing aircraft and would have made a huge difference in the maritime and other domains.

RADAR STATION

The latest version of the Thales/Racal Searchwater 2000 multimode frequency agile I-band radar looked out to 200nm in the following modes:

Maritime reconnaissance (trials showed an order of magnitude in increased detectability of submarine masts) looking for returns from objects on the sea surface from supertankers down to a tiny chunk of metal out to tens of miles.

Weather (severity of the weather, seen on the next page, is indicated by different colours corresponding nominally with varying intensities of rainfall rates/cloud density)

Air-to-air (anti-collision) designed to detect other aircraft that might conflict with themselves. Not so critical as in the MR2 days since the aircraft had TCAS (traffic collision avoidance system), a transponder-based safety piece of kit.

Interrogation and processing of responses from search and rescue transponder (SART), a new system of waterproof transponders which produced a return on certain radar frequencies.

D band IFF, the old reliable 'identification friend or foe' system

Several synthetic aperture radar imaging and surveillance modes. This is a system where many images of the same area are processed together to form a more accurate and revealing three-dimensional image.

It had the ability to fuse or interweave some of the modes and displays, being much more capable than the MR2 Searchwater which it replaced and that was still the best maritime radar in the world!

ALTERNATE RADAR MODES

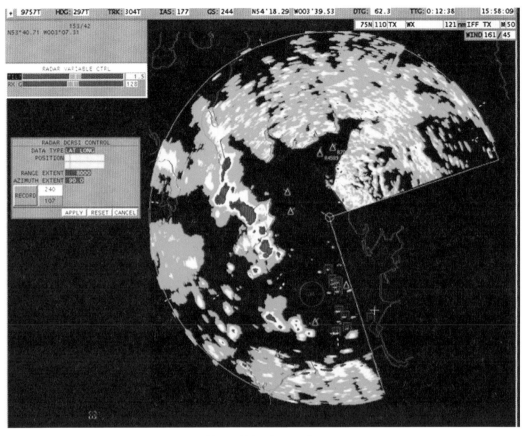

Above: Weather radar
Below left: Search display with A1 scope (outline of selected target) to left
Below middle: SAR display
Below right: SAR display

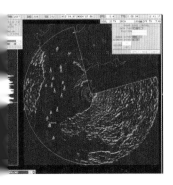  

ESM STATION

Above: ESM station
Below left: Main ESM display
Below right: MAD display also controlled by ESM

ESM – this position managed several sensors described here:

The Israeli Elta EL/L-8300 UK was the ESM system fitted to the MRA4, an evolution of the ALR-2001 fitted to the Australian AP-3 Orion. It utilised twenty-eight aerials (compared to eight of the MR2) – four arrays of six antennas at the nose, tail and wingtips plus the spinner (enhanced DF and analysis for ELINT) which was under the fuselage behind the bomb doors.

MAD (magnetic anomaly detector) simply utilised the existing MR2 system but integrated it into the TCS and provided for the 'trace' (seen here top left) to be shown on five of the crew screens.

The aircraft was fitted with the latest integrated defensive system called DASS, defensive aids subsystem, to permit missions in hostile theatres of operations. This consisted of a radar warning receiver, a missile approach warner (MAWS), a towed radar decoy, chaff dispensers and infrared countermeasures flares.

RWR (radar warning receiver) – Lockheed Martin Enhanced ALR-56M(v) which provided warning of threats radiating RF energy in C/D and E through to K bands.

MAWS (missile approach warning system) – six Sanders AAR-57 sensors provided warning of missile threats.

CFDS (chaff and flare dispensing system) – W. Vinten Enhanced Vicon 78, provided chaff and flare countermeasures protection.

TG/TRD - Racal/Raytheon AJS ALE-50(v), provided active RF countermeasures against threat radars. The TRD (towed radar decoy) was streamed behind the aircraft in response to certain

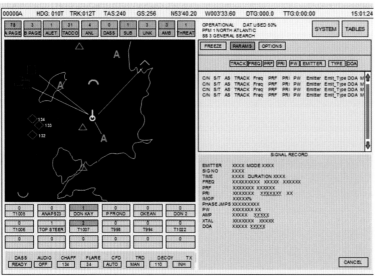

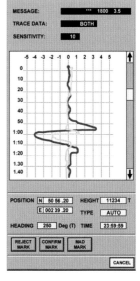

threats and was used to create a more attractive radar signature compared with that of the aircraft, designed to seduce radar missiles away.

The system was integrated and controlled to perform the required response strategy which initiated RF jamming, chaff/flare dispension and/or manoeuvres individually or with a coordinated aircraft response. Overall a massive leap forward in capability over the MR2, possibly the greatest step amongst the sensors.

ACOUSTICS STATION

The acoustics was derived from the same Canadian machine used in the final development of the MR2, albeit both had grown in different directions. The AQS970 was vitally sixty-four-buoy capable, was multi-static capable and was able to ping up to four CAMBS buoys simultaneously. It processed all the sonobuoys from the MR2 inventory, presented the operators with digital signal processing, historical data storage and data fusion (i.e. combining fix data from several sonobuoys) and analysis tools. Due in part to the tremendous integration of the MRA4 and the better working practices employed with the 970, the lead wet would electronically pass the submarine position to the tacco1 for discussion instead of the protracted discussions held between the tac team on the MR2 to result in that same submarine position.

There were some issues whereby the AQS971 (MR2) was considered more capable but in the first few years of the MRA4 these mainly software developments would have caught up. As per the rest of the MRA4 sensors, this was an excellent piece of equipment and combined with the experience of the two operators would have made a formidable collective team.

Additionally and something missing from the MR2, the MRA4 acousticians were fully communication capable with the ability to operate the two HF and five U/VHF radios. They also had their own window – at last! Work was in progress to allow them better control over the EOSDS also, a system that had migrated to the tac rail.

NIGHT HUNTER EOSDS
OPERATED BY TACCO 2

EOSDS – Northrop Grumman night hunter electro optical surveillance and detection system enabled auto-search and detection of targets in TV, medium and long wave infrared. The images were available at five crew workstations, controlled via the TCS control while full turret control was kept at the tacco 2 position through the handgrip assembly. Images could be transmitted from the aircraft and recordings could be analysed post flight.

Advantages were:
Retractable turret which eliminated drag
Auto-tracking of targets
360° azimuth and +15° to -100° elevation
IR and TV pictures could be fused
Hand-held camera photography was still planned to be used by opening the beam window, the images could be transmitted on SHF SATCOM after on-screen editing.
Full recording capability.

ROTARY LAUNCHERS   SONOBUOY RACKS

ORDNANCE AREA

The stores management system was a development of the American-built F/A18 fighter/bomber system. The two pressurized sonobuoy launchers were refurbished MR2 items. The four 'ten shot' rotary launchers were new; the racks enabled 350 sonobuoys to be carried internally.

WEAPONS BAY

The aircraft could carry in the weapons bay a variety of options including fuel tanks if required, torpedoes including the latest BAE Systems lightweight Stingray anti-submarine torpedo and many other different weapons. The aircraft carried and could use the latest sonobuoys. The wings were fitted with two additional hard points so that there could be four weapons pylons. The aircraft could carry Boeing AGM-84 Harpoon anti-ship missiles, Storm Shadow cruise missiles or AIM-9 Sidewinder air-to-air missiles. To manage the weapons and stores carried by the aircraft it was fitted with the Smiths stores management system.

A special feature of the design was that provision was made for new sensors, stores and other equip-

MRA4 with Sidewinders

Above: MRA4 with four Storm Shadows
Below: MRA4 firing infrared countermeasure flares

ment so that the aircraft would not have to be grounded for long periods of time to accept new facilities, as had happened in the case of the upgrade of the Nimrod from MR1 to MR2.

NEW SYSTEMS AND AIRCRAFT CAPABILITY

To demonstrate what a vast improvement the MRA4 would have been on the MR2 from a performance viewpoint, this picture overleaf compares the two aircrafts' search and rescue coverage. At a given distance the search endurance on station was virtually doubled.

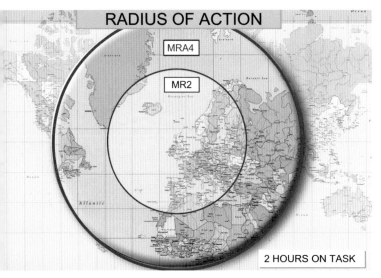

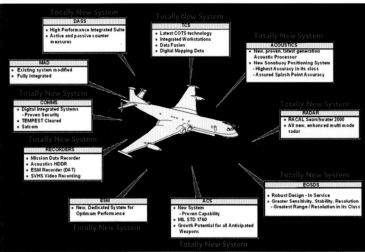

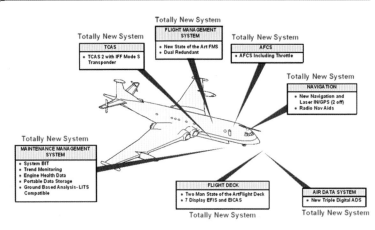

Top: Range/endurance comparison between the MRA4 and MR2

Above and right: The much improved MRA4

DEVELOPMENT PROGRAMME

With the specification for the aircraft agreed BAe needed to put in a bid which met the MoD budget availability. Competitive tendering took place beginning in January 1985 with Boeing with their P7, a development of the Boeing 737, as BAe's main competitor but also Lockheed with their P3 Orion prop jet was involved. The ministry and Treasury buzz phrase at the time was COTS (commercial off the shelf) and their view in the case of the Nimrod was that it would be cheaper to use the existing fuselages than have a new design; consequently BAe very understandably based their bid on this premise though undoubtedly they would have preferred to design a new aircraft altogether. At the time BAe regarded the programme as a 'must win' as they had recently lost the Hercules upgrade programme to an American firm and they felt it important to secure this one. MoD had set a budget of approximately £2bn and this figure conditioned BAe's bid. In retrospect it is clear that BAe under-estimated the cost of re-winging and re-engining the aircraft by about 25% and based the time scale on previous refurbishing programmes; they did not appreciate the difficulty of having to use forty-year-old fuselages with the brand new computer-designed wings. It was probably this key factor which caused increasing delays and spiralling costs and which finally resulted in the cancellation of the project. The phrase that has been used in this situation is that the MoD asked for a golden apple and the firm offered them one, a situation once described as a conspiracy of optimism.

The firm was awarded the contract for the MRA4, initially called Nimrod 2000, in December 1996 with a contract for twenty-one aircraft using existing MR2 fuselages; however, the number was reduced to eighteen in 2002 due to the perceived increased capa-

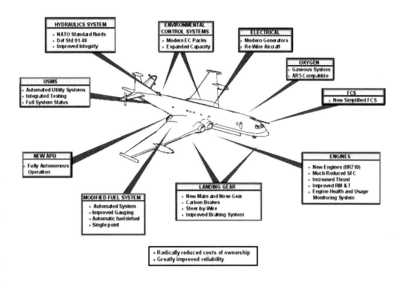

bility of the MRA4 with its new equipment. The expected in-service date was to be 2003.

The original Nimrod programme had been bid and won by the Manchester division of Hawker Siddeley and, as has been said, was an outstanding success. Hawker Siddeley was the prime contractor, the bid was fixed price and the aircraft was delivered on time and on budget. However, by the time the MRA4 came along Hawker Siddeley had become BAe and the centre of expertise and internal political power had shifted to Warton. Furthermore the Comet design teams at Hatfield and Hawarden had long since gone. The Manchester design office had moved to Woodford from Chadderton and no longer had the necessary expertise and computer capability for modern aircraft design. The MRA4 bid was therefore submitted to MoD by the British Aerospace Military Systems division based at Warton, without the core Comet expertise that existed when the Nimrod MR1 was bid; redesigning the wing and increasing the wing area made the MRA4 in effect a new aircraft structurally and aerodynamically. The project director and chief engineer were based at Warton. Woodford maintained the design authority of the MR2 and R1 fleets but not the MRA4.

The whole programme was very demanding both from an airframe and an avionics view-point notwithstanding the operational experience of the earlier MR2 aircraft and the reconnaissance MR1s. However, whilst BAe were clearly aware of the software challenges of making all the sensors work and then integrating the information, it is obvious that they underestimated the task of designing and fitting the new engines. Computer-aided design was used for the new wing but the practical difficulty was that though the fuselage keels were

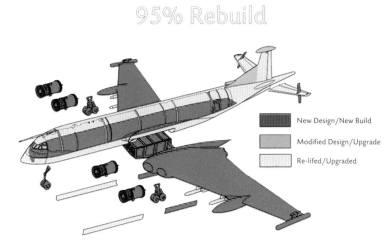

jig built, some of the frames were not quite 'square' with the fuselage. After the mating of the first aircraft, the attachment points of the wing were specified as 'drill to fit' and at the time of cancellation ten of the eleven wings had been attached successfully.

The decision was taken to sub-contract the redesign of the inner wing with the new engines to BAe at Filton because of their world class capability with the Airbus wings. The original manufacture of the inner wings was done at Avro's factory at Chadderton, North Manchester and the outer wings were built by BAe Prestwick, but the remaining six sets were all done at Woodford. The wing design was shifted to Prestwick in 2001 but Filton remained fully responsible until the first mate-ups had been completed successfully.

FRA/Serco at Hurn in 1997 were tasked with re-lifeing the forty-year-old fuselages for a further twenty-five years. To this end the first three MRA4 fuselages were stripped at Kinloss and flown down to Bournemouth in an Antonov 124. Programme slippage was announced in 1999 so that the in-service date, seventh aircraft delivered, was changed to early 2005 with BAe carrying the blame. Because of the slippage and the fact that BAe Woodford was running out of work, it was decided not to renew the FRA contract but to move the work to Woodford and the fuselages were flown there to take over that task. The BAe project management team and build support design team which had been at Hurn also moved back to Woodford to deal with manufacturing change requests. The net result of these management and design changes combined with the problems of the wing design resulted in a slippage of two years.

Nimrod fuselages at Kinloss being transported to Hurn

The delay may have been compounded by the fact that BAE Systems, formerly British Aerospace, wanted to bid a variant of the MRA4 for the US Navy's multimission maritime aircraft (MMA) programme. BAe however failed to get a US partner for the programme and withdrew from the project.

Final assembly of the first MRA4 began in September 2000 when the first completed wing was delivered from Chadderton. As already stated, the wings had been designed using computer-aided design but the teams re-lifeing the fuselage had used different design software which

Nimrod fuselage and Antonov (*Crown copyright*)

caused more problems. Not surprisingly, when the first set of wings were 'offered up' to the fuse-lage there was considerable difficulty fitting them because of the lack of precision build of the original fuselages as mentioned earlier. It is interesting to remember that when Woodford under-took the Victor MR2 tanker conversions in the early 1970s, the engineers took the precaution of ensuring that the wings, when they were modified, went back onto the same fuselage from which they were taken because it was realised at that time that each aircraft was different. No such pre-cautions could be taken nor were measurements made when the MR2 wings were removed to be replaced by MRA4 wings and special modifications were required to fit the first set of wings.

The timetable of the MRA4 slipping to the right can best be demonstrated by the fact that though the final assembly of the first MRA4 began in September 2000, power was not put on the aircraft until December 2001. It was two years later before the aircraft was able to stand on its own wheels and it wasn't until April 2004 that the engines could be started; finally on 26 August 2004 the aircraft took to the air in the hands of John Turner, Avro's chief test pilot who flew it to Warton to begin an extensive flight-test programme.

In parallel with the building of the airframe the crucial design of the mission system was being optimised. Boeing selected Raytheon in 1998 to provide the model 960 computer for the aircraft including the workstations and this was followed by Aerosystems International Link 11 datalink systems to connect them. CAE in 2000 was awarded a contract by Boeing to up-grade the magnetic anomaly detection system so that it could use the latest detection version.

The delay in the programme and increase in costs had severe financial implications. Originally the MRA4 programme had been fixed price but in February 2003 BAe and MoD announced that the contract would be changed to target cost incentive fee (TCIF). This meant the design and development part of the programme was separated from the production phase. BAe took an extra charge of £500m of which the MoD provided £270m. It is averred that this contract change was made to prevent BAe leaving the programme but it is difficult to believe that BAe would have withdrawn at this stage. Also in 2003 the required operation capability was reduced.

While all this was going on the handling of the aircraft was being evaluated on an old HS 146 simulator at Woodford. Unfortunately while flight simulation worked well for the Eurofighter fly-by-wire system, it failed when trying to simulate venerable cable and pulley connections be-tween the control column and the power controls. Inadequate allowance was made in the redesign of the wing for the effect of having to rerun the aileron control cables to accommodate the new engines. Furthermore, increasing the size of the wing was fundamentally destabilising so that more powerful controls and stabilisation were required in pitch and yaw. It was clear that the aileron wheel forces would have to be evaluated in flight as would the elevator forces because there was a nose up trim change with the application of power.

John Turner, Avro's chief test pilot, after the first flight of the MRA4 remarked that the aircraft 'flew exactly as expected' which delighted the media but was bad news for the cognoscenti since the unaccept-ably high aileron wheel control forces and inadequate elevator control had been predicted by the flight-test department. In fact, initially the aileron control forces required two hands to make small control move-ments. In addition the wheel brakes that were fitted were so powerful that it was necessary automatically to modulate the maximum braking on landing to

Cold weather trials at Eglin AFB

prevent the pilot breaking the aircraft.

The aileron wheel forces were gradually reduced by improving the control runs and pulleys. However it was found that the nose-up trim change with power approaching the stall was unacceptable from a handling viewpoint and so it was necessary to fit stick pushers. The second MRA4 flew in December 2004 and its programme was to develop the mission systems. In fact the RAF was very much involved in the flight trials of both aircraft providing aircrew experts to develop the mission systems. In 2005 the first aircraft carried out the necessary handling trials and rectifications that were required and the second aircraft went to Sicily and successfully completed hot weather trials. The third aircraft joined the programme in August 2005. Also in 2005 BAe at Brough received the structural test specimen. In September 2006 the second aircraft went to Eglin in Florida for the cold weather trials but because of outstanding tests on the fuel and navigation systems the aircraft had to go via the Azores and Maine; it returned in November via the Azores having successfully completed all its trials.

By February 2007 the MRA4 aircraft had accumulated 200 hours and the first fully equipped aircraft for the RAF was at Warton. During 2007 the aircraft operated from Kinloss, flew at the Royal International Tattoo at Fairford and released a Stingray torpedo at the Aberporth range to prove the new stores-release system. In 2008 the first MRA4 went to Nashville, Tennessee for icing trials.

Because the avionics was so advanced compared with the MR2, or any other aircraft in the world for that matter, and because it was working so successfully I have described the performance of the system at the time the project was cancelled.

There seems to be little doubt that there were no real problems with the complete system and that the aircraft was ready to be operated in any of its core roles. Though the latest gear had not been tested against a live submarine the operators were confident that it would have performed well after 'tuning up' and getting experience.

Of course the way the data was handled on the aircraft was very different from the MR2 in that there were multifunction displays at the operator positions so the 'targets' could be seen by all the sensor operators, unlike the MR2 where only the tactical navigator could 'see' the whole picture.

To go into some detail, a lot of time and effort was spent successfully ensuring the correct display and dissemination of tactical information around the system and also that this information could be transmitted on data links. Unlike the MR2 where each sensor/system operated largely autonomously, with the MRA4, the data was 'centrally owned' and available to everyone from the outset; this meant that the operators had to be considerably more aware of the overall impact of their individual actions. A very real advantage was that the tactical navigator could display for example a hostile track to all the operators.

A great deal of the testing was on how the system handled, processed and displayed target/track data and this was only possible because the sensors were able to detect/collect the target data even at this early stage of development. Detailed checks were of course carried out on the ESM sensors and clearly it was an enormous jump, comparable to when the MR2 fitted the computer-based Yellowgate system leaving the early ARAR/ARAX system behind.

On the MR2 there was an enormous amount of conversation between the sensor operators and the tac nav in chasing submarines or other targets. The buzz words on the MRA4 were 'data fusion' and old MR2 hands were amazed at how quiet the intercom was when chasing targets compared with the older aircraft. The system worked!

The MRA4 had all the benefit of the upgrades that had been made to the sonobuoy systems on the MR2 fleet and most of the development time and energy was spent on evaluating the best way to operate the system and the interactions between the systems and the operators. Unfortunately for financial reasons the sonobuoy work stations could only display acoustics data to the operator and not have a fully working multifunctional display but had the aircraft entered service this restriction would probably have been resolved.

On 10 March 2010 the Ministry of Defence accepted the fourth aircraft at BAe Woodford as being cleared by Boscombe Down as ready to train crews. The aircraft moved to Warton for the RAF crews to receive transition training. Two days earlier the second full RAF aircraft had made its first flight. By October 2010 the aircraft had completed its trials and was with Boscombe for clearance. The test aircraft had flown about 650 flights and 1,900 hours.

Notwithstanding the flying that the aircraft had been doing proving the airframe and the mission system, the programme had been slipping to the right and the cost of the project had increased dramatically. The view of the incoming Coalition Government was that the Labour Government faced with these ever-rising costs should have cancelled the programme much earlier instead of reducing the number of aircraft from eighteen to nine and there can be little doubt that there is

The author has a flight in an advanced simulator

considerable justification for this view. As mentioned, by now the aircraft was working, Kinloss was completely kitted out for the new aircraft both in buildings and flight simulators, two each for the rear crew and for the pilots with real time interconnection. The crews and supporting operational teams were therefore completely ready for the aircraft. In fact the day after the cancellation I was able to tour Kinloss and fly in the superb simulator which was for me an unforgettable experience.

Perhaps it is interesting to compare the Nimrod MRA4 development programme with some American ones. The Boeing P-8 costs are estimated at £4.9bn and £134m per aircraft which makes £6bn for a nine-aircraft fleet so that the Nimrod cost of £4bn for an eight-aircraft fleet was cheap by comparison, particularly taking into account the tax return to the government and the fact that the MRA4 would possibly have been the operational equivalent of two P-8s. The programme slippage was very bad news but again looking across the water the USAF started trying to replace their P-3s in 1989 and the P-8 is still a long way from being in service. The facts are that because of the size of the US defense budget, it is easier for costs and slippages of these magnitudes to be absorbed in the USA than it is for the UK to handle such delays and increases in costs.

Bearing in mind that a training release had been issued to the RAF, that the brand new mission system was working with all its sensors, that some of the crews were trained and Kinloss was ready, it was a complete shock that the Coalition Government decided to cancel the project altogether. Apparently BAe Sysems were not told until ten minutes before the announcement that the programme was going to be terminated, despite the fact that BAe had spent and were continuing to spend a large amount of their shareholders' money supporting the programme.

It is likely that there were other reasons besides the well advertised financial ones for stopping the MRA4. There were some difficult safety issues that needed decisions which officials may not have wanted to take and these could have affected the advice they gave the politicians. The problem was that while the programme was slipping new aviation safety standards were being formulated which were more onerous for new aircraft to meet and MoD regulators were wondering whether the MRA4 should be forced to comply with these new standards. In particular there was the question of the failure case for engines being buried in the wings instead of being on pods and also there was an aileron safety case which had not been considered at the time of the design. Normally these issues are dealt with by excusing old aircraft from having to comply with new rules but the basic safety of the Nimrod had been severely questioned by the 2009 publication of the Haddon-Cave report on the accident in Afghanistan. Cancelling the aircraft would remove the need for uncomfortable decisions to be made.

Apparently the Coalition Government was told that there were outstanding aircraft problems that were estimated to take at least another eighteen months to fix so the earliest possible entry into service would have been 2012. Given this information the view seems to have been that the programme was going to be costly to complete and that it would be

MRA4s at Woodford ready to go

cheaper in the end to terminate it and instead buy the less capable Boeing P-8 aircraft when it became ready. Apparently it was thought that there would be an added political advantage to this approach since it would clearly demonstrate that the government was no longer prepared to keep programmes that slipped uncontrollably in time and escalated in cost, conveniently forgetting that in this case they had agreed to the extended programme by getting BAE Systems to share in the escalating costs.

There will inevitably be different views on what the government should have done, but it is an unpalatable fact that by its act of cancelling the MRA4 it has left the UK, a maritime nation, without a reconnaissance aircraft. In addition, the UK ground forces need the capability of a Nimrod MRA4 with its advanced optical system; unmanned aerial vehicles (UAVs) may have a part to play but it is difficult to believe that in the forseeable future they can ever be as flexible and responsive to events on the ground as a properly manned and equipped aircraft. The government also chose to ignore the fact that they had a partner in the programme, their chief defence contractor BAE Systems, who had put £1.1 bn of their shareholders' money into the project. Not to inform BAE of the cancellation when the aircraft was already working and was available for immediate use makes one question the ethics of the procedures. The politicians had to work on the information they received since they were not able to evaluate the system completely in the time available; it would seem that from what they were told they may have been encouraged to cancel the project but whether the project should have been stopped will always be a matter for debate. In reality, the bulk of the money had already been spent, the aircraft was ready and the industrial and social expense of cancelling the project resulting in thousands of redundancies was almost certainly ignored.

A few weeks after the cancellation the government, trying to justify their cancellation of the aircraft, allegedly leaked a document to the *Sunday Times* detailing all the things that were wrong with the aircraft. Most of the accusations were either old incidents long since cured, minor items being rectified, incorrect or items that were planned to be done in the normal way after the initial release for the aircraft had been given but that is the way of all governments when trying to justify their decisions. However as expected, perhaps unduly influenced by the Haddon-Cave report, the government also chose to doubt the safety of the aircraft which sounds

Scrapping MRA4s – note the screens to hide the precipitate nature of the job

unarguable to those who do not understand that there is no such thing as absolute safety, that safety is a matter of balancing risks and it is ridiculous to expect, for example, an old Boeing 737 to comply with some of the rules applied to an Airbus 380.

Like the TSR2 cancellation forty-five years earlier, the government inexcusably rushed to scrap the perfectly good airframes so that their decision could not be reversed. Had they delayed the decision Nimrod could have been used almost immediately in the Middle East since the aircraft with all its sensors were working and the crews were trained. They might have avoided the ignominy of having to reverse the decision to ground the Nimrod R1s two weeks before the official closing ceremony.

Had an administrator been called in to manage the cancellation, consideration would have been given to minimise the financial consequences. Clearly one option would have been to sell the airframes to a friendly power and recover some of the money that had been spent; presumably the government shied away from this approach as they were afraid they would have looked foolish. However selling the aircraft would have prevented the loss of jobs caused by the cancellation since the firms involved in the project would have had to continue supporting the purchasing air force. One can't help feeling that the cancellation and the way it was handled left a lot to be desired.

EPILOGUE

The Nimrod more than lived up to its name, it was indeed a mighty hunter, finding submarines, locating vessels in distress, supporting the Falklands campaign and, in later years, helping our troops in battles on the ground. Over the years its equipment was continually updated and the Royal Air Force with its dedicated crews made it work superbly.

The aircraft was incredibly reliable and helped to safeguard these shores for decades with very few accidents. Regrettably, it had one tragic accident while it was supporting our troops in Afghanistan but, sad though that was, all aircraft have accidents and this one was a typical one, a combination of circumstances which resulted in disaster. It is easy to criticize after the event but in doing so care must be taken to consider all the possibilities and not focus on just some of the issues (see conclusions, Chapter 8). It is my personal view that the life of the Nimrod has been shortened unnecessarily because of the reaction to this accident and maybe it will be possible one day to tell the whole story.

Though I flew most of the Nimrods that were built I never had the good fortune to operate the aircraft on missions, but from everything I have heard I believe the sensors on the aircraft were every bit as good as competing aircraft and the Searchwater radar made other countries jealous. Furthermore in our competitions against the RAAF and RNZAF Orions we won many more times than we lost so perhaps it isn't altogether surprising that in all my many communications whilst writing this book, I've only received one message disparaging the aircraft.

Nothing is perfect in this world but in designing and operating the Nimrod for so many years with superb crews we have a lot to be proud of. It is indeed more than a shame that the MRA4, which, when finally completed was almost certainly the best reconnaissance aircraft in the world, should have been cancelled so finally and abruptly – leaving the country without the capabilities of anti-submarine warfare, long-range maritime reconnaissance, long-range search and rescue, and the ability to fulfil its international commitments. I am reminded of the poem:

> '….for you are not wanted here,
> and that was all the farewell…'
>
> A.E.Houseman
> *A Shropshire lad*

Surely after over forty years of dedicated service in the defence of the realm, the aircraft and its crews deserve a better epitaph.

APPENDIX 1

A TYPICAL DAY IN THE LIFE OF A LATTER DAY NIMROD MR2 CREW, BY JUSTIN MORRIS

To get the most out of the aircraft during a day as many flights as possible had to be squeezed in, whether that was three short trips or two long ones. The north of Scotland in mid-summer often heralded wonderfully bright mornings at 4am though. Anything mildly sociable, timings-wise was referred to as 'Gentlemans', ie a civilised time of the day. More often than not the crew would arrive in dribs and drabs at operations at the same sort of time to be met by those on the crew stood at the front of the building who'd forgotten their door pass card. On the way to the cold brief there was a chance of some caffeine at the vending machine for those folk not ingratiated with the ops staff enough to cadge one for free. There were always some who had been there a wee while as they couldn't sleep due to nerves because of the importance of the task, bawling babies or time-zone faff due to using the GMT clock.

The cold brief was just that, turn up at work cold to discover what was happening that trip. More often than not it was a training sortie for which the crew mostly determined their own plan but the moniker stuck. Most of the brief was given by contemporaries, friends and colleagues who were on their ground tour, which encouraged a very comfortable feel to the whole thing. A little bit of banter was already developing but first up was the met man (person), mostly someone dyed-in-the-wool who'd been at Kinloss forever but sometimes a new face. The crew took this bit very seriously as it was vitally important to them. The perils of the weather can never be underestimated in the context of maritime aviation.

Many types of mission could be presented at the drop of a hat in changing times but normally it would be pretty much known what was coming. Training was good in most respects, a crew could normally determine what they needed to achieve and what they fancied doing that day. So many different disciplines and mission types were demanded of the MR2 that it was necessary to try and stay abreast of things as much as possible. The Americans generally had a different squadron for each task, a Sqn in Iceland perhaps would be the duty ASW Sqn and one in Puerto Rico would be slated for anti-drug smuggling work. A Nimrod crew was the poor relation, having so few assets they had to be able to do the lot, quite often in one sortie! A directed task was always very exciting as it meant there was a job to do 'in defence of the Realm' and the whole chain of command was energised to resolve a problem or intruder or go and win a war. Going to find a submarine, a surface ship, a drug running fisherman or a yachtsman adrift called upon many different skills and had to be practised to remain the acknowledged world experts at these endeavours. Sounds a little over-confident but it was true.

When the extensive weather brief was over the met man (person) would leave the room for the rest of the brief to continue. All sorts of stuff, airfield and navigation-aids states, diversion airfield information, a/c availability and equipment states, details about the area, intelligence and recent history, specific sensor information and stop-press type items. Fastballs could be thrown in at any time, an area change normally for weather reasons could force a complete mission re-think or the 'checkers' might come along (more of them later). A lot of this was briefed via a computer system called MSS (mission support system) which had grown with the Nimrod and other aircraft since the 1970s, built by Thales (pronounced Tallies). This system became the backbone of many military operations, never quite the master but certainly the jack of ALL trades. The powers that be often confused MSS for something that the MRA4 could undertake a mission without – incorrect. The machine was a huge part of Nimrod life, even replaying the mission tapes to fully reconstruct a sortie. At the end of the cold brief the captain would normally stand up, re-iterate the salient facts and state what and when the crew was to do. For a training mission that might be running over the main task and talking about the main brief time, ie how long the crew all had to collate the available information to do a complete run through in the same room, say, ninety minutes later.

The crew then dispersed to their various responsibilities; these were many and varied but the description here is what might happen for a regular training sortie. The operators of the wet, sonobuoys/acoustics, and dry teams, radar/ESM, would have plenty to get on with; whoever was the most junior guy normally looked after the in-flight rations, some might say the most important job of the lot. He'd check with catering that everything was ok with the previous day's order and any last minute changes were correct. Was it to be wraps or rolls, salads or curries, chilli or pizza? Was there enough coffee or stale doughnuts in the rations bag, that most terrible of life forms? When one put a hand in the enormous (unrefridgerated) bag would it discover the three-year-old mayonnaise jar? Other items had to be looked after, the safety equipment section had to be visited to ensure all the crew kit was laid out; headsets, 'Mae Wests' (life preservers), tool boxes, immersion suits; any passengers coming along had to be fully suited up with everything to keep them warm and safe.

Friendly naval units, coastguard ships or merchantmen had to be called or investigated, their courses plotted out and mapped. Some of this indeed could be done the previous day as per other aircraft types but the maritime world was much more fluid and in any case generally involved a full day previously too.

The intelligence situation also had to be fully exploited, not just the feeds received from elsewhere but that of our own, which other crews had de-briefed previously too. There were books and publications by the shelf load to pore through to ensure nothing was missed and although the whole crew were all in the same building everyone had to be made aware of what was occurring before the main brief. This meant everyone gravitating back towards the flight planning room, a large airy place with enormous windows looking out over the airfield, where the flight deck crew (P1, P2, Eng) and tac team (N1, N2, AEO) hung out. There they'd spread all their charts across the big planning tables and start wielding dividers, highlighters and felt-tip pens to create a mission. The crew 'execs', captain, first pilot, first nav and lead rear crew operators, would all then crowd around the chart to discuss what was to be, make sure the plan was evolved, sound, achievable and sensible. There were many ways of doing this, with the luxury of having many good brains gathered around the table. Developed techniques were used and lists of methods to ensure there was a sound plan as there were many, many different tasks, needs, injects, things to factor in, differing requirements that all had to somehow interact without threatening the safety of the crew – which was easily done at 200ft over an unforgiving ocean.

Inevitably the phone would ring to say the aircraft had gone unserviceable with no spare, or there was a spare which was only partly compatible with the mission, someone needed to go to the Sqn to see the Boss, the met man called to say our diversion airfield had just deteriorated out of limits, the rations man was reporting a delay in getting our order together, or the wife rang to say Gran had died. The bigger the crew the more hazards were possible. That Harrier pilot on his own was looking awfully smug by now. Human factors was invented in maritime surely….

At the allotted time the crew would gather in the briefing room and begin the main brief. Aided by the duty MSS operator the captain would state the mission essentials again for the record, followed by one of the pilots with the Met and Jet, a brief resumé of what had been talked of before with the weather, how it affected the trip and what had changed. By this time the Eng was at the aircraft doing his extensive checks so the same pilot briefed the Jet, what was fitted, what wasn't, what worked, what was broken, the sonobuoy load and a lot of other stuff. The routine (route) nav then briefed the route to the area, waypoints, altitudes, fuels and all the traditional navigation type details for what was quite a 'manual' aircraft, which required prodding furiously to be accurate. The route nav had many other auxiliary tasks too to remove some of the pressure from the often maxed-out tac nav. Next came the lead dry to brief all the above-water details, latest intelligence on the targets and how they would be found with the various sensors he managed. Next was the lead wet to do the same for the below-water targets and info on the sensors he managed, electro-optics latterly. The tac nav was next, to pull all the information together for the main thrust of the day, specifically what was to happen and how to do it, with all the gotchas in-between. This was the make or break sometimes as frequently the tac nav drove the mission from the back end, Nimrod pilots often being expensive taxi drivers (albeit good ones). Finally the AEO briefed all the communications info and admin details. He also ran the emergencies being kind of the spare man so these and any passenger requirements were spoken about here. The AEO was mostly the person under the least pressure during the trip so was able to see the 'Big Picture' instead of having to 'fight' a piece of equipment. It was often said a good one was invaluable but a bad one wasn't worth his weight in fuel. Normally this whole period in the briefing room was a quiet time, there weren't many interruptions. The door was opened sometimes by someone unsure of where they should be and we'd all hold our breath, expecting it to be the ops officer to say we'd been scrambled on SAR, to forget all that had gone before and to get in the air immediately which if we were lucky on a good day would take ten minutes.

All the while the added pressure of having the Checkers present had to be endured. As flying hours dwindled inexorably due to various cuts and different problems faced the crew the very real issues of getting rusty due to lack of practice became evident. In the flying business this is inherently dangerous and ever-present supervision seemed to be the way to manage it. With the paucity of flying these guys needed their hours too, whether it be the STT (squadron training team) or the dreaded Staneval (standards evaluation unit). The STT were guys drawn from each trade of the best of the on-average eight crews per squadron to form a small unit with their own office to educate, train and check their own crews, on a regular basis. At least once every year, more often twice yearly, the Staneval came along to check a crew with little or no notice. These were the best of all the squadron's operators and expected high things of those they oversaw, every little error to be debriefed in minute detail to keep everyone on their toes. Some were nervous of different aspects of these weeks; the air check where safety breaches were an unacceptable mark on one's career, the simulator check where everything could be replicated in one mission to properly fry one's brain or the endless 'chalk and talk' sessions, magiboard in front of a collection of people and dry marker pen in hand. In the latter circumstance, sometimes a couple of days worth of it, the checker would say something like 'draw me the entire wiring diagram of the ninth circuit board of the wibble-frizznit gromit valve box' or something like that – and would throw a pen at one of the audience. Woe betide if one hadn't studied that book the night before!

Away on detachment, or on ops in the desert recently, all these things were slightly different without the infrastructure of home. Unfamiliar airfields and accommodation, temporary, borrowed or shared office facilities, little or no ops and met support, sorting rations and other details meant that operating overseas (and sometimes UK) was a challenge. Often though it was a bit of a release from the binds of home and as much of a challenge as it was to run a large aircraft detachment, the crew was on their own to do what they were good at without hindrance. They could certainly jump in the jet and go do a job for the most part but to do it properly and effectively was sometimes another matter.

Back at Kinloss, all the preparation complete, the crew and kit assembled downstairs to await the bus. Once on board, importantly, the junior guy checked everything was on the bus, a mountain of equipment; strong boxes, bags full of secret books, cryptographic material, rationing, kit and lots more – the checklist had to be complete before the bus could move off to the flight line. After arriving at the aircraft the captain's job would be to exit the bus, climb the steps and check the thing was fit for purpose. If he didn't have both hands full before leaving the bus a barrage of abuse would generally see an about turn to collect some more kit (this would be repeated for other officers on the crew also until they one day got the point). His silhouette would walk past the two windows to the galley where the crew chief was often to be found and then after a brief chat turn and thrust an upturned thumb (vastly important maritime tradition) through the open doorway to signal all was fine to get on board.

Mostly the crew wanted nothing other than to be airborne but sometimes didn't even get this far, the Flt Eng or the chief would meet the bus as it rolled up with whatever news there was; jet unserviceable, not enough fuel had been put in yet, etc. In this circumstance an executive decision would be made by the captain as to what to do according to the situation, occasionally influenced by the deafening chant of DFM! from the crew, meaning they'd been at least an hour since a meal and needed a 'delayed flight meal' at the respective messes to tide them over. In any case excepting at the risk of human life a DFM was considered a huge victory for a crew, something for free, a definite win in the daily grind. Nothing at all to do with thirteen guys thinking of nothing but their stomachs!

Once actually on the plane the work started in earnest, obviously each person knowing exactly what they had to achieve. They moved about the cabin as a fluid, the lack of room and lots of bodies surrounded by equipment and kit coupled with many sharp edges everywhere meant they had to be able to interact physically very well. The constant pushing and shoving, jostling and weaving amongst ourselves in such a cramped environment led to a natural closeness, we had to get on, to live out of each other's pockets.

The labour intensive ways in which the Nimrod worked meant that very quickly a new member to any crew learnt that they had to be a sociable person, be able to communicate well and above all else rapidly become not just a team member but a team player. In other aircraft fleets this was not necessarily so but Nimrod people were in each other's faces, were families within families (a team within a crew within a squadron within a station) and were incredibly tightly knit. They learned each other's strengths and weaknesses through all the evolutions of working incredibly hard together, constantly pitting their wits against and with each other, through harsh and pleasant debriefs and sometimes in the most trying of circumstances. Above all of this, they were a constituted crew with personnel changes happening only occasionally, as opposed to most other multi-crew environments where individuals were selected to fly together only for that trip. They were therefore a family, thirteen people all in the game together to do the best they could. All of this was a contributor to how well Nimrod aircrew mixed together, at home, on detachment, in war.

Preparing the aircraft for a full mission internally took a good thirty minutes, on top of the forty-five minutes the engineer had already spent doing his own thing, checking the wings were still screwed on etc. As well as we maintained the aircraft and got it to work, reliability was sometimes a problem. Best practice, often controversially, was deemed therefore to turn on the sensor to check it was ok and then turn it off. One might argue that each cycling of the power was another one closer to the death of that particular black box of electronics, an argument that held some water, but if that box did have an underlying serious snag one really needed to know. Each individual piece of equipment had its own foibles, things to look out for, things on certain days it wouldn't be happy with. Education and experience taught the operators how best to massage the kit to get the best out of it, what could and couldn't be done and, more importantly what could and couldn't be accepted. Some of the snags were fine and would go away with a little warmth, some needed to be fixed.

Sometimes the groundcrew, when faced with a challenging problem, would only have their maintenance procedures (MPs) to fall back on and wouldn't have the benefit of decades of aircrew experience. This only happened now and again and is possibly over-simplifying some of the issues, but the guys' hands were sometimes tied. Anyhow, it was necessary to be pretty sure all the equipment was ok, not least in accordance with the go/no-go book, which advised on all sorts of mission on what was the accepted minimum from various items. Some of the kit had BIT (built-in test) which helped run checks through the whole chain of black boxes, some of the kit just had lots of settings and number crunching to carry out and this all took a while. If there was a short transit to the operating area then a ground load was required too, the tac nav signalling the sonobuoy load to ordnance and a couple of guys loading up to fourteen buoys to save time later on. There were often passengers to brief too, get them strapped in safely.

During this evolution there was normally someone dishing out the rations. On cold days the vats of steaming hot drink were very welcome – if the water tank contents hadn't frozen – sometimes keeping flying gloves on until things started to warm up was prudent. If an item of kit was being waited for before the start then that was a good time to take a break, roll firmly in one hand, cup of tea in the other, in the galley mainly, a good chance to relax for one of the only times in the day. Meanwhile, other crewmembers of groundcrew were under pressure to effect a solution up and down the aircraft while everyone else stood in the way in the already cramped middle of the jet.

Soon though it would be time to get airborne and everyone took their places for the start. Once everything was acceptably serviceable and individual intercoms and oxygen were fine, then everyone checked in ready to go. There were many checks to go through, mostly for the flight deck but soon enough Air Traffic were called for start clearance and the crew chief checked on intercom outside if he was happy before the engines were started. Once he'd said *"Crew chief's on"* and cleared the crew to close the bomb doors he'd say:

"Steps and ground equipment are clear of the aircraft, chocks are in on the port side, beacon lights are on and strobing red, APU door is open, fire cover's in place you are clear to start the APU!"

The first item to fire up would be the APU (auxiliary power unit) with a whooooosh, which this aircraft needed to provide air to turn the engines. This was the motor that was used in the jet-powered Rover BRM racing car but that's another story. Once the APU had stabilised, the pilots opened up the cross-feed air pipe using air assist switches and asked for clearance to start main engines in order 3,4,2,1 to expose the groundcrew to the least danger but also for convenience (unless in the desert sometimes or with an air-start trolley under starboard wing so we would start 2,1,3,4). The chief would clear each individual start when he was sure fire cover was there and he was in a position of control and could see the rotation of the compressor. To start the first engine the pilot would say 'button' as he podged the button and the eng would say 'air valve' as the air valve kicked in. This was sometimes the first stumbling block of the day as sticky air valves weren't uncommon and the chief would pick up the big rubber chock to give it a thwack (frowned upon latterly). After numbers 3 and 4 were started (steam often rising from the exhausts after a heavy night of rain) with their generators on and they were confident that they could take the aircraft power load the GPU would be switched off and the call would be *"clear ground power"*. The power lead was removed by the boys and girls, the GPU set towed away, the chief would give clearance for 2 and 1: *"Ground power disconnected and clear of the aircraft start number two, then one.* Once they were started the after-start checks would be carried out and the flying controls were checked, *"Flying control checks, on the Blue, rudder port, neutral, starboard, neutral. Ailerons, port up starboard down, neutral, neutral, starboard up, port down, neutral, neutral. Elevators up, neutral, down, neutral.* The pilots would then throw the changeover levers to green and do the whole lot again. Then: *"Clear airbrakes, airbrakes travelling, airbrakes out, travelling, airbrakes in and flush. Flaps selected to 60, flaps travelling down together, flaps all at 60, flaps travelling up together, flaps at twenty, set, checked.* The chief's final declaration before disconnect: *"All ground equipment removed from the aircraft, all hatches and panels will be closed and secured on my disconnect, which way are you turning?* (he couldn't hear the radios so was unaware of which runway the crew were headed for). Then would come: *"Have a nice flight, see you in 6 hours, you are clear to taxi".*

As the chief walked away he'd indicate to the marshaller which way to signal and hold up his intercom lead for the port beam operator to confirm that he had unplugged. Unusually this aircraft had beam windows, a bubble-shaped window a dozen feet or so behind the pilots for observation purposes whilst 'on-task' but very useful on the ground as two extra sets of eyes to avoid bumping into things. Two of the junior rear-crew would occupy these positions until released when approaching controlled airspace in the climb, keeping their eyes open for hazards but additionally enjoying the fantastic views whilst chasing the clouds through the skies. Some of their time would be spent mopping up the rainwater until the pressurisation sealed the windows fully.

Of course at any time the jet could have broken down, be it any one of the things really required that day, whether it was the most minor of equipment or something more serious. For a mission to succeed there were so many interminable 'ducks' that had to be 'in a row'. If there was a spare aircraft then a 'bag drag' would ensue and all the kit would be gathered up, prepared and sorted out, and with half a ton of rations dragged across the tarmac to the next plane – if it was close. If it was on the other side of the airfield then another bus would be required. The spare broke more than a few times too, that made for a long day.

It was soon time to taxi out, a check of the brakes on both hydraulics systems, the pilots and navs had to swap navigation equipment settings, all the radio settings, fully brief the emergency reactions and what was expected from air traffic as well as the climbout and transit information. As the aircraft trundled past ATC at no more than 10 kts someone would say hi to them and swap waves. There'd be more rafts of checks on the way to generally runway 26 (until they changed it to 25 with the earth's magnetic field – how confusing!), dip out of view of ATC behind Hangar 7 and call 'two minutes' to enable Kinloss to call Lossiemouth and ask for the departure clearance as they were the local ATC centre.

Line-up clearance would enable the crew to take ownership of the runway, bring the aircraft to a full stop for a final brake check and evacuate any air that might still be in the fuel lines. Take-off clearance would come in and the beam window operators would be cleared to face forwards, tighten the seat straps and prepare to go. The pilots would advance the throttles to the firewall, passing 87% on the way where the bleed straps would close to give that almost Vulcan-like howl and they'd be off, roaring to 80 kts for rudder authority over the nosewheel steering, V1 and rotate, free of the shackles, up into the delirious blue!

The non-handling pilot would raise the undercarriage, check all was well and call Air Traffic: "*Airborne, stud 3*" to tell them they were safely up and were switching to the pre-selected frequency under rotary dial on V/UHF Box 2 to call Lossiemouth, whilst the AEO in the back called Operations to let them know too.

Circuit leaving checks:
"*Red pump - Off*
Rudder limiter – Normal
Landing lamps - Off
Bomb bay heating – On" (changed latterly to 'Remaining Off')

As all the aviation stuff was occurring in the front the rear crew were preparing sensors and other items of kit, carrying out safety walkround checks of the fuselage, putting cameras, documents and books in position from their stowages and latterly with the Wescam, examining the external aircraft surfaces for anything out of order. The beam operators were doing this simultaneously, whilst carrying out the more important task of looking for other conflicting aircraft. This was sometimes a little difficult whilst trying to ignore the beautiful scenery, the sunlight peeping through the clouds and admiring the aircraft chasing wisps of clouds through the sky. Obviously the water boiler would be on at this stage for another pot of tea. Towards Flight Level 245 (24,500 feet) they'd be approaching controlled airspace when the beams would be released for other duties, the radar hopefully released from collision warning for surface search before this time.

On an all-sensor ASW mission more often than not the MAD would need calibrating (known as a MAD comp), meaning to compensate it to account for all the manoeuvres the crew would be performing that trip. This meant turning off known electrical items that interfered with the MAD and allowing the pilots to complete a set of intricate and precise flying procedures to allow the sensor to 'get used' to the aircraft. This was done periodically to ensure that as the MAD slowly became naturally un-calibrated, and indeed items of electrical equipment on board were changed, the sensor was in the best shape to detect a lump of steel in the ocean.

Unfortunately, this had the undesired effect of bringing forward the inevitable air-sickness for those who were prone to it, as all the heavy manoeuvres would simply precede even more of the same later in the trip. For those lucky enough not to suffer, it was a great time to play negative-G astronaut type jumping about games in ordnance for five minutes, whilst not much else was allowed to happen during this period. Very often crews would be getting checked out by one or more persons each trip and this was another opportunity for them to get in the way and ask lots of probing questions.

The radar was generally the primary sensor due in no small part to the obvious safety benefits of being able to have a good set of eyes in any weather. Given a regular overt all-sensor sortie type the radar would be employed to provide an anti-collision service before descending into the particular area of ocean the crew were operating in (above). This was to check that there was no danger of conflicting with other civilian aircraft, helicopters and indeed other MPA.

The next priority before entering the area would be to generate a surface picture or 'radar plot' of the contacts in the area.

At distance obviously a small contact such as a yacht or submarine mast wouldn't be located as there was a sliding scale as to what the radar set could detect, so only when much closer could the crew be confident that everything had been 'seen' from supertankers down to the smallest objects. Therefore, depending on the mission the position of the aircraft would be changed, if large contacts were being searched for the crew would stand off at, sometimes over a hundred miles away, deliberately to 'declutter' the radar operator's screen or remove all the contacts he wasn't interested in. If small contacts were being sought the crew would conduct their search 'close-in', either flying from contact to contact or flying one of the different types of search, typically sweeping from one side of the area to the other whilst creeping forward to ensure complete security of the search, ie covering every bit of the sea surface. If the situation allowed the best height for radar detection would be considered, as swell and wave height might determine flying higher to 'look into' the sea. Other weather conditions and radar propagation effects might influence how the crew carried out a radar task.

If the sortie was covert or the mission demanded it then acoustics would become the primary sensor and the aircraft would be set up for this, with less or even no emphasis on radar. Depending on quite how 'silent' the aircraft needed to be, the radios would be silenced, the radar would be off and it might even be necessary to turn off all the external lights and use the window blinds to stop the internal lights showing. During an acoustics sortie the sensor would be used to check the RF in the area to see if there were any one else's sonobuoys transmitting that could be poached or listened to covertly. The crew would have already decided where to lay their pattern of sonobuoys depending on what the perceived submarine mission was and how he was likely to operate to give the MPA the best chance of detecting him.

The MAD sensor was a remarkable bit of kit, enabling another method of classifying a blip on the radar or acoustics screen to an object of several hundreds of tons made of steel. "Mad Mark" would be the cry as the operator shouted above everything else being said on intercom, to enable the aircraft to be thrown into a steep turn to get back to the same spot to prosecute the target. During daylight to optimise for MAD the aircraft would be flown at 200 feet over the sea, the MOA (minimum on-task altitude). At night this became 300 feet for an increased safety margin but during these manoeuvres the pilots would pull up to 500 feet to allow full freedom to rack the mighty Nimrod around the sky as by now the submariners had heard the roar of four Spey engines and were aware that their worst nightmare was about to come true. They had to employ all their skill to evade and the Nimrod crew had to do the same to not lose the submarine.

ESM would be used the whole time generally to add to the sortie, providing information to confirm or deny other intelligence. It could certainly become the primary sensor if it detected an emitter that pinpointed a particular unit that was being sought. In all of these scenarios, if the crew detected something they were interested in there were set procedures and tactics for every action depending on the situation. These tactics, the flexibility of the platform and the ability of the crew was what combined to make the Nimrod normally the very best tool for the job. It might have been that the submarine was detected rapidly and a Stingray torpedo took the edge off his day, it may have been the case that days and days were needed to get to that position if the intelligence was lacking or the submarine was more of a slippery adversary. Wartime ASuW was generally thought of as being a long job, the crew having to remain many miles from the threat due to his missile capability and needing many missions and crews to slowly gather the information on the opposition over a period of time.

During some busy sorties the crew would sometimes run out of bodies when all the sensors were required and manned and then say a submarine mast was detected meaning often a camera run. One of the acoustic operators and the radio man would then have to leave their position to take the pictures as there simply weren't enough people to cope. Loading the buoys in ordnance had a similar toll. This all had another effect – no rations! If everyone was busy then the tcapot wouldn't go round the aircraft, the meals wouldn't get cooked and the crew could go several hours without sustenance, a traumatic time for the 'pie-munchers'.

The ability to concoct amazing meals from the tiny Nimrod galley was legendary, pre-cooked fare being the norm meaning chicken curry for breakfast at 3am or sausage rolls with chilli sauce accompanied by jammy dodgers, arctic roll and dairy cream sponge! More exotic locations might mean beef satay skewers or meat samosas, club sandwiches, huge beefburgers and ice cream, the Americas would inevitably produce KFC buckets, Subway sandwiches, Oreo cookies and MandM sweeties! If the intercom was busy and an unwanted catering intrusion was likely to provoke a rebuke then the 'galley bitch' at that time would whisper unannounced "Tea or Coffee" to try to avoid the captain's stern reply. If the chosen lull was short-lived then the comment went unnoticed but otherwise many of the crew would voice equally quietly their opinion of what hot drink should be next, followed by most of the rest. This usually provided a little light relief as the reason behind these moments were normally busy, tense periods of work.

When it was time to set out for home, or on an important trip all the 'on-task' fuel had been used to prudent limit of endurance (PLE), meaning there was only enough to get back plus sensible diversion fuel, then the aircraft would get tidied up, the last of the meals would be put in the oven and the crew would set about wrapping things up. Radar would be switched to collision warning, acoustics would monitor their sonobuoys until out of RF range and configure the Wescam for the transit back, the pilots and engineer would relight those engines shut down for fuel economy and with the navs would discuss Air Traffic and destination airfield details and the beams would be manned once more for that extra bit of safety.

Very rare was the trip where the pilots didn't 'need' to get some circuits and bumps in at the end. Obviously they had stats to upkeep the same as the rest of the crew but theirs were naturally a little critical to safety. Specific pilot training sorties were regularly laid on but any time in the air was playtime for the pilots. Invariably this would entail lots of groans and grumbles from the rear-crew but the pilots had very thick skin, especially when it came to the inevitable critique of their landing technique.

Putting it all to bed was often a protracted evolution too, meaning for some a lot of debriefing still to go. The mission debrief entailed many things, not least beforehand including telling the groundcrew what had been broken, proffering opinions and ensuring it was written up correctly for the remedial work. Upon arriving back at operations before the debrief proper could start all the kit needed to be signed back, returned to its original locations or locked away again. Several of the teams on the crew, depending on their type would need to debrief their side of the action, either to brief the next crew, the wider maritime community, the RAF/MOD hierarchy or simply for the history books. The wet team would debrief all the acoustic 'signature' details in the MAAU (latterly the A3 section) before the analysts there would replay the mission or 'spin the tapes'. This entailed long hours running the acoustic data through a processor at several times real time to enable a quick turnaround. If the mission was important enough then these same tapes would go to Farnborough for very extensive reconstructions of the whole sortie, coming full circle when these were sometimes briefed back to the crews at Kinloss. The dry team would debrief all the intercepted ESM data before their tapes or flashcards were stripped by the MSS and the information archived and passed on to the Air Warfare Centre at Wadding-ton. The longest session was normally for the AEO to get the Form Purple or MISREP filled out, both types of debrief form, often a very lengthy task.

And when it was all over we would all drift away to our homes and pick up our lives again hopefully as if nothing had happened! Sometimes if the timing was right or it had been a par-ticularly stressful evolution then a quick beer and a calm-down would be in order, otherwise it was thoughts of the next day – which might be to do the same all over again …..or maybe not!

APPENDIX 2

GLOSSARY AND ACRONYMS

AAR	Air to Air refuelling
ACINT	Acoustic Intelligence and identification of sound source.
AEW	Airborne Early Warning is a facility which enables all aircraft that are flying to be examined on an airborne display by an AEW aircraft and to be classified as friendly or enemy. Furthermore the aircraft must have the capability of controlling friendly aircraft and enabling them to 'attack' possible foes.
AIP	Air Independent Propulsion
ARAR/ARAX	Electronic Support Measures ESM
ASDIC	Initial echo-sounding sonar equipment. No acronym.
ASR	1) Air Sea Rescue 2) Air Staff Requirement is a document written by the RAF to give an indication of what will be required to help defend the UK.
ASUW	Anti-Surface Unit Warfare.
ASV	Air-to-Surface Vessel.
ASW	Anti-Submarine Warfare.
AUTEC	Atlantic Underwater Test and Evaluation Center
AWACS	Airborne Warning and Control System is an AEW aircraft.
CPA	Closest Point of Approach.
DASS	Defensive Aids Sub-System.
DRC	Disappearing Radar Contact.
Dry Team	The Nimrod crew members that looked after the radar, ESM, radios were called the dry team.
ECM	Electronic Countermeasures are electrical or electronic devices designed to trick or deceive radar, sonar or other detection systems. When fitted to aircraft it is installed to prevent attack.
ELINT	Electronic Intelligence implying security classification.
EOSDS	Northrop Grumman Night Hunter Electro Optical Surveillance and Detection System enabling ground imaging day and night.
ESM/ELINT	Electronic Support Measures is a system that listens to all radio signals and identifies the source of the transmissions from a large database.
ESM advantage	A submarine can hear an active sonobuoy pinging at a greater range than the aircraft can hear a reflected return from the submarine.
FASS	Fore and Aft Scanning System.
FLIR	Forward Looking Infra Red enables targets to be visible at night.
GOO	Gulf of Oman.
Honkers	A stew prepared on the Nimrod consisting of tinned steak, vegetables and anything else within range all put into a pot and served steaming hot in foil trays and eaten with a plastic spoon.

IFF	Identification Friend or Foe enables an aircraft to transmit an identification which is identifiable on radar screens.
ITP	Instruction to Proceed.
IUSS	Integrated Undersea Surveillance System is a developed version of SOSUS, below, for tracking submarines.
JAAC	Joint Acoustic Analysis Centre.
JTIDS	Joint Tactical Information Distribution System.
Link 11	Battlefield communication system which enables data to be transferred between co-operating defence units.
MAAU	Maritime Acoustic Analysis Unit.
MAD	Magnetic Anomaly Detector
MAWS	Missile Approach Warning System.
MOD	Ministry of Defence.
MOD(PE)	Ministry of Defence Procurement Executive.
MPA	Marine Patrol Aircraft.
MSA	Mission System Avionics is the combination of different electronic sensors to enable a target to be identified, located and attacked.
NATO	North Atlantic Treaty Organisation.
NLS	Nimrod Line Squadron comprises the engineers and servicing team for the aircraft.
PLE	Prudent Limit of Endurance.
PSAB	Prince Sultan Air Base, Saudi Arabia.
RAE	Royal Aircraft Establishment.
RSRE	Royal Signals and Radar Establishment.
SAM	Surface-to-air missile.
SIGINT	Signal Intelligence implying security classification.
Sonobuoy	A floating electronic device which enables location of submarines by listening to underwater sounds possibly transmitting as well.
SOSUS	Sound Surveillance System is a chain of very sensitive line of fixed hydrophones laid between Greenland, Iceland and the UK to detect submarines.
SSBN	Submersible Ship Ballistic missile Nuclear.
SSGN	Submersible Ship Guided missile Nuclear.
SSK	Submersible Ship Hunter Killer.
SUS	Signal Underwater Sound.
TACAN	Tactical Air Navigation System is a navigation system showing distance and bearing from a radio beacon.
TICMS	Thermal Imaging Common Module System.
Wet Team	The Nimrod crewmembers that looked after the sonobuoys and cameras were called the wet team.
WSOp	Weapon System Operator (S) wct, (EW) dry, (L) linguist R1.

APPENDIX 3

NIMROD TIME LINES

September 1958	NATO specification for long-range maritime aircraft.
July 1963	AST 357 issued, calling for a sophisticated jet aircraft to replace the Shackleton by 1972.
October 1963	Hawker Siddeley submits MR aircraft feasibility study.
April 1964	Hawker Siddeley submits proposal based on HS.800 version of Trident airliner.
4 June 1964	ASR 381 issued, calling for cheaper and more rapid Shackleton replacement.
June 1964	Design of HS.801 based on Comet 4 airliner begins.
July 1964	HS.801 offered to meet ASR 381.
February 1965	Decision to order HS.801 announced.
June 1965	Hawker Siddeley receives Instruction to Proceed (ITP).
January 1966	Fixed price contract placed for 38 Nimrod MR.Mk 1s.
23 May 1967	First flight of Spey-engined prototype (XV148).
31 July 1967	First flight of Avon-engined prototype (XV147).
28 June 1968	Maiden flight of first production Nimrod MR.Mk 1 (XV226).
2 October 1969	First production MR.Mk1 (XV230) delivered to RAF – 236 OCU at St Mawgan.
27 October 1969	First overseas flight, Gibraltar.
October 1969	Order placed for three R.Mk 1 ELINT versions.
27 November 1969	RAF Strike Command absorbs Coastal Command.
October 1970	RAF Kinloss (201 Sqn) begins conversion to Nimrod.
7 July 1971	First R.Mk 1 (XW664) delivered to 51 Sqn as an 'empty shell'.
January 1972	Second batch of eight MR.Mk 1s announced.
1973	Project definition for Nimrod AEW version carried out.
21 October 1973	Flight trials begin of mission-equipped R.Mk 1s.
10 May 1974	51 Sqn formally commissioned with Nimrod R.Mk.1.

1975	Work starts on MR.Mk 2 upgrade.
31 March 1977	Nimrod AEW chosen to meet British AEW requirement.
28 June 1977	Converted Comet 4C (XW626) begins AEW radar trials.
13 February 1979	First production MR.Mk 2 conversion flight (XV236).
31 March 1979	203 Sqn leaves Malta.
23 August 1979	Redelivery of first upgraded MR.Mk 2 to RAF.
1980	Major avionics update for R.Mk 1s carried out.
16 July 1980	First flight of first development AEW.Mk 3 (XZ286).
9 March 1982	First production AEW.Mk 3 first flight.
14 April 1982	Work starts on in-flight refuelling probe installation design for MR.Mk 2.
27 April 1982	First probe-equipped MR.Mk 2P flies (XV229).
29 May 1982	First carriage of AIM-9 Sidewinder missiles (XV229).
early 1982	Initial planned Nimrod AEW service entry date.
1984	First AEW aircraft delivered to 8 Sqn for crew training.
Spring 1985	ESM wingtip pods introduced to MR.Mk 2.
1985	Upgrade of 35 MR.1 aircraft to MR.2 standard completed.
September 1986	AEW competition reopened by MoD.
December 1986	E-3 Sentry selected as winner, Nimrod AEW.Mk 3 cancelled.
1993	Request for information for Replacement Maritime Patrol Aircraft (RMPA) to meet ASR 420.
April 1994	Installation of 'Starwindow' avionics update for R.Mk 1 commences.
1995	Bids submitted for RMPA.
15 May 1995	R.Mk 1 XW666 ditches after catastrophic engine fire.
25 July 1996	Nimrod 2000 wins RMPA competition.
2 December 1996	Fixed-price contract awarded to BAE Systems for Nimrod 2000 development.
14 February 1997	First of three Nimrod fuselages delivered to FR Aviation at Bournemouth.
early 1998	Nimrod 2000 renamed Nimrod MRA.4.
March 1998	Santiago air display, Chile, drop to dismasted yacht.
late 1998	Nimrod MRA.4 programme reviewed due to poor progress.

1999	Nimrod MRA.4 contract re-negotiated – three years slip in delivery to service.
1999	First BR.710-48 engine deliveries for Nimrod MRA.4.
January 2000	First fuselage returned to Woodford.
19 December 2001	Electrical 'power on' for first MRA.4.
2002	Initial planned delivery date for MRA.4.
March 2002	Engines installed in first MRA.4.
February 2003	Programe restructured again – further delay to in-service date.
21 July 2004	MRA.4 order reduced to 'about twelve'.
26 August 2004	First flight of MRA.4 first prototype (ZJ516).
15 December 2004	Second prototype (ZJ518) first flight.
August 2005	Third aircraft joined programme.
2005	Structural test specimen, Brough.
September 2006	MRA.4 successful cold weather trials.
2 September 2006	Nimrod MR.2 XV 230 crashed Afghanistan.
28 October 2009	Haddon-Cave report published.
10 March 2010	Training clearance of MRA.4 to RAF.
31 March 2010	Last operational flight.
October 2010	MRA.4 trials finished, Boscombe for clearance.
19 October 2010	MRA.4 project cancelled.
31 March 2011	MOD planned to stop operating Nimrod R1s.
28 June 2011	Last flight Comet R1s.

APPENDIX 4

COMPARISON BETWEEN MRA4 AND MR2

	MRA4	MR2
CREW	10	12
LENGTH	38.6 m (126 ft 9 in)	38.65 m (126 ft 9 in)
WINGSPAN	38.71 m (127 ft)	35.00 m (114 ft 10 in)
EMPTY WEIGHT	46,500 kg (102,515 lb)	39,009 kg (86,000 lb)
MAX TAKEOFF WEIGHT	105,376 kg (232,315 lb)	87,090 kg (192,000 lb)
POWERPLANT	4× Rolls-Royce BR710 turbo-fans, 68.97 kN (15,500 lbf) each	4× Rolls-Royce Spey low by-pass 54.09 kN (12,160 lbf) each
MAXIMUM SPEED	Mach 0.77, 496 kn (571 mph, 918 km/h)	Mach 0.77, 498kn(573 mph, 923 km/h)
RANGE	11,119 km (6,910 mi)	8,340km (5,180 mi)
SERVICE CEILING	12,800 m (42,000 ft)	13,411 m (44,000 ft)
AVIONICS	Searchwater 2000 improved radar. Two CDC/Ultra UYS503 / AQS970 acoustics for monitoring 64 buoys. CAE improved MAD. ELTA ELL-8300UK ESM DASS with MAWS. Integrated multimode workstations. Northrop Grumman 'Nighthunter' Electro Optic Search & Detection System in turret (EOSDS) inc real time video transmission. Design provision for expansion	Searchwater Radar. Ferranti 1600D computer. Two Ultra AQS971 acoustic processor for monitoring 32 buoys. CAE MAD. Loral 'Yellowgate' ESM. DASS with MAWS. Link 11 Datalink. L-3 Wescam MX-15 electro-optical turret plus realtime video to ground streaming.

	MRA4	MR2
ARMAMENT		
WING HARDPOINTS	4× under-wing pylon stations and an internal bomb bay with a capacity of 22,000 lb (10,000 kg)	2× under-wing pylon stations and an internal bomb bay with a capacity of 20,000 lb (9,100 kg)
MISSILES	Air-to-air missile: 2× AIM-9 Sidewinder. Air-to-surface missile: AGM-65 Maverick, AGM-84 Harpoon, Storm Shadow	Air-to-air missile: 2× AIM-9 Sidewinder (non-standard in RAF service, only mounted on the MR2 during the Falklands War). Air-to-surface missile: Nord AS.12, Martel missile, AGM-65 Maverick, AGM-84 Harpoon
BOMBS	deleted	Depth charges, US-owned B57 nuclear depth bombs (until 1992)
TORPEDOES	Air-dropped Stingray torpedoes	Air-dropped Stingray torpedoes
MINES (probably not in reality)	Naval Mines	Naval Mines
SONOBUOYS & LAUNCHERS	Full Range of buoys. Four 10 shot rotary launchers plus 2 pressurised single buoy launchers	Full Range of buoys. Two 6 shot rotary launchers plus 2 pressurised single buoy launchers

APPENDIX 5

MOD DEFINED TASKS FOR THE NIMROD

- Defending the United Kingdom and its Overseas Territories.
- Providing strategic intelligence.
- Providing nuclear deterrence.
- Supporting civil emergency organisations in times of crisis.
- Defending the interests of the United Kingdom by strategically projecting power and through expeditionary interventions.
- Providing a defence contribution to UK influence.
- Providing security for stabilisation.

INDEX

221